APRI
VIRGIN
REME

APRIL 16th: VIRGINIA TECH REMEMBERS

Edited by Roland Lazenby
With Kevin Cupp, Suzanne Higgs,
Omar Maglalang, Laura Massey,
Tricia Sangalang, Courtney Thomas,
and Neal Turnage

A PLUME BOOK

PLUME
Published by Penguin Group
Penguin Group (USA) Inc., 375 Hudson Street, New York, New York 10014, USA • Penguin Group (Canada), 90 Eglinton Avenue East, Suite 700, Toronto, Ontario, Canada M4P 2Y3 (a division of Pearson Penguin Canada Inc.) • Penguin Books Ltd., 80 Strand, London WC2R 0RL, England • Penguin Ireland, 25 St. Stephen's Green, Dublin 2, Ireland (a division of Penguin Books Ltd.) • Penguin Group (Australia), 250 Camberwell Road, Camberwell, Victoria 3124, Australia (a division of Pearson Australia Group Pty. Ltd.) • Penguin Books India Pvt. Ltd., 11 Community Centre, Panchsheel Park, New Delhi - 110 017, India • Penguin Group (NZ), 67 Apollo Drive, Rosedale, North Shore 0745, Auckland, New Zealand (a division of Pearson New Zealand Ltd.) • Penguin Books (South Africa) (Pty.) Ltd., 24 Sturdee Avenue, Rosebank, Johannesburg 2196, South Africa

Penguin Books Ltd., Registered Offices: 80 Strand, London WC2R 0RL, England

First published by Plume, a member of Penguin Group (USA) Inc.

First Printing, September 2007
10 9 8 7 6 5 4 3 2 1

CIP data is available.
ISBN 978-0-452-28934-5

Printed in the United States of America
Set in Minion

Contents

About This Book

This book was put together in the long, difficult days after April 16, 2007.

It's easier to define this book by what it isn't.

It isn't an "official" book. It isn't sanctioned by the university.

This book offers little insight into the mind of the killer. We include content about Seung-Hui Cho, but he isn't our focus.

Likewise, this book is not an investigation of Virginia Tech's administration or its decisions on that fateful Monday. Nor is it a defense of the university administration. A commission impaneled by Virginia governor Tim Kaine is investigating those issues.

This book attempts to report the powerful emotional record of the events of April 16 and the aftermath, and even that by nature is a fragmented story. The shooting deaths of thirty-two students and faculty (and the injuries to an additional twenty-five) on that Monday shattered the Virginia Tech community into millions of emotional shards. In this book we've recovered some of those shards and present them to the reader. We have done that for two reasons: First, to honor the victims and their extraordinary lives; second, to try to understand ourselves and what we are experiencing in the wake of these horrific events.

There are those who say we should not have attempted to write this book, that it is too soon. They may well be right. We struggled each day as we gathered the information for it. Half of the time we were overwhelmed by the difficult nature of the information and considered abandoning the project. The other half of the time we were inspired by the actions of the people we were writing about. As a result we consider this book extremely important.

It is a debate we will face right up until press time. If you are reading this, it probably means we decided to publish the manuscript. On the other hand, you may be reading this material years after the event because we chose to archive it in the Virginia Tech Library.

Either way, our approach will have been the same. We attempt to view the events through the eyes and work of student journalists from planetblacksburg.com and *Collegiate Times,* Virginia Tech's century-old newspaper.

But the book involves many more perspectives. As a result, it is presented in an oral history format, with the voices of students, faculty, and others telling the story along with the student journalists. Thus, the text reflects the words of many people from the Virginia Tech community.

Twenty-year-old Derek O'Dell somehow managed to get up off the floor of his decimated German class in Norris Hall, tend to his wounds, address the media, and work to honor the classmates and instructor he lost. He also found time in the weeks after to pen seven thousand words of remembrance for this book.

Likewise, numerous people from the broader Tech community, including friends and relatives of the victims, have given their thoughts and recollections.

There has been a tremendous assist from faculty and university staff members, including Dr. Ishwar Puri, professor and head of the distinguished Department of Engineering Science and Mechanics that was hit especially hard by the shootings; Dr. Ezra "Bud" Brown, alumni distinguished professor of mathematics and a pillar of the university; Dr. Sam Riley, pioneering professor in the Department of Communication; Dr. John Chermak, an instructor in the Department of Geosciences, who took the time to speak in depth about the courage of his neighbor and friend, Kevin Granata; and Jenna Lazenby Nelson, the former manager of the Virginia Tech news bureau in the office of University Relations.

In addition, I must personally cite the work of the student journalists who have been so strong and good and true in their efforts to conduct often highly emotional interviews and gather precious information.

A number of them are Planet Blacksburg staff members and yet others are or were *Collegiate Times* staffers. Kevin Cupp, Suzanne Higgs, Omar Maglalang, Laura Massey, Tricia Sangalang, and Neal Turnage worked tirelessly on this project. They were aided by the efforts of Andrew Mager, Courtney Thomas, Amy Kovac (of BigLickU.com), and several others.

In addition, we must mention the numerous *Collegiate Times* reporters who contributed the profiles of the victims. They include Kevin Anderson, Michael Berger, Kim Berkey, Caroline Black, Emerson Blais, Robert Bowman, Rosanna Brown, James Carty, Laurel Colella, David Covucci, Janelle Frazier, David Grant, Saira Haider, Alexandra Hemenway, Drew Jackson, Joe Kendall, Katelyn Lau, Ryan McConnell, Meg Miller, John Rhoads, Michelle Rivera, T. Rees Shapiro, Amie Steele, Teresa Tobat, and Duncan Vick.

At Penguin's Plume imprint we must thank editor in chief Cherise Davis and her staff (especially Jennifer Risser and Norina

Frabotta), who have believed in the value and importance of this remembrance. Then there's Matthew Carnicelli, who originally envisioned this project and asked me to do it.

I also must thank Cathy Hudgins, a family counselor with much insight into the circumstances who helped us through many difficult moments and decisions. We also must thank all of the people who submitted essays for this project. Many of them did so despite much personal difficulty.

It has been an immense effort by many people, all of us heartbroken yet lifted up by the courage displayed by special people like Derek O'Dell, whose example helped brace a grieving community on April 16 and in the difficult days that followed.

Our efforts, humbled by the circumstances, are dedicated to them.

Roland Lazenby
June 1, 2007

PART I

APRIL 16th

CHAPTER 1

Unimaginable Nightmare

The scenario is destined to be studied in crisis management and law enforcement circles for years to come: Police are called to a major college campus to investigate an early-morning shooting in a large dorm. Found shot and near death are two people—an African-American male, a resident adviser (student dorm counselor), and a Caucasian female student. Police learn that the student had been dropped off at the dorm by her boyfriend, who attends nearby Radford University, just minutes before the shootings. What seems an obvious domestic case is anything but. While police race to track down the boyfriend for questioning, the real killer, a homicidally deranged loner, is on the loose and about to execute a plan that he has spent months preparing. He wants to murder as many people as possible, then manipulate the media into airing on network and cable television his incoherent manifesto and the *Natural Born Killer*–style photos and video he has taken of himself. With police pursuing the other lead, the killer has time to visit the local post office to mail his media presentation to NBC. Then he finishes the plan. He has selected an old building on campus because it has just a few escape routes. He can chain the doors on the exits to the building and quickly trap the people inside. He knows the second floor of the building is filled with students in their classes. He also knows that the classroom doors have no locks. The occupants will be defenseless. The classroom windows are too small in many cases to exit through, and their position on the second floor means that some students will hesitate to jump. He plans to move quickly, using the shock effect to execute as many people as possible before authorities can respond. To do this, he has selected two common handguns, one is a light .22-caliber Walther, the other a 9mm Glock, a light, powerful instrument of destruction that reloads easily and quickly. He has taken a common student backpack and loaded it with hundreds of rounds of ammunition.

Sounds too fantastic to believe, doesn't it?

In Blacksburg, Virginia?

Ezra "Bud" Brown, alumni distinguished professor of mathematics: It was this atmosphere at Virginia Tech, and it was this atmosphere in Blacksburg, that great big major university in a gorgeous setting in the middle of that pretty little sleepy little safe town . . .

Jenna Lazenby Nelson, Virginia Tech news bureau manager: I had lived in Annapolis, Maryland, and worked in Washington, D.C., during 9/11. I was at home the morning that two planes flew into the Twin Towers and then another into the Pentagon. I knew that bad things happened in our world. I knew that evil is inevitable in our society, oftentimes without any explanation. However, I never for a moment thought that a tragedy of this proportion could happen in Blacksburg, Virginia, to our Hokie Nation, to an institution where I had myself studied, and on a campus that I knew well and loved.

Blacksburg is the kind of place that could go several years without recording a homicide. The school's athletics teams and consequently its fans are known as Hokies, a term with no literal meaning derived from a century-old cheer. A search of records seemed to confirm that the last time a "Hokie" had been charged with murder was 1980, when a former walk-on football player named Stephen Epperly was arrested in the death of Radford University coed Gina Hall (one Tech student was charged with involuntary manslaughter in 2006). Still, the peace of the little college town had been shattered on the first day of classes in August 2006 when a hospital security guard and a Montgomery County sheriff's deputy were shot to death while trying to apprehend an escapee. That incident had sparked a campus-wide lockdown and set the community on edge, a sense of unease that would be revived in April by two unexplained bomb threats.

The university took a low-key approach in reporting these bomb threats, which in turn left some students with an almost casual attitude toward them.

None of that came close to preparing Blacksburg for Seung-Hui Cho's fury.

West Ambler Johnston

In an event fogged in unanswered questions and confusion, the first shootings present perhaps the biggest mystery of all. Why Emily Hilscher? Why Room 4040 of West Ambler Johnston? The coed dorm, with seven floors and almost nine hundred residents, is one of Tech's largest.

After better than a month of investigation, Virginia State Police superintendent William Flaherty would concede that detectives had been unable to find a motive or any connection between Seung-Hui Cho and Hilscher or any of his other victims. One investigator said police could only speculate that Cho had been stalking Hilscher, just as he had stalked other female students in 2005.

"It's as mind-boggling to me as it is to you," Flaherty told reporters in May. A witness recalled seeing Cho outside West Ambler Johnston about 6:45 that morning. About 7:00, Hilscher was dropped off by her boyfriend and went into the dorm. Virginia Tech police chief Wendell Flinchum said that the killer probably didn't see her enter the dorm.

Records show that Virginia Tech Police were called to Hilscher's dorm room around 7:15 that morning, ostensibly by reports that someone had fallen out of a bunkbed and been injured. Numerous press reports had offered wild speculation that the killer and Hilscher had once dated, but no clear connection exists. Some reports have indicated that Cho had gone from room to room on the fourth floor of the dorm until he found her. Resident adviser Ryan Clark, who lived next door, came to check on a noise that sounded like gunfire. A senior with a 4.0 average in three majors, Clark became the shooter's second victim.

Other students were awakened by the noise and thought it was the sound of the wind slamming shut open doors. Many more slept right through it.

Records show that the Virginia Tech Rescue Squad was dispatched to the dorm at 7:21 a.m. The unit responded at 7:24 and arrived two minutes later. Squad members began treatment at 7:29 and determined that Hilscher's chances of survival were greater than Clark's. At 7:31, a second ambulance arrived for Clark. A minute later, a call went out for all members of the university rescue squad to respond to West Ambler Johnston. The squad's Unit No. 3, with an emergency medical technician, arrived at 7:35. A minute later, the squad captain notified Montgomery Regional Hospital that one victim was in cardiac arrest. At 7:43, the ambulance departed for the hospital with Hilscher. At 7:48, the rescue squad requested air rescue from Carilion Roanoke Memorial Hospital. Stiff winds that day made medevac helicopter rescue extremely problematic. At 7:49, the squad's second ambulance left for the hospital with Clark.

Kristina Ticknor left the dorm that morning without learning there had been a shooting on the very floor where she lived. She would later note that she had awakened at 7:15, around the time a 911 call had gone out. She had known nothing about it and was told nothing about it on her way to class.

> **Kristina Ticknor, West Ambler Johnston resident:** I woke up and made my usual sleepy stumble to the bathroom down the hallway. Not a soul was in sight, and the halls were as quiet as any normal morning during the school week. After finishing my morning routine I headed out to go tutor at about 7:50. I was stopped on my normal route toward the elevators by the housekeeper, who casually informed me that I couldn't exit through those doors. No explanation was given, and I simply turned around and went out a different door.

> **Omar Maglalang, Virginia Tech student:** Kristina told me how she found it odd that the housekeeper told her to leave through a different door as she was walking out of her room to go to class that day. She didn't understand why the housekeeper would be so secretive about what happened near the fourth-floor elevators. She had never felt that way before about her residence, and she knew she felt something weird about the way the housekeeper told her to use a different exit.

Kristina Ticknor: As I made my way around the outside of the building, walking toward Lane Stadium, the morning air was quiet and still, without any noise of cop cars or ambulances.

Kevin Lancaster, West Ambler Johnston resident: I woke up at eight and had breakfast in the corner lounge of the second floor of West Ambler Johnston. One thing did stick out that was unusual: about fifteen police cars that several people noticed outside the study lounge window. We all just figured there was a bomb threat and figured everything was okay. After leaving for class, a friend of mine returned saying that he was told to return to his room. After some discussion we basically convinced each other to go ahead and go to class since the doors nearest our rooms were not blocked off. As we left we were told by another friend that a janitor had told him that two people had been shot in the building on the fourth floor. Halfway believing him we continued on our walk to classes in Squires and Randolph.

Kristina Ticknor: It wasn't until shortly after nine when the first fear hit me. My cell phone started to buzz during the middle of my media writing class as my roommate and several of my hall-mates were calling me. I knew something was wrong, because it was very odd that so many of my close friends would be trying to get in touch with me at such an early hour. I finally received a text message from my roommate that provided me with my first piece of information. There had been an "incident" on the floor of our dorm and they had been told not to return to their rooms, but nothing more. Later I found out that the residents of the fourth floor were awakened at approximately 8:30 by the housekeeper, who knocked on all their doors frantically instructing them to head to the third-floor crossover lounge for a meeting. At the meeting they were told that there had been an "incident," but to still go about their day and head to class.

When my roommate asked the residential adviser whether everything would be okay, she replied, "I think you're safe, but I'm not sure."

University officials had one thing going for them. The shootings in West Ambler Johnston had brought dozens of state police and local law officers to campus.

On the other hand, authorities had no idea what was about to unfold. Even worse, it was about to happen just as thousands of students and faculty were converging onto campus for the start of the day's third class at 10:10 a.m.

Sam Riley, communication professor: Around 9 a.m., give or take a few minutes, I was taking my income taxes to be postmarked and mailed at Blacksburg's downtown post office. Just before I reached the building's steps, I noticed a strange-looking young man of college age coming out of the post office in my direction. I don't recall what he was wearing, possibly because my eyes were immediately drawn to his face, which appeared dazed and slack-jawed. It is not at all unusual to see college students who look dazed at such an early hour after having been on a bender the night before. I nodded and spoke to him as we passed; he gaped at me silently in return. I remember saying to myself as I went up the post office steps some such sentiment as, "Great Lord! That's the most deranged-looking individual I've seen in a long time." As I reached the door, three police cars with sirens screaming came down Main Street headed toward the campus at an unusually high rate of speed. I got my taxes in the mail with a postmark showing I was on time, and as I was about to leave the building, a local businessman asked me if I knew there had been a shooting on campus.

Ezra "Bud" Brown, mathematics professor: The wind had been blowing in Blacksburg for five solid days with hardly any letup, and the Monday morning of April 16 arrived with no indication that it would stop. At eight that morning the barometric pressure was extremely low, but the sun was shining and it was a beautiful day as I walked from my home near the Blacksburg Library to my office in McBryde Hall. I needed to prepare for my Tuesday classes, the one at 11:00 in 211 Patton and the one at 12:30 in 211 Norris. My office is right in the middle of the side of McBryde Hall that faces Norris Hall. Shortly after 9 a.m., I looked out the window and saw a sheriff's car by a tree just outside of Holden Hall, between McBryde and Norris. And then a colleague came running into my office, saying something about a shooting going on in Norris Hall. I then saw police officers running toward Norris, and remained glued to my window, thinking, "What could this possibly be?"

Brittney Asbury, Virginia Tech sophomore: I parked my car and we continued to chat about our weekend and how much we really hated Mondays. The three of us had gotten to the sidewalk and were getting ready to cross the street to begin our walk through the academic side of campus when we heard several sirens. I looked up and saw three police cars getting ready to turn on the road we were trying to cross. Immediately we all began to joke that there was another bomb threat on campus (we had already had two the previous week). The cars pulled up onto an access road that leads in behind several of the academic buildings that face the Prices Fork parking lot. The cops quickly jumped out and started running toward the direction of the Drillfield, holding assault rifles in their hands. My father has been a police officer for longer than I have been alive, so I have grown familiar with police officers and why they do the things they do. As I watched the officers creep up the hill I begin to realize they were not responding to a bomb threat. None of them was in tactical gear, and the way they were walking and creeping down behind buildings gave me the sick feeling that they were looking for a shooter. As the three of us stood there unsure of what to do, a feeling of deep sadness began to creep over me. I'm not sure if it is because, for the first time in my life, I had seen what it is my father does when he gets called out, and that got to me, or if deep down I knew that something terrible had happened to the place I call home. Finally, after what seemed like forever, we saw several students running toward the parking lot saying someone had been shot on campus. I told them I know, someone was apparently shot in West AJ that morning. I was quickly told no, there is a hostage situation in Norris. It was then things began to get more and more confusing.

Ezra "Bud" Brown: As I watched the events outside of Norris Hall unfold, there was a knock at my open door and Sam Abboud, a member of the Hillcrest Honors Residential Community, came into the room. "Have you heard about the shooting at West AJ? Somebody shot an RA (resident adviser) and another student around seven this morning!" I had not heard; Sam and his friend Michael Miracle from Hillcrest told me that McBryde was locked down, and asked if they could stay in my office for the time being? Of course they could, and while acts of unspeakable carnage were happening not two hundred feet away, there I was, blithely talking to students about a couple of interesting mathematical puzzles. Occasionally I looked out the window and would see several groups of students racing out of Norris Hall with their arms raised, running toward the Drillfield. Again, I thought, "Two students shot? Are they dead? What next?"

Norris Hall is an older building with a jutting right wing that houses engineering laboratories on the first floor, classrooms on the second floor, and a mix of classrooms and offices on the third floor.

In Room 207, thirty-five-year-old instructor Christopher "Jamie" Bishop, liked by his students for his easy smile and long hair that was often tied back in a ponytail, had arrived early for class, as usual.

> **Derek O'Dell, student in Bishop's Introductory German class:** Herr Bishop (Herr B, as we called him) talked with us in English mixed with German prior to class. That morning we talked about baseball as the season had just started a few weeks earlier. Jamie Bishop was an Atlanta Braves fan and Michael Pohle and I were both Philadelphia Phillies fans. This, of course, caused a little conflict as they were in the same division. Michael and I were both miserable as the Phillies had started out the season as usual with only one win and . . . too many losses. Michael and I both blamed the Braves for the Phillies' disastrous start this season. Herr B brushed it off and simply stated the Phillies will never be as good as the Braves. Then class started.

"It's a small class, about twenty-five people," student Erin Sheehan would later tell the *Collegiate Times,* the campus newspaper. "And I would say no more than two people didn't show up, were absent."

> **Derek O'Dell:** We were learning how to use the correct grammar in German when quoting someone. It started out as a normal class, nothing out of the ordinary until fifteen minutes into class, when a short-haired male cracked the door slightly and peeked his head into the room. Something that seemed relatively normal, maybe a lost student searching for a class. Then the door opened again, about ten or fifteen seconds later. What appeared to be the same person looking into the class again as if he had forgotten what he had seen just a few moments earlier. This was pretty weird, even warranted a

few thoughts as to who this person was. I quickly dismissed it as a lost student and continued paying attention to the lesson Herr B was giving. Herr Bishop's PowerPoint presentations were always entertaining and captivating, to say the least. So for something to draw my attention away from his lecture was relatively rare.

"The teacher stopped because he was bothered by this twice," Sheehan recalled, "and we all thought it was a little bit funny. . . . It was strange that someone at this point in the semester would be lost, looking for a class."

Some have speculated that after peeking in the classrooms, the killer retreated to the first floor to chain and lock the exits. An accounting exam was being given on the third floor of Norris, and one of the first finished was Daniel Stumpf, twenty-one. He headed downstairs with the idea of going to a nearby coffee shop, but Stumpf got to the first floor and found all the double-door exits chained and locked from the inside. He and another student asked Norris housekeeper Pam Tickle why the door was locked. "I was dust-mopping the hall, and when I got to the end, a student was trying to get out the door, but it had a chain around it with a lock," Tickle later recalled for *People* magazine. "That was weird. I've never seen that. The student said, 'What's going on?' I said, 'I don't know, but I'm going to call my boss.' "

Moments later a professor walked up and said she had found a note taped to the door that warned: "Open the doors and a bomb will go off."

As more people left the accounting exam on the third floor, they, too, encountered the locked doors on the first floor.

Ashley Brohawn, Virginia Tech student: [taking the accounting exam on the third floor] One of the girls got down there after the doors had been locked and she thought it was construction, too, so she's thinking, "Okay, there's construction around. Maybe the construction workers blocked this exit off because they're doing something and they don't want us to go out this way." She later told us that she started going back up the stairs and two guys came running down; one of them had been shot and they hid in a office down on the first floor. And they were giving him first aid and he went into shock.

Ishwar Puri, professor and chair of the Department of Engineering Science and Mechanics: There was this burst of sort of repetitive noise, for lack of a better word, sort of construction noise.

Ashley Brohawn: All of a sudden we start hearing this sound that sounded like hammers, and there were construction sites all around, so we continued taking our test, and I even remember looking up at the teacher like, "How do they expect us to finish this test with this noise going on?"

Ishwar Puri: It was followed by that sort of repetitive one, two, three sounds. It sounded like a nail gun: pop pop pop, pop pop pop, pop pop pop. I was in my office, which is on the second floor of Norris Hall. Joyce Smith (one of the department secretaries) came by and said, "You know, what you just heard were gunshots." There's been so much construction on this side of campus that I thought it was some kind of construction device.

The noise distracted students in Room 205, where doctoral student Haiyan Cheng was serving as a substitute for a professor out of town at a conference. Student Theresa Walsh later recalled that she looked at her watch upon hearing the noise. It read 9:40. Some early sources told interviewers that the incident began to unfold shortly after 9:30; however, Virginia Tech police chief Wendell Flinchum said the first 911 call came in "nine-fortyish."

"Basically, after the initial gunshots I heard a scream," Zach Petkewicz, a student in Room 205, later recalled for reporters. "I didn't know if the gunshot—I didn't know it was gunshots at first until I heard that scream. It all kind of sunk in."

"Once we heard the screams, there were no longer any questions about what was happening," said student Andrey Andreyev.

Walsh looked into the hallway to see who or what was making the noise. Haiyan Cheng also looked outside. "I'm the closest one to the door so I got up and went in the hallway," Walsh recalled.

Haiyan Cheng told the *Washington Post*: "All we saw was across the hall there were two classrooms with both doors closed. And then suddenly, from one room, a guy came walking out of the door with a gun in his hand."

Theresa Walsh, student in Room 205: I literally went out into the hallway, like two or three feet into the hallway. We all thought it was jackhammering. We had heard no more than ten shots. So it was like the first room he was in. And then I got out into the hallway to yell at the construction workers but that ended up not being it. At that point you could start smelling the gunpowder and you could hear the screams. You begin to put two and two together and you're like, "This can't be what this is." And at that point I looked across the hall at Dr. [Liviu] Librescu's class, and I looked at him and he was in the doorway. All of his students were behind him, he was like holding them inside the classroom, and he's a short man. I just saw the look on his face and it was like he knew exactly what was going on. That's when I realized that it really is this. Then, out of the corner of my eye, I caught a glimpse of something. At this point the TA [teaching assistant], Haiyan Cheng, had come up behind me in the doorway and had gasped. I looked up the hallway and the shooter had come out of the room and he was walking toward us. When he walked out, he walked out in almost like a trance, like as if he had no cares in the world. He was just doing what he was doing. He never said one word; he had a blank look on his face. And that makes it kind of hard to identify a person if they don't have any specific characteristics. Plus, looking down the barrel of a gun, you're not thinking, "Well, he's about five foot something." You know what I mean? He was just really blank and that made it difficult to get his image. I still can see what he looks like. And he got about three and a half to four feet away and he started raising his gun. He got it to about shoulder level and right before he shot we just kinda threw ourselves back into the room. Then he shot and he missed. And then we slammed the door and that's when one of our classmates yelled to barricade the door. It's so weird. I have this problem—my mom says it's a problem, I say it's a good thing—where I react to things without thinking about it. It actually saved my life. I've played a lot of sports. I played varsity softball here at Tech and I remember one time a teammate of mine got smashed in the face. She tried to break up a double play and got a ball right to the jaw, she broke it and there was blood all over the place. I'm the kind of person that really doesn't like the sight of blood, but since it had just happened I remember ripping the gauze and helping my trainer to stop the bleeding. Didn't think until later the next day, "Ew. That was ugly. That was just gross." So when I saw his gun I thought, "Oh my God, this is real." At that moment the only thing I could do was react to it. I got my TA into the classroom and warned everyone to slam the door. I don't know what I was thinking; I just did it. When he raised his gun to shoot—I don't know how, to this day I still question how—he missed. He shouldn't have missed. I mean he was three and a half to four feet away. There's no way he would have missed. It's something that is unexplainable. I remember just reacting, never thinking. I didn't start thinking about it until a few days later when the shock stopped. When I made it back into the classroom I remember being very calm, and the only thing that was not calm about me was my hands. My hands shake anyway, but this time they were frantically shaking.

Zach Petkewicz later told CNN that like the rest of the students, he ducked for cover. The best place he could find was behind the teacher's podium, then it struck him that such a plan probably meant certain death. "There was nothing stopping this guy from just coming in. And so I said, 'We need to barricade this door,'" Petkewicz recalled. "I was completely scared out of my mind originally, just went into a cowering position, and then just realized you have got to do something."

Theresa Walsh: Two guys grabbed a table, like a teacher's table, which is like nothing, and threw it against the door. Meanwhile I was yelling for everyone to get down, that he had a gun, he was shooting. I was pulling people, my classmates, to the ground. I don't know why, I just did. Then I went to the back of the room to call 911 and that's when they barricaded the door. And he came to our classroom next.

"One of our classmates, Zach, says, 'We need to block the door, he's coming for our classroom next,'" Lisa Kaiser, another student in the class, told reporters. "And we threw a table up against the door, and sure enough, two seconds after we threw that table against the door he was at our handle trying to get in, pushing against the door. . . . He had tried twice to push it open and they were like stronger than him. I mean, four people or so, pushing on the table."

"He tried to force his way in, got the door to open up about six inches, and then we just lunged at it and closed it back up," Petkewicz said. "And that's when he backed up and shot twice into the middle of the door, thinking we were up against it, trying to get him out. A couple of my classmates were on the phone with 911 the whole time while all this was going on. We—I could hear police shouting all around the building. I mean, they were there really fast. It was just a matter of getting up and getting to us and getting this guy out of—out of the picture."

The killer's shots into the door didn't hit anyone. "We were lying on the ground and they were going over us," Kaiser explained.

> **Theresa Walsh:** He tried getting into the door and he nudged it with his shoulder, but he was unsuccessful because everyone was on their stomachs holding the legs of the table, pushing it up against the door. And then he stepped back and shot twice through the door. One bullet hit the podium and the other one went out the window. At this point, through all that was happening I was talking to Haiyan and I was like, "Ms. Cheng, do your ears hurt? Do your ears hurt?" because he was close when he shot at us and I had lost part of my hearing after he shot. So I didn't know how loud I was being. Loud enough to hear myself talking because I really couldn't hear anything. It was so weird, I couldn't hear the bullet go out the window because my ears were still ringing. I mean, a nine millimeter is not a quiet gun.

"You could feel the bullets, like you could feel . . . the vibrations of each gunshot . . . ," Theresa Walsh recalled. "He shot, bam, bam, bam, bam, and he didn't stop until his clip was empty and you heard the clip hit the ground right outside our door. He reloaded and started again."

"I was up against the side holding this desk up against there, and

I just heard his clip drop to the ground," Petkewicz told CNN. "He reloaded, and I thought he was coming back for a second round and trying to get his way in there. And, I mean—he didn't say a word. He just turned and kept firing down the hall and didn't try to get back in."

Theresa Walsh: I called 911 immediately to tell them all I'd seen just in case I started forgetting. It seemed like they didn't know about it. Now I don't know if I was the first one to call, but it seemed like I was because they asked, "What building are you in?" and I was like, "We're in *Norris*. Why aren't you guys here?" This had been going on for what seemed like forever when really it had only been like ten minutes or so. Also, my phone had cut off and I had lost service. Then other people in the class started calling 911, but I told them I got it. We didn't need everyone calling 911. So I called back and they said, "Yes, we've gotten reports about it. What room are you in?" I tried describing Norris; it's an *L* shape. I mean, how do you describe it depending on which door you go in?

In Room 205, the students maintained a measure of composure.

Theresa Walsh: Surprisingly, no one was freaking out and running around. There were people crying and upset. After I called 911 I tried calling my parents. I had just finished talking to my mom at 9:05; I was late to my class. Then right after I got off the phone with her apparently the power went out in my house and I couldn't get in touch with her again. So I had to call my sister who lives twenty-five minutes away to drive through there. I live in upstate New York and they were in a state of emergency. They had a snowstorm and were under like two feet of snow. She had to drive through the snow to go to my parents' house to tell them what had happened because they had no TV and knew nothing of what was going on. After I finally got in touch with [my sister] I started going around to everyone in the classroom asking if they were okay and they were. Some of the guys in the class and one of the girls were still holding the door shut. I asked if they were okay or needed to swap out and they were like, "No, we're good, we're good." Then I turned to my teacher and asked, "Are you okay?" and she said, "Yeah." There's this one guy in the class who's a little bit older, a PhD student. I remember asking him if he had family and he did. I told him, "If I were you I'd call them right now." Because there were a lot of people who were so stunned that they couldn't think to use their cell phones to call out. Also, a lot of us had to be quiet because we didn't want him to think there were still people in the room. So a lot of people were very calm yet very frightened. Not calm in the sense that everything's okay, but that scared calm, just quiet.

The killer had pressed on to other rooms on the second floor of Norris Hall, and like everyone else in the building, the students in Room 205 listened through the door. "The only silence you heard the entire time throughout the shooting was when he had to reload," Walsh said.

Theresa Walsh: They always say that [in a crisis] one person will freeze, somebody will run around like a chicken with its head cut off, and somebody reacts. I saw all of that in our classroom. You saw people running to the back of the room, getting underneath the desks. You saw people who stood there in the line of fire who could've gotten hit but didn't because we shut the door. They just stood there and froze. And you saw people reacting like how I ran into the room or like my classmate Zach [Petkewicz] who reacted to help barricade the door. It's really weird when you're put in that horrible situation to actually see those things occur.

Up on the third floor of Norris, the students taking the accounting exam were just learning what the noise really was.

Ashley Brohawn: All of a sudden one of the female classmates who had finished taking the test early had gone downstairs and she came running back up telling us that someone was downstairs shooting people. She was kind of panicked, like I thought she was having an asthma attack or something. She was having trouble breathing, she was in tears, crying. And she had said that when she got down to the second-floor landing, some guy had dove through the doors to get away from the shots, and that's when she ran back upstairs to tell us. And my teacher, James Yardley, went out into the hallway, and was still kind of like "Are you sure?" because we were all still like "What?" She came up around 9:43 or 9:44, I know that because the teacher put up on the board, "You have 15 minutes left to take your test."

Ishwar Puri: I'm literally responsible for Norris Hall. You know, Norris Hall does not have any emergency alarm system. It's an old building. So we have these air-blown horns; in case of a fire or some other emergency my administrative officers and I are supposed to run up and down Norris Hall blowing these horns, yelling "Fire!" or some such, or "Evacuate!"

An hour earlier a friend had called Ishwar Puri to tell him there had been a double homicide on campus.

Ishwar Puri: This was before the university announced a thing. I suppose there's a sort of an informal telegraph system on campus. There's a call that came into my office, and one of the secretarial staff took it, and it's actually the information we had, that it was a "lovers' spat." Immediately I didn't make a connection, because a

> lovers' spat double homicide seemed to indicate someone was shot and then they killed themselves. Just a few minutes later outside my office, I could see policemen behind a pickup truck actually between Randolph and Norris Hall. There was a policeman crouched behind that with his gun drawn. And soon thereafter, I saw a SWAT team run by Norris Hall. They were dressed with helmets.

The noise carried to nearby Pamplin Hall, where freshman Hector Takahashi and other students were talking about the administration email. "Then all of a sudden, we were like, 'Whoa—were those shots?' " he later recalled. The gunfire came in two quick bursts, then a fusillade, maybe three dozen shots.

About 9:45, university president Charles Steger was meeting with administrators in Burruss Hall, trying to decide how to respond to the shootings in West Ambler Johnston when aides notified him that shooting had erupted next door in Norris Hall. Steger thought he heard gunshots. The university president looked out the window and saw police surrounding Norris, realized what it was, and, thinking that a shooter might target his own office, ordered security to lock the doors to his office. "I thought it could be a target," he later told *Newsweek*.

Alec Calhoun, a twenty-year-old junior in Norris Room 204 for a lecture on solid mechanics, later recalled that he was startled to hear "what sounded like an enormous hammer" next door in Room 206.

Park Chang-Min, a twenty-seven-year-old engineering student, told reporters that he was sitting in the back of Room 206 when the killer stepped into the room and shot fifty-one-year-old Professor G. V. Loganathan. "He shot the professor and then started to shoot at us. In the blink of an eye it turned into a nightmare," Park later told reporters. "I didn't even feel the bullet hit me in the chest and arm."

The killer had apparently donned a disguise. "He hid his face behind a mask and had his brown-colored cap lowered to his eyes. He wore glasses and something like a black ammo jacket," Park told reporters from his hospital bed. "We were only minutes into the class. There were about fifteen students in the room. I was sitting in the back. The man came in with two handguns and a lot of ammo. He shot the professor first and spread bullets toward us. In a moment, the room turned into a bloody hell."

The graduate class in advanced hydrology in 206 had thirteen students, including Guillermo Colman, thirty-eight, who was shot in the head and shoulder. He later told friends that the killer "started going right down the row. Bam. Bam. Bam." Colman survived because he was covered by the body of Partahi Lumbantoruan, an Indonesian doctoral student who was shot and killed. The attack killed nine of the thirteen graduate students in Room 206. The survivors included Colman, Park Chang-Min, and Nathanial Krause, who were wounded, and Lee Hixon, who fell on the floor and pretended to be dead.

Students in the classrooms across the hall heard the noise, including Clay Violand, a twenty-year-old junior, in the French class taught by Jocelyn Couture-Nowak in Room 207. "About halfway through class we heard the noises," Violand told *Time* magazine. "Someone said something like, 'It's probably just construction.' The noises didn't stop. The teacher stiffened up and said, 'That's not what I think it is, is it?' "

On the third floor, a student from the class taking the accounting exam went across the hall to speak with engineering professor Kevin Granata.

Ashley Brohawn: None of us had even known about the first shootings that happened. We were all in class before the emails actually got sent out. And my teacher came back across the hall and told us, "Okay, let's go across the hall to Kevin Granata's room, Office 307." I remember looking out the windows, seeing people just walking by normally, and I'm like, "Are you sure there's someone down there shooting?" I would have thought people would, you know, be running away or something. And all of a sudden I see them all stop and freeze and just book it the other way, and so that's when we were like, "Okay, something's going wrong here." And we saw the police drive up and that's when we went across to 307 and locked ourselves in. My teacher and Kevin Granata, they were both in the office at the time, and we could hear gunshots, screams, and everything. Granata went on his computer to see if the homepage had said anything about it because none of us really had gone down there other than that one girl. We were still unsure as to what was happening and he checked his email and that's when he found out about the first shootings. He decided to leave to see if he could go down and stop what was happening. I think my teacher was kind of like "Don't do that," but from what I understand, Granata was ex-military or something, so he just went down and that was the last time we saw him.

John Chermak, Virginia Tech instructor and Granata neighbor: Knowing Kevin—I know him fairly well and his character—I didn't have a good feeling about him getting out of there because I knew that he would try to do something to stop it. If he could do something, he was going to try and do something. He's the kind of person to do that. I always jokingly call him Dudley Do Right. So I had a feeling that he may have tried to intervene. Unfortunately my feeling was correct. After the facts came out, we learned he took a class from across his office and brought them into his office and locked them in his office and went downstairs. He was on the third floor at the time, and he went downstairs. Knowing Kevin's character, as I expected, he wasn't in one of those classrooms, but he tried to go help. There are people that had no choice, but he decided . . . he made a decision that he went downstairs to help.

Ishwar Puri: Kevin asked the business students to essentially stay in his office while he went to investigate, which is what he and Wally Grant were trying to see, what was going on, and trying to help. My understanding, anecdotally of course, is that he was shot in front of the French class.

The two ESM professors were later cited for their bravery, for going to the shooting and trying to help. Granata was killed and Grant seriously wounded. Upstairs on the third floor, the students locked in Granata's office were terrified by the noise from below.

Ashley Brohawn: People were calling on their cell phones, calling their parents. A few girls were crying and we were kind of like, "Shh, shut up, shut up, we don't want him hearing!" But they were panicked so they didn't quite listen, but it was, you know, panicked.

The killer, who had emptied his guns on the graduate engineering class in Room 206, reloaded.

Across the hall in Room 207, Jamie Bishop was teaching the German class. "I remember looking at my phone. It was about 9:40," sophomore Trey Perkins told MSNBC. "We started hearing some loud pops. None of us thought it was gunshots. It was not loud like that."

Having heard the noise, Bishop had looked in the hallway but saw nothing. He shut the door, and one of his students suggested that he place something in front of the door just in case the noise was really gunfire.

> **Derek O'Dell:** The lecture continued without interruption until around 9:35 a.m. At that point we heard some loud banging noises, sounding almost like some hammering every second on concrete blocks. Herr B stopped the lecture and started to try and figure out what these noises were. There had been construction going on in the next building over for the past couple months. It seemed very unusual that these noises were so close to where we were, even sounding as if they were on our floor. Someone in the class thought out loud that they were gunshots, but Herr B and others said they weren't loud enough to be gunshots. We sort of were in the process of coming to a class consensus about these noises being construction hammering, when an Asian male wearing a maroon hat, black jacket over a tan ammunition vest, and jeans swung open the door and entered our classroom, Norris 207.

"All of a sudden a door just opened real fast, a guy came in with a gun. I mean, he was very, very deliberate. He didn't say anything. Just came in and started firing," student Garrett Evans later told reporters.

> **Derek O'Dell:** The sound of gunshots started echoing in the small classroom even before the wooden door had hit the doorstop. Herr B was standing at the front and center of the room. The shooter took aim at him first, while still standing in the door frame.

"He shot our teacher," Trey Perkins, twenty, from Yorktown, Virginia, recalled. "And then we all got on the ground real quick."

The killer then turned his weapons on the students. O'Dell, a twenty-year-old from Roanoke, Virginia, sat in the classroom's second row. "He was very calm, very determined, methodical in his killing. He shot as he opened the door. He was going along the front row shooting people," O'Dell told reporters.

> **Derek O'Dell:** I heard two shots go off then saw the gunman's arm swing around the room. He started firing once it stopped on the student sitting right next to the door. At point-blank range he fired a shot into this young man's face. He ended up surviving, thankfully. He then proceeded to fire at the people in the front rows and near the door. I was shot sometime in this period. As soon as I saw him swing the gun around and fire the third shot, I began to frantically try and get underneath my desk. At first it almost seemed like the shooter might have been firing blanks or rubber bullets. Then I saw the bullet casing fly out of the gun and my professor fall.

"He never said a word the whole time. I've never seen a straighter face," Trey Perkins said. "There were a couple of screams, but for the most part it was eerily silent, other than the gunfire."

"He was just a normal-looking kid, Asian, but he had on a Boy Scout–type outfit. He wore a tan button-up vest, and this black vest, maybe it was for ammo or something," Erin Sheehan said in a media interview. "He seemed very thorough about it, getting everyone down," she said. "I was screaming 'oh my God' and then I realized I should stop because he'll know I'm alive."

> **Derek O'Dell:** As he swung the gun around his eyes fixated on the people in the front row for a split second. As the barrel of the gun and the shooter's eyes moved back across the room, he briefly

> stopped on me. I saw into his eyes, his face darkened by the shadow from his maroon cap. They seemed completely black and there appeared to be emptiness behind them. Sometimes you can look into a person's eyes and see their life story and the hardships they've encountered. With his there was nothing. They didn't even seem to be that angry, and the fiery, fierce look that you might expect in a person who is willing to kill until they're stopped was eerily absent. The gunshots continued to echo off the cinder-block walls. With each echo it seemed like someone was getting closer to death, like the room would get darker and darker and the life was almost getting sucked out of the room. He proceeded to walk calmly and methodically around to the window side of the room away from the door. He never said a thing the entire time, just a calm, methodical demeanor determined to kill as many of us as he could. He continued firing until the room lay motionless. The loud echoing sounds of gunshots had ceased and now all that was left were the moaning of injured people. I had scrambled to the back of the room underneath the desks after I saw the first few shots.

Erin Sheehan lay among the shot students on the floor and hoped the killer would think she was dead. "I saw bullets hit people's bodies. There was blood everywhere," she told reporters.

At the back of the class, Trey Perkins lay behind overturned desks. "I'm not sure how long it lasted," he later recalled. "It felt like a really long time but it was probably only about a minute or so. He didn't say a single word the whole time. He stopped to reload twice. The shots seemed to last forever."

The killer fired several more rounds then went back into the hallway. "He walked out of the door, went back, started shooting again, bang, bang, bang, other rooms," Garrett Evans, who was shot in the leg, recalled for reporters.

Derek O'Dell: He left our room, the door open, and went down the hall and we heard more gunshots. As soon as I heard more shots, I jumped to the top of the desk I was under, and made my way as fast as I could to the front of the room. Most of this was on top of the desks, as the two aisleways were strewn with backpacks and belongings and sadly a few of my classmates. They had been shot and lay motionless, fallen out of their seats. I was up at the front of the room and shut the door as quickly as I could after I heard more shots fired down the hall. I feared that class was facing the same fate that we had encountered a few moments earlier. In all he was probably in our room less than one minute, maybe around forty-five seconds. It seemed like an eternity, especially when it replays through my mind.

O'Dell and Katelyn Carney rushed to the door and shut it, putting their feet against it to hold it in place while lying on the floor so that if the killer returned and fired through the door, the shots would maybe pass over them.

Derek O'Dell: I was at the windowless wooden door with my tennis shoe wedged at the base where the carpet and door met below the door handle. At this point I finally realized what this numbness in my arm was. I had been shot, and now my arm was bleeding. I took off my brown leather belt and wrapped underneath my fleece jacket just above my right bicep. I pulled it tight in my teeth and tried to stop the blood flow. The shots from down the hall were still reverberating through the hall and even would shake the door as each shot was fired. I pulled my cell phone out of my pocket and dialed 911. The responder answered and I said, "There is a man with a gun shooting and there are a lot of people down in my room." I told the responder my location and a description of the shooter. At this point the shooting had stopped at the end of the hall. I could hear footsteps coming closer down the hall. Now Katelyn was at the

> door helping barricade with our bodies. The desks were too light and the podium was bolted to the floor. It was our only option in the amount of time—only about two minutes—that we had before he came back to our door. Trey and Erin, who were both uninjured, tried to get help out of the second-story windows and tried to figure some way out of this classroom. Trey tended to a classmate who was shot in the thigh, and tried to stop the bleeding.

An Eagle Scout, Perkins turned his efforts to treating the wounded as best he could while Erin Sheehan went to the window to yell for help.

"I told people that were still up and conscious, 'Just be quiet because we don't want him to think there are people in here because he'll come back in,' " Perkins said.

> **Derek O'Dell:** We heard the steps stop outside our door, then the door handle rotated down. He was back again. This time he met resistance as he tried to get into the room. He tried to force his way into the room and my foot moved back an inch or two from where it was. He had gotten the door open enough to see we were still alive and behind the door. We managed to force the door shut again and the handle rotated to its resting position again. It seemed like we had stopped him, until we heard a shot fired and a bullet came through the door. Katelyn and I were both crouching; I was where the hinges were with our legs stretched across the bottom, and Katelyn was near the other side of the door with her hands pushed up near the handle of the door. The first bullet came through above the handle, then they started getting lower. He continued to fire four or five more shots. Katelyn was hit in the hand in the first couple shots. Then the bullets started coming through closer to my side of the door. I prayed quietly that they would stop. The last bullet came through my unzipped jacket right over the cross I wear on a chain.

It had passed through my open jacket and not hit me. God had answered my prayers and the shots had stopped temporarily. He left our room and went the other way down the hall and we heard more gunfire from the direction of the first shots.

In Room 204, Professor Liviu Librescu had looked out into the hallway and realized the circumstances. He shut the door and braced it with his body to stall the gunman and give his students time to get through the windows and drop to the ground below. Richard Mallalieu, twenty-three, from Luray, Virginia, said the class was viewing a virtual project when the noise started.

"I was in a mechanics class, engineering class," said student Josh Wargo. "We were sitting in class and all of a sudden heard loud banging noises and thought it could be construction. We could hear people screaming 'Oh my God!' from next door . . . and everyone started to panic."

"It started about nine-thirtyish. I put my head out to see what was going on. I heard a girl scream and it sounded like gunshots," said twenty-three-year-old Matt Webster.

A group of Librescu's students rushed to the windows toward the back of the class and began punching and kicking them out. The two-story drop seemed precipitous, but it quickly became clear as the gunfire sounded nearer, that it was the best option. Richard Mallalieu said the "steady pop, pop, pop, pop" convinced them it was time to jump. One girl landed on her back; another student fell and broke both legs. Mallalieu dangled from the windowsill and then let go to help shorten his fall.

Karla Rothenberg: I was on my way to my 10:10 economics class in Robeson. It was about 9:45 a.m. and I was walking toward the tunnel behind Burruss Hall. As I walked up the steps beside Patton Hall I noticed that quad to be very empty and eerie. I was actually on the phone with my mother—as I am every morning at that time—and she was informing me of the "shooting incident" outside of West AJ earlier that morning. My mother is a huge worrier, and since we had two bomb threats she checked the Virginia Tech website every morning to make sure nothing was happening. Thankfully, she had read the homepage that morning and was able to let me know about West AJ or I would have been completely clueless on what I was about to see. As I walked between Patton and Norris halls I noticed two young men. One was crawling very slowly and the other looked as if he was jumping out of a tree. I thought this was very odd but continued walking, thinking they were doing some sort of surveying-type project—don't ask me why I thought this. As I was watching those two, I told my mom, "Oh, I hear the sirens over at West AJ." However, I was wrong. Those sirens were coming right to where I was. Within seconds, a gray-haired man opened the door to Patton Hall and screamed for me to get off the quad and get inside the building. At this point I pretty much froze, realized what was happening, and told my mom, "Oh my God, someone was just shot in front of me!" and then hung up on her. To this day, I'm not sure if those two people had been shot or if they were just injured from jumping out the window, but some reports say that the last two students to jump out of Professor Librescu's room were shot and I think it is very likely those were the only two students I saw. I started to run toward Patton and my worst recurring nightmare came true: I was running and I felt like I wasn't moving. My initial thought was that a gunman was in that quad shooting people and the only ones out there were those two boys and myself. I have never been so scared in my life.

The numerous police in and around campus had gotten to Norris Hall quickly but were apparently stymied by the locks the killer had placed on the door. Other factors, such as a lack of protective gear, may have played a role as well. Virginia State Police sergeant Matthew Brannock told *Newsweek* that he felt vulnerable without his bulletproof vest. Brannock said he first took cover behind his car, then advanced to a breezeway connected to Norris. He told the magazine that when the shooting stopped he entered the building.

Up in Room 204, the last few students were trying to get Librescu to abandon the door to save himself. "We had heard the gunfire coming from the classroom behind us, and we just reacted to it and headed for the windows," Caroline Merrey later told reporters. "Professor Librescu never made an attempt to leave . . . I really don't think me or my other classmates would be here if it wasn't for him."

She looked back before she jumped and Librescu was still holding the door.

"His English was not good, and it must have been hard for him to communicate in this situation, so he talked to us with his hands. He used his hands to tell us to get back. We heard the sounds getting closer. The shots were moving toward us, down the hallway," said student Andrey Andreyev, who tried to pull Librescu away from the door. "He pushed me back. He stood at the door and wouldn't move. He pushed me toward the back of the room, a corner. He himself would not move. He just stood there."

One of the other remaining students, twenty-year-old Alex Calhoun, thought to turn over desks to create a hideout, then realized that his best hope was to jump. He jumped and made it to safety, but the two students who jumped after him were shot when the killer ran to the window and fired outside. The killer gained entry by shooting the seventy-six-year-old Librescu through the closed door. Once inside, the killer shot the professor at point-blank range. Matt

Webster and three other students remained in the room when Librescu was killed. The gunman then shot a female student and turned the gun on Webster, who had curled up on the floor. The shot grazed Webster's head before coming to rest in his upper right arm. "I lay there and let him think he had done his job," Webster later told reporters. "I wasn't moving at all, hoping he wouldn't come back."

The shooter left and apparently returned to the German classroom.

> **Derek O'Dell:** There was about another two minutes before he returned for the last time. I sat there at the door looking around at the carnage he had caused and just imagined what he might have done in the other classrooms that he had entered. I sat there barricading the door, hearing the gunshots go off in the other rooms, and fearing that he might return again. I sat there in shock glancing at the side of the room near the door. I wanted to help all of those who couldn't help themselves, all of those who had fallen on the floor, bleeding out. I figured being a Biology major and wanting to be a veterinarian qualified me as the best bet in helping my classmates and professor until VT rescue arrived. It was hard to sit there knowing that he might return and open the door again and finish what he had started in our room. I was torn and I still do not know if I could have helped them more by staying at the door, or by helping staunch the bleeding.

With O'Dell, Erin Sheehan, and Katelyn Carney holding the door for dear life, Trey Perkins attempted to treat the wounded. Classmate Garrett Evans had been shot in both legs. Perkins tied his pullover sweater around one leg and Evans's tank top to tie off the other. Nearby, a female classmate had been shot in the mouth, so

Perkins held a sweatshirt over her face. As O'Dell was dialing 911 again, the killer returned.

"I guess he heard us still talking," said Sheehan.

Derek O'Dell: He returned one last time. I was still at the door with my foot wedged at the bottom, but this time I had tried to avoid leaving the core part of my body in the path of potential bullets that might come through the door. I only had my left leg and my two arms pushed up against the lower half of the door, the other leg . . . using it to brace my body. Katelyn was still able to help blockade the door with her other hand and legs. This time I think Trey was helping us, too. He tried to force his way into the room again, but he could not turn the handle far enough to unlatch the door.

"The door opened about three inches and I saw his face," Evans later told the media. "I thought he would put the gun through and shoot, but they pushed the door closed. Bang, bang, four shots through the door."

"Fortunately, we were lying down and weren't in front of the door," Perkins said.

"It was almost like you had to fight for your life. If you didn't, you died," O'Dell told reporters afterward.

"I saw Satan at work and God at work at the same time. Evil, evil spirit was going through that boy, that shooter. I know, I felt it. I felt God move me away so he didn't shoot me in my head," Evans said.

Derek O'Dell: He gave up on forcing his way in with his body and fired two shots into the door. Both of these were fired higher up the door and had missed anyone inside the class. He then gave up trying to get into our class and headed back down the hall toward the

French class. We heard no more than ten shots after he left our door before the gunfire stopped.

From there the killer paid one last visit to Room 206, where he shot more students. Guillermo Colman and Lee Hixon played dead and miraculously survived. Police finally managed to blast the locks on the doors and entered the building. Hearing the blast on the doors, the killer knew it was time to take his own life.

Brannock, the state police sergeant, told *Newsweek* he entered Norris and was immediately taken aback by "the amount of blood in the hallway . . . There were bodies all over. It was just overwhelming. I had never been in a war environment, but I thought, this must be what it's like. Disaster and chaos. People screaming and crying, sobbing out in panic."

The responders—police, rescue squad personnel, emergency workers, investigators—all would say the same things over and over again after viewing the scene:

"I can't get what I saw out of my mind."

"This has changed my life forever."

"It took a long while after everything became quiet before police entered the room," said Park Chang-Min. "They said, 'Anyone who is okay, raise their hands.' Me and two others got up. All the others were either lying facedown on their desks or sprawled on the floor."

Derek O'Dell: We heard yelling in the hall from the direction of the first shots that were fired. It sounded like police officers.

Ashley Brohawn: After being locked in Kevin Granata's office for about five to seven minutes, we started hearing yelling in the hall, but we couldn't quite tell if it was the police or what. Someone knocked on the door so my teacher cracked it just a little bit and it was the police and they kicked open the door and aimed their guns at us and told us to put our hands on our head and just run and don't take any of our stuff with us. I was fine in the office until the police came with the guns, that was when my breaking point was. Police were lined all the way outside the building, all the way up the stairwell in the hallway. And they were all aiming their guns at us and they told us to put our hands on our head and just run until we got across the Drillfield, so that's what we did. We didn't have anyone leading us. They were kind of like, "Go, go, go." There was a ton of them out there as well. And we jumped down, there's a little ledge right there, we all jumped down there, and ran. Once we hit the sidewalk, one of the cops was there asking us if any of us had seen it, the person, or if we knew anything. It was like a quick like, "Did anyone see anything?" You know, and then after that when we were all "No, no, we don't know." We booked it across the Drillfield and didn't stop until we got across.

Karla Rothenberg: We sat inside Patton for a while and watched everything that was happening. It was terrifying. My mother felt so fortunate that I found out what was happening before most, and she was able to get ahold of me before all of the phone lines were tied up. I watched doors being breached and a few students from the German class run out—I recognized them in their news interviews later that day. Shortly after they released them, two SWAT officers came into our building to find the entrance to the roof. At that point, I began to panic thinking they're going to have a shoot, out between Norris and Patton and I'd be right in the middle. However, right after that an officer ran in the building and told us to leave. We all walked outside (via the Drillfield entrance of Patton, not the Norris side) and were very nervous and confused about where they wanted us to go and why they were making us go out into harm's way. As soon as we walked outside of the building an officer who was kneeling behind his vehicle with his gun drawn by McBryde screamed "*Run!*" At that point, I ran like I've never ran before. It was horrifying.

Jason Haggard, Tech student: I was coming out of a 9 a.m. class in McBryde through the exit that oversees the parking lot area between Holden, Norris, and Randolph. When we first tried to exit the building people were hovering around the door. There were police. The police were protecting all the exits to Holden and Norris so we guessed that the shooter was in one of those two buildings. Then we saw people in groups of eight or ten being transported across, and then we saw an older white gentleman, probably a professor, holding his arm. And we guessed he was shot, there was blood coming out of his arm pretty bad. He came out of Randolph. We saw a girl being carried away on a rolling stretcher. There was a lot of blood and she was carried away in an ambulance. A few minutes later another ambulance came, but we didn't know where they ran to. Then they brought another body out. For a little while it was stagnant and we saw a few paramedics covered in blood, and then we realized it wasn't just a couple people hurt across campus.

Theresa Walsh: You could kind of tell he was done, that he had killed himself, because it was a very awkward silence. But also the police were coming through and were screaming.

Derek O'Dell: The shooting had stopped and I only heard police officers. I decided to open the door and look quickly to see if the police were out in the hall. I stuck my head out in the hall, and almost instantaneously I saw the officers focus their guns on me. I think I was the first one out of any of the rooms on the second floor. Everyone else's barricades of the doors had eventually given way to the fury of gunfire. Once I saw the police and all their guns focused on me, I immediately brought my head back into the safety of the classroom. The officers didn't know what the shooter looked like, which room the shooter might have been in, or how many shooters there might have been. I realized this when they said to me, "Come out with your hands up." I followed their orders and came out with one arm up in the air while still holding my belt in my mouth and my injured right arm down. I came out with Trey, Katelyn, and Erin, who were all able to walk out under their own power. We quickly made our way behind the police line of about eight officers all armed, some with shotguns and some with Kevlar vests on. Two officers led the four of us from my class down the stairwell to the front door. We encountered one of the chains he had used on the front door. This one was still locked and intact. The officer with a shotgun blew the lock off with one shot and we then ran as fast as we could out of the building. Katelyn and I were shot and bleeding so we tried to find an ambulance. We were some of the first out of the building and the first to an ambulance. There were three or four ambulances near McBryde Hall. Our exit from Norris was the one that faces the Drillfield, so our journey to an ambulance was about two hundred yards. They were trying to figure out who was worse, so it took about five minutes before my ambulance went to Montgomery Regional.

The shooting was over, but the great surge of fear and horror had just begun to course through the Tech community and campus. One of the custodial staff in Norris Hall told police that he was sure there was a second shooter. Police searched the building as if a second shooter might be present. With these concerns, many classes across campus would remain on lockdown for more than two hours.

Ishwar Puri: One of our professors comes out and says something like, "Excuse me." And I immediately hear several police voices saying, "Freeze! Turn yourself toward the window. Put your hands up." Things of that nature. And the professor told me later that he had six guns pointing at him, and he was patted down, etcetera. When we were evacuated, there was a state trooper who asked our custodian, "Are you sure that you saw a second person?" They were concerned in the beginning that there were two gunmen in the building. That gunman could have been any one of us.

The police thoroughly searched the building and identified any survivors among the bodies. That process kept many in Norris Hall and surrounding academic buildings locked in their rooms until after eleven.

Ishwar Puri: Then we were evacuated and I remember telling the staff and the students, "Put your hands out. Don't take anything with you." I remember coming out and I remember seeing Vince Houston, he's a campus police officer, and, boy, was I glad to see him. He says, "Oh, I'm very happy to see you." I guess he knew I was in the building. He and I served on the Race and Institution Task Force together.

Amid all the carnage police found on the second floor of Norris Hall, there was a pocket of safety, Room 205, where the students had been able to hold the door from the beginning.

Theresa Walsh: I think we were the last classroom that could be moved out of Norris. We were definitely the last one on that hallway. So police were screaming and swearing to get the "F" down and "Where is he?" We remember them yelling, "We've got the shooter," and that they were looking for another one just in case. Being a police officer in Blacksburg and looking at the scene you'd have to be thinking that one man could not possibly have done all this. They went through all the classrooms and when they got to ours they were not allowed to open the door. We had to let them in. All my classmates were asking, "How do we know if it's going to be the police?" I suggested they check the shoes since they all would be the same, kind of uniform. All the guys that were holding the door would look under it for multiple boots. We asked them to identify themselves and they did as officer such and such or sergeant such and such. When they came into the room we had to go to the back of the classroom and had to have our hands up and they asked if there was a shooter in here.

Ruiqi Zhang: We were told to get our hands in the air . . . then we were escorted out of Norris into Randolph. They just wanted to make sure everybody was okay and the gunman wasn't in the room. We were told to stay put until the situation cleared up. I was questioned by the authorities as a witness. I think we were the only classroom in the hallway where everybody was all right. We acted really quickly and like I've said, God was definitely watching out for us. We did everything right. Otherwise, maybe I wouldn't be here right now. My adrenaline is still going. I'm just glad that we got out okay. I can't imagine what the others involved might be going through.

Theresa Walsh: They finally cleared the hallway and we had to go in a single-file line. We had a police officer in the front and on the side and behind us. Then we ran out of Norris the long way and had to run through the hall which had a huge bloodstain in the middle with a smear mark that was at least twenty feet long and an inch wide. I remember I didn't want to look, but a part of me wanted to make sure other people were okay. I looked in the classroom that the shooter had come out of [initially] which I think was 206 or 208.

This was running by; we weren't just jogging by either, we were sprinting. I was the last one out. I looked in that classroom and saw at least seven bodies not moving. The worst part about it was the first body I saw was a kid who had been sitting in the same exact seat as I sit in my class. I sit right next to the door on the front row, and if the shooter had come into our classroom I probably would have been the first one to get picked off. It was hard looking in there, but I think I was in adrenaline mode. I was in shock mode for four days. Part of me still hasn't dealt with it; I can't really feel it. I remember feeling like, "Did this really happen? Is this real?" There were people not moving in there. TV does not do justice to what actually occurs in real life.

Tommy McDearis, pastor, Blacksburg Baptist Church; chaplain, Blacksburg Police Department: I made it a point to be there at Norris Hall with the other chaplains while the police officers were bringing the bodies out of the building. It was an awful event, an awful scene. I wanted to be there for all those officers that needed to talk and to give them the opportunity to do that. There's just a myriad of feelings coming out of that. There was a lot of intense sadness, intense anger. A lot of it was just bewilderment. And they were professionals; they were doing their jobs. They were doing them very well, but it was tough. It was a hard time.

Ishwar Puri: I later got my cell phone bill. There's a call at 9:48 to my wife saying something's going on. I called my wife, who's a middle school teacher in Blacksburg Middle School, just to tell her, "Look, there's been an incident in Norris Hall. You're probably going to hear about this." And she said, "Well, we've been wondering about it because we've been in lockdown since morning." So all the local area high schools, middle schools, elementary schools were locked down since morning.

Beth Levinson, Ishwar Puri's wife; Blacksburg Middle School teacher: During my second-period class, we had an announcement that we were going on lockdown. That means that we lock our doors, and since we're in a pod, there's four classrooms that we need to account for so we also have to lock the doors for our pod. I initially thought, "Oh, this is just one of those drills" because I'm just usually unaware about them; I told the kids that I was sure it was just a drill that I didn't know about. So it just went on and I had the kids do their work. And then, that period ended, and the principal announced that we were still on lockdown and that we needed to close our blinds. So I just closed the blinds, and I kept going. At some point, my husband called me, and he just said, "There's something going on in Norris." So I thought, "Oh, this is why we're on lockdown." He was calling me like every ten or fifteen minutes, and he was just saying, "I think there's a shoot-out between someone in our building and the police" because he was just locked in his office and didn't know what was going on. I was locked in the school, and we were told to have our computers off, TVs off, radios off; they didn't want these kids knowing anything. I was in the room with the department head of mechanical engineering's son, and half of the kids in my class somehow are involved with Tech; the last thing you want is to be locked in a classroom with kids flipping out. Some of the kids knew for some reason that there had been a shooting in West AJ earlier. We still really did not know what was going on, and we were told not to tell anybody what's going on if we knew. When my husband called to tell me about a shoot-out, I told him to stay down because it was really scary.

Ishwar Puri: As I was talking to her, I saw Wally Grant, one of our professors, one of the faculty members in my department, being escorted by a police officer toward Hancock Hall; and it looked as though he'd been injured. He was holding his arm up to his head. I said, "Oh my God. I think he's been shot." But I didn't believe it. I mean, shot? That's incredible.

Beth Levinson: Now it was almost lunchtime, and we were on lockdown with the same kids. Ish had told me that Wally Grant had been shot and that he was getting really more and more nervous, but I was sort of still in the mind-set of keeping the kids busy. And I wasn't panicking or anything. When lunch came, everybody was getting dismissed for lunch and the kids were all chatting about what was going on. Somehow, it got out that something had happened at Tech because parents were text messaging their kids saying that they're okay. Ish just said that I had to call Linda Granata to ask her if Kevin went in to work or if she knows where he is. So I thought that, since they couldn't find Kevin, I said, "Oh, Kevin's probably in an ambulance just helping somebody." My husband also said that he thinks Liviu had been shot. Then he said he needed to go to the hospital to see the kids who have been shot. So I was like "The kids who have been shot? What?" So there was this huge gap between thinking there was this shoot-out between some guy and the cops. Now all of a sudden, kids have been shot. They can't find Kevin, and Liviu's been shot. The math teacher, who had actually been absent, came in crying and said, "Oh my gosh, they said this is the biggest shooting in history." And then it hit me.

Jenna Lazenby Nelson, news bureau manager, Office of University Relations: The next half hour seemed eerily familiar to the shootings and lockdown on the first day of school. I sat in the media building with my coworkers, watching the television, listening to the police scanner, discussing the situation and awaiting further direction from Burruss Hall. Same as the August shootings, my phone began to ring incessantly, as national media editors and reporters wanted somebody to interview. My response was the same. "At this point I cannot comment on the situation. I'll have to take your name and number and have somebody get back with you." It was a little after ten when I first received news that the situation might be worse than I ever could have imagined. I was in a coworker's office when it came across their police scanner. "Thirty-one black." Of course, not being familiar with police jargon, that meant nothing to me, but my coworker had been listening to police scanners long enough to know what it meant. In shock I walked down the hall to the closest TV. The local news was reporting one dead and seven or eight injured. As I started to recount to others what had come across the scanner, nobody seemed to believe me. I don't think anybody could believe or wanted to believe that somehow thirty-one people were dead on our campus. Then there it was again. "Thirty-one black" came across the police scanner. Almost concurrently the body count began to rise on the television. As I watched the TV footage of police officers running around campus, just moments from my office, and listened to the sounds of the police sirens outside my building, for a moment I thought I was in a dream. However, when a coworker stepped into the office and said, "Looks like we have a Columbine on our hands," I knew that it wasn't a dream. It was a nightmare, and the August shootings didn't come close to what this situation was.

Brittney Asbury: When we flipped the channel to CNN they reported that there were thirty-two fatalities. We shook it off and thought they had gotten confused, because they were getting their information from the local station that kept saying casualties. We all knew there was no way there were thirty-two people killed.

Jason Haggard, senior Mechanical Engineering major: It's almost surreal. . . . It's almost too much to take in. It's just almost not real, not happening. It's just Blacksburg; it's just Virginia Tech.

Neal Turnage, Planet Blacksburg sports editor: We stopped in the Schultz dining hall at 9:45 so we could open our laptops and check our email. At that time we saw the email notice that the campus was being shut down. I looked over my shoulder and saw a custodian locking the front doors of the building. Not wanting to miss my wife Ashley's flight at the airport in Roanoke, we quickly shut our laptops and rushed out the back doors to the parking lot. It still didn't occur to us that we were in any real danger. From that point we left campus and started our trip to the airport. It was about that time that we started to catch on that this might be really serious. Before we even made it to the interstate we saw multiple police cars speeding toward campus. Once we made it to the interstate the mood started to get very unsettling. More and more police cars flew past us toward Blacksburg as we traveled in the other direction. Then came the ambulances. One. Two. Three. Four. Five. Six. It was clear this was not an isolated domestic dispute but an instance of someone "going postal." Ashley called her office and found out that Burruss Hall was shut down and the workers and families visiting the university were locked inside but safe. She heard that the hospital in Blacksburg was no longer accepting patients.

Ishwar Puri: We were sent to Randolph Hall, where there were just clusters of people standing around. I thought, "Oh my God. I've got faculty members, staff, and students in that building. What if they were hurt?" So I got hold of Scott Case, my assistant chair, and I said, "Scott, we've got to set up a command center, and we've got to find out who's in that building who might have been in harm's way." We didn't have any laptops or computers because we'd left everything in Norris, but we had a couple of students, including some who jumped out of the building. They'd been evacuated to Randolph. And so the students loaned us their computers. Thank God we have a wireless campus. We went into one of the Mechanical Engineering Department offices and requested a little command center or cubicle and we were given one so we could use the Xerox machine. Scott fired up one of the laptops, got on the banner, found out which engineering science and mechanics class was there in Norris Hall, and who was teaching it, Liviu Librescu. We downloaded the list of students, and we now had their phone numbers, because most of them had chosen to provide the university with phone numbers. So then we developed a script for our phone calls. This is our undergraduate coordinator; Scott Case, who's the associate department head; myself; and a few students, undergraduate students who were there. The script was: "We understand there has been an incident in Norris Hall. Have you heard from such-and-such?" Some of the numbers might have been cell phone numbers, some of the numbers might have been parents' numbers. We were hoping the kids would call their parents if they'd survived.

As the department head of engineering science and mechanics, Ishwar Puri began to realize that he possibly had a number of faculty and students injured or affected by the incident. So he requested permission to leave to go to Montgomery Regional Hospital to check on those injured.

Ezra "Bud" Brown: Eventually a uniformed officer knocked on the door, informed us that they were closing McBryde Hall and telling us that we should go home. Sam and his friend left, a few minutes later my wife, Jo, called, and I heard her say such things as "Virginia Tech is on CNN . . . a shooting in Norris Hall . . . are you okay?" "Yes, I'm fine. They closed McBryde, and I'll be home soon." A short while later, I looked out and saw that the frenzied activity outside Norris had stopped. People were walking, not running. As I walked home, I saw what seemed like dozens of police cars—actually hundreds—and began to realize that something really horrific had happened. I got home, hugged and kissed my wife, walked into our den, and watched CNN in slack-jawed amazement. My sense of astonishment and horror rose with each new report about the number of slain students and faculty members . . . after which my mind became blank. I had no recollection of the rest of That Day until days later when I asked my wife, "What did I do on the afternoon of April 16?"

CHAPTER 2

Planet Blacksburg

The old line is that journalism is the first draft of history. At Virginia Tech that Monday, April 16, 2007, journalism became the first step in a community's long, bitter grieving process. Yet to begin working, student journalists first had to somehow conquer their fears.

Roland Lazenby, journalism instructor: I always tell my journalism students at Virginia Tech that "tragedy" is one of the most overworked words in the language of news. "What is a tragedy?" I ask. "A play by Shakespeare," they say, intoning the answer I've sought to instill in them. "You don't need to tell the reader something's a tragedy," I tell them. "When something rises to the level of tragedy, the reader will know it. The reader is perfectly capable of deciding what's a tragedy without your hyping it." I've taught three media writing, or basic journalism, courses for each of the past sixteen semesters at Virginia Tech. Like clockwork each semester, I've run about a hundred young students through the rigors of the trade. Get the facts, I tell them. "If your mother says she loves you, check it out. Make sure. Get confirmation from a second source. Ask your daddy, or somebody else who really knows." I tell them about the pain of making mistakes, that I did things as a reporter for which I will surely burn in hell. They stare back at me like I've lost my mind. "Now they know," as good friend Marcus Morris told me after the event.

Tricia Sangalang, media writing student: Class began promptly at 9:05 in Shanks 160, a computer lab. Roland Lazenby began talking about press releases in a vehement tone, keeping all twenty or so of us engaged in the discussion, well, as attentive as college students can be at that hour of the morning with computers sitting in front of them. I often checked my email and perused Facebook periodically through class discussions simply because the computer was accessible in front of me.

Roland Lazenby: I had arrived earlier that morning and opened the heavy, spring-loaded door to Shanks Hall Room 160 and jammed a rubber doorstop in place to keep it wide open. I'd had a running battle with the university for two years about the doorstops. [Without them] the doors would quickly close and lock automatically after each person entered. Access was granted only by a three-number code, which meant that students entering class constantly knocked, forcing me to get up from my work and let each one in. I had quickly decided to use a stop to prop open the door, which worked fine for a couple of years, until the university decided that was no longer appropriate. One of the supervisors for Shanks Hall issued a directive that the doors should remain locked all the time. I ignored the directive and continued to prop open the door so students could get into my class. It wasn't too long before building custodians began confiscating the stops, which ignited a running battle of sorts. I'd put a stop under the door, and they would quietly take it away the next morning. "I can't believe this is higher education," I'd complain, just loud enough to keep my students smiling. Strangely, I arrived at the start of school this year and discovered I'd won the test of wills. There at the entrance to my classroom was a brand-new university-issued stop. Stranger still, the first day of classes for the 2006–07 school year was the first time we'd ever really needed the locked doors. A shooter had supposedly killed a security officer and a policeman and was loose on campus that August day. Word raced through the student body that the shooter was terrorizing the campus just yards from my room. The kids were glad for the heavy locked doors that day, although we later learned that the shooter had actually been hiding across campus on a remote athletic field. That day had impressed on me that safety is an annoying concept, right up until the exact moment that you really need it. Funny how quickly that little lesson faded from my mind. Eight months later I had forgotten it entirely.

Omar Maglalang, media writing student: Lazenby left the room briefly but came back to pass out several press release sheets. By this time my classroom was filling up with countless students looking tired and restless like me. After passing out the sheets, class started approximately 9:05 a.m.

Roland Lazenby: I had actually arrived about eight the morning of April 16 to do some extra copying for a new lesson I had to distribute to my students. The halls of Shanks and most other academic buildings are mostly deserted that time of day. Kids prefer to take classes at midday or later, after they've had a little time to sleep in. I always figure the students who take the early classes have a little extra pluck. Sure enough, I walked into class that Monday and found my usual group bright-eyed and ready to go. I rewarded them with a talk about agenda-setting and the business of public relations. I'm a boisterous, often rambling, lecturer, striding about the classroom when I see their eyes going half-mast so that I don't lose them altogether.

Omar Maglalang: I believe it was a lecture on how to write opinion pieces, but I'm not quite sure. We didn't start talking about public relations until near the end of class. I often wondered the symbolic nature of these blurs of time in my mind. Why are some scenes like this one forgotten from my memory and where did they go?

Roland Lazenby: Upon my arrival at work that morning, I had learned that there had been a shooting at the dorm West Ambler Johnston, commonly called West AJ, that housed about nine hundred students. Frankly I was preoccupied with the busy week ahead and the morning lecture and thought little of it, even though the university had already been shaken by a couple of recent bomb threats. Some of the students, however, were already cutting their eyes nervously as class started.

Kristina Ticknor, media writing student: A student sitting in front of her computer informed the professor of a recent email she had just received at 9:26 that read: "A shooting incident occurred at West Ambler Johnston earlier this morning. Police are on the scene and are investigating. The university community is urged to be cautious and are asked to contact Virginia Tech Police if you observe anything suspicious or with information on the case." With this news the professor was shocked. He told students to take a pause in the class instruction and to contact any family and friends who might be concerned. I text messaged my roommate and a few hall-mates to let them know that I was safe in class.

Tricia Sangalang: At 9:50 a.m. another email was sent. "A gunman is loose on campus. Stay in buildings until further notice. Stay away from all windows." My eyes widened. I went numb. I sat in my chair, with my back to the large glass windows of the classroom, and I wondered who I should call and how I should react. I quickly texted one of my roommates who I knew had a class at 10:10 telling her to stay home.

Roland Lazenby: Not long after that, a frightened-looking woman, a university employee, came to the door at Shanks 160 and said the earlier shooting incident had worsened and moved to nearby academic buildings, that a shooter or shooters might be loose on campus. I looked at the door propped wide open, kicked away the stop, and quickly shut it. Moments later, those students sitting near the big windows of our ground floor, corner room said they thought they maybe heard some shots. I told them to get away from the windows, to move across the room and get on the floor. I told one of my students to make sure the classroom's back door was locked. Then I switched out the lights. If the shooters were nearby, no sense in giving them any clue the room was occupied. The twenty students huddled together and looked very frightened. I decided to keep lecturing, usually a perfect sedative. But after about ten minutes it became clear that was only adding to their torture. The students were understandably upset.

Tricia Sangalang: Students frantically gathered their belongings and sat on the floor behind the center row of tables. I took out my cell phone, and as I attempted to press the buttons, my fingers, usually quite nimble when I text or make a phone call, became almost too stiff to dial the numbers. "Contacts." "Mom work." I said, in the calmest voice I could, "There was a shooting on campus. But I just wanted to call and tell you that I'm okay." My mom, completely unaware something had happened, asked where I was and who I was with. I assured her I was safe in my classroom among my classmates and teacher.

Kristina Ticknor: It was at this point when I truly became petrified. I sent my boyfriend a text message that read, "I'm safe. Gunman loose on campus. Someone shot on my floor of the dorm." The professor attempted at continuing our class discussion at first, not knowing quite how to handle this news. After the two recent bomb threats, little did our class know the magnitude of tragedy that was occurring two buildings over.

Kevin Lancaster, media writing student: After continuing to teach without the lights on, Roland Lazenby finally told us to get away from the windows and we moved to one side of the room after students received an email about a gunman being on campus. Having to do so really got my heart going, realizing that this was really happening.

Kristina Ticknor: Sitting on the floor, we listened to the police sirens and indistinct loudspeaker announcing that we should stay inside until further notice. The message repeated over and over as we sat there waiting for information and any sign of relief. I knew that if I didn't call my mother, she would soon turn on the television and see the news. When I called her from under my desk, the first words out of my mouth were "Mom, I'm safe." I wanted her to at least know that before I relayed to her the horror that was unfolding outside my classroom walls. Other friends began calling me to check that I was okay. A close childhood friend and resident of the sixth floor of West Ambler Johnston told me that she risked her life by running to the fourth floor to check on me after hearing the news of the first two shootings.

Tricia Sangalang: Classmates began receiving text messages and instant messages informing them that more shootings were taking place in Norris, an engineering building not too far from Shanks Hall, where my class was located.

Kristina Ticknor: The numbers began to grow exponentially. Five to seven shots had been fired. . . . A professor was wounded. . . . Someone had come out of Burruss Hall bleeding . . . ten confirmed dead . . . twenty confirmed dead. It wasn't until my professor heard the news of twenty to thirty confirmed deaths when I truly saw the terror in his eyes, as he slammed his hands on the desk and demanded that his students confirm their sources. Being a professional reporter, it was my professor's instinct to react to the situation by turning our classroom into a bustling newsroom. He figured it would help us get our minds off of the tragedy and fear that we were experiencing.

Roland Lazenby: After the August shootings and lockdown I had been disappointed that I hadn't pushed my students to begin reporting on the incident. I decided on this morning that I wasn't going to have more regrets about inaction. The Virginia Tech community needed information, and we were going to provide it. We had the ideal vehicle, too. A year earlier, one of my students, Andrew Mager, and I had started up a student-run news website, planetblacksburg.com. "We'll get information and start posting on our site," I told the students. Some of them understandably seemed frozen with fear. Others, though, got on the computers in the classroom and started searching for details online. I told others to start phoning the state police dispatchers, local hospitals, university officials, anyone who could tell us what was happening.

Tricia Sangalang: I instantaneously went into "reporter" mode. With an innumerable amount of questions running through my head, I wanted to know what was really happening beyond the walls of that classroom. Who were the students who were shot in AJ? What does the shooter look like? Were there any witnesses? I didn't want to believe hearsay about how many victims there were or where the most recent shootings had occurred. I wanted to find out for myself.

Roland Lazenby: Throughout the morning, university officials made a series of garbled turnouts on some sort of emergency public address system. They were absurdly inaudible. I kept stepping outside my classroom, then out of the building trying to pick up what the university was saying to us. "This is like some strange scene from one of those TV documentaries about one of those bullet-pocked Baghdad neighborhoods," I remember thinking.

Two anxious hours went by, with some students working the phones, others writing up their findings, and yet another feeding the edited copy via email to our webmaster who was locked down near Norris Hall. Because Andy Mager had been so good with Google Analytics, planetblacksburg.com was immediately available across the globe to anyone doing online searches for breaking news. Soon the BBC, NPR, CNN, and numerous major newspapers were linking to the little student-run site.

Kristina Ticknor: I was told to get in touch with friends who had heard something about the shootings in West Ambler Johnston. That was when I informed my teacher that I, in fact, was a resident from the fourth floor, and had been walking around minutes after the first event. Immediately the interview spotlight was flipped onto me, and I recounted my morning to a fellow student. As the classroom became frenzied in a search for information, I decided to stop cowering beneath my computer and to start figuring things out myself.

Tricia Sangalang: In a few minutes, that classroom, that computer lab, became a newsroom. Students were interviewing other students, others were calling friends they could get in contact with . . . we wanted information.

The same was true for the staff of the *Collegiate Times*, Virginia Tech's student newspaper. Robert Bowman, the paper's managing editor, had an eight o'clock class that morning, then dropped by the newspaper's offices where the editorial adviser, Kelly Furnas, told him of the early shootings in West Ambler Johnston. Like others around campus, he had read the administration's emails and heard the turnouts on the campus PA system. A noon press conference had been hastily called for university president Charles Steger, Tech police chief Wendell Flinchum, and university PR vice president Larry Hincker to address reporters, so Bowman made his way there.

Robert Bowman, *Collegiate Times* editor: Before the first press conference at noon, there were reports of one killed and one injured. CNN reported eight casualties. I never imagined what I would hear, sitting in the Holtzman Conference Center. Flinchum, Hincker, and Steger talked before opening up for questions. One of the first questions was of a body count. Twenty dead. The room gasped.

Reacting to the announcement, the *Collegiate Times* editors hustled to call in the newspaper's staff to its offices in Squires Hall.

Robert Bowman: In the *CT* newsroom, reporters were busy finding stories, finding names, and finding pictures. The phones were constantly ringing as different news outlets tried to get more information or a few interviews. Some *CT* reporters were trying to get a list of names of the departed. This was by far the most difficult part. We searched Facebook pages, mostly, and tried finding friends of victims who could verify the names of those lost. After getting adequate verification, we posted those names and pictures on our website. There was absolutely no room for error. It was reported that nytimes.com linked the *CT*'s website for a list of names of the deceased. We were not motivated by competition, but by getting information available to the students as soon as possible.

> **Michelle Rivera:** Toward 1 to 2 p.m., I got a text from my news editor with the *Collegiate Times.* I was recently hired on as a news reporter and was therefore very surprised when I was told to come into the news office because I was needed there. I admit that it felt good to feel needed, it felt good that someone needed something from me because sitting there, watching the news, not knowing what to do or how to act or what to feel made me feel worse than I ever have before.

As with Planet Blacksburg, *Collegiate Times* reporters would work into the late-night hours putting the stories together that first day.

> **Michelle Rivera:** Everyone was busy. Other news crews wanted to come in and see how the *CT* was handling this crisis, what the office was like at this time. The phone was going crazy and no one seemed to know what to do with it: a bunch of different people would answer it and would have to give it to someone else, they'd say "it's London," or "it's NBC" or some other newspaper or news channel. Everyone was so busy, so flustered, and so dedicated to getting things done. It looked like a real-live newsroom, and I felt completely useless. The two boys I initially met up with were Web guys and disappeared somewhere and the other reporter was given the phone. Then the webmaster came up to me and said he needed a brief. Honestly, I didn't know how to write a brief—he said write two or three sentences on a few facts, and so I just turned the three-to-five-word scribbles into sentences and gave it back to him.

Before the day was out, Rivera would complete her first full story for the *Collegiate Times.*

> **Michelle Rivera:** My first news article ever written on the day in the newsroom was given to me. I was to write about how down-

town merchants felt about what had happened, and it didn't occur to me at that point to go downtown and do on-site interviews, but they were mostly closed anyway. I went into the hallway with my computer and called up all the businesses and asked all the ones that were there where they were, what they were doing, how they heard, and their reaction to what had happened that morning. I was incredibly amazed at how open and honest everyone I spoke with was. I had been terrified that they would hang up on me after hearing my introduction: Hi, my name is Michelle Rivera and I'm with the *Collegiate Times* . . . etcetera. I'd ask them how they were, tell them I was writing an article on this subject, and would they mind answering a few questions for me? I was new to the whole thing and didn't even know how to approach before, but now? In this circumstance? How was I supposed to ask people how they felt about what happened that morning? How was I supposed to ask them anything about that morning when I couldn't even think about it myself? I was absolutely dreading that the people I called would think I was insensitive, would tell me I was a horrible person for talking to them about this, report me to somebody, would do anything at all but answer a few questions or tell me what they felt like sharing. I'm always surprised how friendly people are, how willing the community is to share information and how understanding they are. After that I went back into the newsroom and wrote about how the downtown merchants were all supportive, because that's what they were. That is the only impression I have ever gotten since that afternoon and to this day. I have never in my life seen such a supporting community.

In nearby Shanks Hall, Planet Blacksburg reporters were pursuing their own stories on the shootings. Several of them were students from the media writing class who stayed after the lockdown ended. The students who decided to report began gathering information and feeding it to editor Suzanne Higgs, who was writing the main story.

> **Suzanne Higgs:** I'm scared to start talking about this because I'm afraid it will all come back to me, which it is supposed to, but that doesn't mean it's a good thing. I feel cold because I distanced myself from it. After we moved away from the windows, and some students were lying on the floor, I finally moved into the head honcho seat and began searching for updates online. Others began reporting as well. We had no TV, only the Internet for information. Some people were getting updates from friends and parents, and my mom and cousin, who was in Boston, were emailing me news stories I could look to for information.

Higgs continued to update the story as she got information from the reporters. Then she would email her updated versions to Kevin Cupp, Planet Blacksburg's webmaster. There was only one problem. Cupp was smack dab in the middle of the situation himself because he left class and headed over to Norris Hall to find out what had happened there. But that didn't prevent him from receiving stories and posting them on planetblacksburg.com.

> **Kevin Cupp:** I got into the atrium of Pamplin Hall and saw everyone just standing around by the door; I went down there to find two cops with guns right outside the window, ready to catch a shooter they thought was still on the loose. The cops were hustling everyone outside to quickly get inside; it was hard to watch the fear on their faces as the cop yelled at them to run for their lives to Pamplin, not knowing what's going on at all. It was then when I sent a message to Twitter.com from my cell phone saying, "Trapped inside of Pamplin, shooter on campus, they won't let us

leave." People told me that was their first indication that something big was happening on campus and that none of the major news networks had even broken the news yet. Bloggers blogged about the post, saying it took their breath away. I got out my laptop and started updating the Planet Blacksburg site with the latest information in collaboration with Roland Lazenby's media writing class via instant messaging, right there in the Pamplin atrium, just the second building over from Norris Hall. At one point, police thought the shooter had come into Pamplin and ran through the bottom part of the atrium (we were in the upper part). So they had us pick up everything and run into a locked classroom. We all thought we were running for our lives as no one knew the shooter's journey had already ended. Needless to say, it was a false alarm. The students had nothing better to do, we didn't have a TV, so they started playing hangman on the chalkboard. I was able to access a live streaming feed of one of the local news stations and got updates live as they were coming in.

That night CBS would present a story on Cupp and Planet Blacksburg and how technology had changed the reporting of news.

Roland Lazenby: My students suddenly realized they were providing information to the world. That day sleepy little Planet Blacksburg got 1 million hits [the next day the number would rise to 1.3 million]. Quickly readers began posting comments on our site, telling my students, "This is way better information than what CNN or Fox or MSNBC has." The posters told my kids over and over again: "Keep up the good work."

Later, Henry Abbott of ESPN.com would link to planetblacksburg.com and declare for his millions of readers: "A lot of the media covering this shooting has felt bizarre to me, even a little exploitative. But this journalistic work, by students, for the university community, and with real-time responses from all concerned? This seems very real and important."

Even before the lockdown was half over, a student in the media writing class was doing a phone interview with CNN. Soon, other news organizations from around the world were emailing PB's student reporters and editors and requesting interviews.

Roland Lazenby: Our dread mushroomed. Working from both a police scanner accessed online and other sources, my students kept hearing that the number of victims was high. Thirty-one people. Thirty-two? Not possible. Wanting yet more information, I slipped out of the building and made my way about seventy-five yards west to the side entrance of Torgersen Hall. A former police reporter, I had worked more than a few crime scenes in my day and figured I could get a better view of things. Standing on each side of the doorway there were two helmeted SWAT guys, their rifles jutting in the air. They looked at me like I was crazy, so I pulled back.

Omar Maglalang: Despite my reluctance to report the news, something inside of me changed drastically an hour after the shootings occurred. I somehow managed to stand up from the floor and make my way onto a seat in front of the computers. The drastic change that occurred within me was a revelation of sorts as I began to feel a sense of responsibility to make others aware about what was happening on campus that day. I stared at the computer for a few minutes not knowing what to do. Then I began looking around national media websites and Facebook to piece together the puzzle. At that point, I went from a shocked state to a reporter. I wanted to dig up the clues. Who was the gunman? How many did he kill? What happened? As hours passed, the death count had increased from twelve to twenty and so on. I couldn't believe that so many people were killed. I checked to gain leads on the identities of the gunman and the victims. We had heard that the shooting in West Ambler Johnston occurred on the fourth floor and involved a resident adviser and a resident. I looked around the Internet trying to figure out the identity of the RA, but I had no luck as many of the people I called were in complete shock about the loss of a friend. I even tried to call a friend who was a resident adviser in the dormitory, but she was told not to disclose the identity of victims to anyone.

Roland Lazenby: Finally, about 12:40, it seemed safe to allow the media writing students to leave class. While most grabbed up their belongings and took off, a half dozen students kept working intently on the phones, then feeding information to Higgs. I asked if any of them wanted to go with me over to Norris Hall to survey the scene.

Omar Maglalang: I felt that there could still be a possibility of danger out there. Who knows what could still be there? The news had reported that the gunman had been killed in Norris. I figured it was a suicide. As I looked around the room, I saw that everyone was busy working on their computers. I looked at my professor one more time, and this time, slowly raised my hand.

Roland Lazenby: Omar Maglalang and I set out to find the story. We didn't have to go far to encounter police lines, but we slipped through when some officers were looking the other way. We had neared Norris before another officer shooed us back, which meant we had to snake our way to the other side of Norris and come through the tunnel at Burruss Hall. On the way, we stopped to talk to ambulance drivers and police officers waiting at the commuter parking lot. We chatted with two Christiansburg officers who had just come from the carnage in Norris Hall. I asked an officer what he thought and was surprised when he immediately launched into the issue of gun control. "We've got to do something about people having access to guns," he said. "I don't know what, but we have to do something."

Omar Maglalang: Yellow caution tape lined the perimeter of Norris, stretching all the way to Burruss Hall. A police officer watched near the back of Norris, and when Lazenby asked him if we could go through the yellow tape, our request was denied. We made our way through Burchard Hall and went to the front of Johnston Student Center. There, we ran into two housekeepers who we found out worked in Norris Hall. They were still wandering around because their car keys had been left in Norris and they couldn't go back in and get them. Pam Tickle, the housekeeper in charge of the second floor where the shootings happened, told us how she and students were locked in a student lounge. It wasn't until near 11 a.m. when she was released by police officers. In that lounge, Tickle heard gunshots. The other housekeeper, Gene Cole, told us that he caught sight of the gunman in Norris Hall. Cole said he came in looking for Tickle, but he was confronted with danger instead. Out of the two housekeepers, Tickle was in deep disarray when we talked to her. She had this aura about her. She seemed utterly shocked by what had happened that morning, and the grief about the killing of thirty people on her housekeeping floor had not yet sunk in. She had experienced such a traumatic event that she only felt a blur of what had happened. I felt sad for her. I couldn't imagine how hard it must've been for her to overcome that close fear after experiencing that. After those interviews, we went to the side of Burruss and found that the tunnel leading to the sidewalk near Norris was not closed. We went through the tunnel and upon arriving to the other side, we found ourselves right beside Norris while grim-faced police officers came and went. The eeriness worsened by the second. I stood gazing at the building. I didn't know if I wanted to cry or be angry. I stood there in complete shock. Maybe I had the same kind of face as Pam Tickle, but thankfully, Lazenby was with me. If I was alone staring at that, emotions would've rung so hard that I would probably not be able to bear it. We stood there staring at the building where such a horrific event took place. The windows were wide open to let air out, but I felt that having them open like that exposed even more the gruesome nature of the events that took place there.

Especially telling were the faces of the officers. They would later tell counselors they had seen things they just couldn't get out of their minds, no matter how hard they tried. Then there were the ringing cell phones in the body bags as they carried out the victims. Desperately ringing cell phones. Unanswered calls from family and friends.

Omar Maglalang: We were actually inside of the yellow tape, so I felt that at any given minute police would stop us and make us turn back to where we came from. But they didn't. There were several different law enforcement officials mulling about in front of Norris at that time, yet it was the same theme in the looks of their faces. Their heads were down. They looked defeated. An evidence collection unit truck pulled up right in front of us. Evidence collectors had the same faces as they brought briefcases from the academic building to the back of the truck. Several state troopers passed us by without a word. They just nodded. They had a look of disbelief. A group of local officers gathered around outside of Norris as well. Members of the SWAT team were circled around but no one talked. They were somber. Downtrodden. Melancholic. That describes what we all felt near Norris Hall that afternoon of April 16. How? Why? The building brought up nothing but questions. How can I even describe something like this? I had serious doubts about how I was going to write the article. I didn't know that being so emotionally attached to my community would somehow affect what I would write. I used my camera phone and took a picture of Norris Hall. Afterward, I went back to Shanks Hall to write. I grabbed a seat in front of a computer and typed my story. It was crunch time for writing the article. Lazenby didn't give me an exact deadline to finish it, but while in front of Norris he said, "You know what to do."

Back in the Shanks "newsroom" Tricia Sangalang, Kevin Tosh, Suzanne Higgs, and others were working away.

Tricia Sangalang: We put down the overhead screen and started playing streaming news from the Internet. Tech was the main, breaking story on every news site. One confirmed death. Emergency medical services (EMS) on the scene. Multiple injuries. I called Carilion Roanoke Memorial Hospital and talked to an ER doctor who said they were preparing for multiple patients. Then I was connected to the spokesperson for the hospital, Eric Earnhardt. He told me there were three patients who arrived earlier, and six more were en route. The hospital was sending additional ambulances to campus for assistance. Once we became aware the shootings happened on the second floor of Norris, a student went on the university website and started looking for the classes that were scheduled in Norris at 9:05. I wrote down each class, logged in on Facebook.com, and added each course as one of my own. Doing so would allow me to click on the course and bring up students who added the course on their profiles. Each click brought up many results, but many students made their profiles limited or private, not allowing people who they weren't "friends" with to view them. The few I could access, however, luckily had their screen names on their contact information. I instant messaged a few, some responded; some said they would rather not answer any questions. One student was more than willing to tell me his story: Computer Engineering major Ruiqi

Zhang. I spoke with Zhang for maybe twenty minutes, and he explained how the students pushed a table in front of the door to block the shooter from entering, expressing his feelings and thoughts during the chaos. "He put two shots through the door," he said, explaining how the shooter tried to shoulder his way into the room but could not. I froze. As a reporter, I needed the information. As a student, as a person, I was just as scared and overstrung as anyone else, but I knew I needed to keep calm.

Omar Maglalang: When I finished typing the story, Lazenby had gotten back in the room. I asked him to edit the story for me before we published it on Planet Blacksburg. A few minutes later, it was up on the site.

Witnesses Recall Memories of Norris Hall Shootings

by Omar Maglalang and Tricia Sangalang
News Staff Writers
April 16, 2007

A typical morning in Norris Hall is pretty quiet for the housekeepers who work there. Most classes do not start until 9 a.m., and various classes from German to Engineering are held there every day.

But on this one day in April, when wind gusts roared like a snowstorm in January, a gunman shattered the quiet nature of the quaint building, which like many at Virginia Tech is constructed with the distinctive "Hokie stone."

Ruiqi Zhang, a junior Computer Engineering major, experienced the incident firsthand in his class on the second floor of Norris.

"A student rushed in and told everybody to get down," said

Zhang. "We put a table against the door and when the gunman tried to shoulder his way in and when he saw that he couldn't, he put two shots through the door.

"It was the scariest moment of my life."

Pam Tickle, who works as a housekeeper in Norris, was moving through another quiet, easy morning at her post in the second floor of Norris when a little after 9:30 a.m., she heard numerous gunshots coming from the hallway.

"We weren't quite sure what happened at first," said Tickle. "We didn't hear anybody screaming, but we heard lots of shots."

Gene Cole, a building worker from the Pulaski County community of Belspring, had heard the shots and was on his way to look for Tickle, when he came around a corner on the second floor of Norris and saw a body on the floor.

"Across the hall, I caught sight of the shooter, and he loaded his gun at me," said Cole. "I ran down the steps to get out of there."

Cole, who has worked for more than twenty years at Virginia Tech, saw bloodied hallways and also a hint of what the suspect looked like. Cole noted that the man had a hat on and was wielding a black automatic handgun.

Meanwhile, Tickle and several Virginia Tech students had rushed to the student lounge on the second floor, locked the door, and waited for police officers to evacuate them.

Their wait would last almost two hours, an anxiety-filled two hours.

"We peeked out the door one time, but more shots were fired," said Tickle. "We stayed in there not knowing what happened. When we heard police out in the hallway after eleven, we let them in. They body searched us, and led us away to evacuate from the building."

Tickle did feel a sense of relief when a little after 10 a.m., she heard an announcer on the radio who said, "Shooter's down!"

Police led Tickle and students in the lounge to Randolph Hall, behind Norris, after the gunman was pronounced dead, and they stayed there until police cleared the area.

"I thank God because he was watching me today," said Tickle.

Tickle has worked for about three years as a housekeeper in Norris. She said she enjoyed the hustle and bustle of students and professors there. She particularly liked the quiet atmosphere and the neat look of the hallways.

By midafternoon, however, yellow caution tape lined the entire perimeter of Norris and the academic buildings around it.

By afternoon, the building was Virginia Tech's own ground zero of sorrow, the bed of yellow tulips in front of the building tossed in the stiff wind, as evidence technicians and other officers came and went from a building that will surely live in infamy. An abandoned red backpack sat next to the entrance and bicycles were also left in a rack nearby, signs of the quiet, carefree student life so terribly shattered.

That student routine and quiet atmosphere was now obliterated as police cars, ambulances, SWAT teams, and investigators mulled about the crime scene.

The stern faces of the evidence collection team and other huddled-up officers in their bulletproof vests seemed stunned at the sight of what had happened in Norris.

Officers gathered outside of the academic building to deal with the particulars of the crime scene while others stood to guard the perimeter with shotguns.

Nick Pheil, an Accounting and Information Systems major, had an exam on the third floor of Norris in the morning. He finished and on his way back to his residence he noticed police officers everywhere. Like many Tech students, he watched and listened as the news worsened by the minute.

"I'm in a state of shock," said Pheil later. "It seemed low-key and contained earlier when they reported one dead, several wounded, but things escalated very quickly when the numbers shot to seventeen and then twenty-two dead. I'm still in a state of shock."

On one of the chilliest days ever on record this month in Blacksburg, the site of Norris Hall will be remembered for the sight of yellow tape lined around its perimeter, blowing in the cold wind, a wind that will break hearts for as long as hearts can be broken.

Omar Maglalang: In a way, I believe that story changed my life. So many emotions came upon me that day and I couldn't truly admit that I handled any of it well. As a reporter, you have to be objective with everything you do. It was hard for me to be as objective. I had been hurt by the murder of several victims in West AJ and Norris Hall. I felt the pain of my fellow Hokie brothers and sisters, who were overcome with so much grief after experiencing the traumatic event. Even the housekeepers I regarded as family. Even the killer himself I regarded as family. Why would a Hokie do something like that to hurt other Hokies? The emotions that went around inside of me that day were unforgettable. They were important in helping me grasp the situation, but it hindered me as well. My life had been changed since that day because I had found a way to handle my emotions. I took a step back and evaluated my thoughts. Were they legitimate? Were they real? If I let my imagination take over, I would be spiraling in a heap of distress. I would not be able to report the news. I would be dumbfounded. Reporting was not an outlet I used to overcome my emotions. It was my sense of responsibility to make everyone aware of what was going on in my quaint little town. It was hopefully my contribution to the community because I knew that if I didn't report, I would feel helpless in a time of tragedy. I wanted to give back to the community that I loved so much. Virginia Tech had literally become my home. It was painful to know that a fellow Hokie like myself had bloodied my own home. It was truly emotional, but I kept reporting to give a sense of hope for the community. I wanted to write articles about the human experience, how people can overcome their grief, and how the community can bond together during the aftermath of the event. I didn't want to be caught up in the violent nature of the killer. I didn't want to be caught up in the national media circus that went on in the days following April 16. I was a student journalist attending the site of a horrific event. I couldn't help but not be a subjective journalist.

Suzanne Higgs: That day was a blur of missed phone calls, callbacks, interviews, updates, emails, and news. I stayed in that seat not trying to make sense of anything, but just being a reporter and telling what happened. That's what we had been taught to do, be objective. It took me two days to even begin processing what happened. It wasn't until I started reading the comments on Planet Blacksburg that I started to really understand it happened here. It happened to my school, my Hokies, my town, and my friends.

Students working for Planet Blacksburg and the *Collegiate Times* put in long hours that first day of reporting. One hindrance to their work became the many interview requests from journalists and media organizations around the world. Because of the Internet, news organizations identified the student journalists as news sources. Within a matter of hours, the student journalists had watched their school transformed by a horrific incident. Then they had become instant international media stars.

Tricia Sangalang: Internationally, they wanted to know what was happening. My email in-box quickly filled with messages from reporters and others asking if they could interview me. A radio station in the UK asked me to come on their show and talk about my experiences that morning. They were the first news media to ask for an interview. Little did I know, many more media would contact me in the following days.

Suzanne Higgs: I remember being excited about talking to so many people across the world. I still feel bad, and I still feel guilty that I was excited that they wanted to talk to me. I had to scold myself at the thoughts of "OMG, CNN wants to talk to me." Under any other circumstances I had the right to be excited, but I felt guilty for days after that because I was glad people wanted to talk to me. To this day I still feel crappy about it, but when I look back and see how far removed I made myself, I understand, but feel no better about it. Talking to radio stations, newspapers, to the BBC, to media outlets in the UK and Ireland and everyone else that contacted me was handled very informatively. At that point they all just wanted to know what was going on, and my personal experience of that day. I didn't have much to tell other than I had been reporting all day, and was still in the same building. They were all very sensitive to the situation, though. Everyone apologized and sent out their thoughts to me and our school. They did ask about contact systems with the school: how we handled it, how I thought the university was handling it. At that time I was just like, I felt safe, they reached us in time, and I was locked in a classroom. Three of us stayed in Shanks 160 for twelve hours that day reporting and searching out information. People all over the world wanted information so we were trying our hardest to provide it to them. Suddenly sleepy little Blacksburg was wide awake.

Courtney Thomas, Planet Blacksburg news editor: The phone was attached to my ear all day and texts came in sometimes faster than I could read them. When I spoke to media I mostly repeated what I had seen and heard on the news. Many of them asked me what students were talking about, how we felt. I recounted my day for many of them. They were disappointed to learn that I had not been on campus and that, no, I didn't hear gunshots or see people jump from windows. No, I'm sorry, none of my friends were shot. Thanks for asking. They were frustrated. Well, do you know anyone who knows someone who was shot or who can't find their friends? No. Thanks again for your concern, but I don't know anyone who's willing to cry for your camera. These people can't be serious. This is what I want to do with my life? Harass people and hope to catch something dramatic live on the air? Granted, I'm cynical by nature, but this was too much. And I wasn't alone on this one. The media were vultures that day. We went downtown to Sharkey's after we left Shanks. Ordered food and beer. I had water. I felt out of it. Dazed. There were reporters in Sharkey's hoping to speak with students. We spoke with someone from the *Los Angeles Times,* and a K92 reporter from Roanoke came over to the table as I was leaving. They couldn't have paid me to say another word about it.

CHAPTER 3
Code Green

Reacting to news that the shooting had spread across campus, Planet Blacksburg reporters began phoning area hospitals that morning for word about shooting victims. It soon became clear that the most serious patients had been sent to Carilion Roanoke Memorial Hospital; however, other ambulances took the injured to Lewis Gale Hospital in Salem and to the Carilion New River Valley Medical Center in Radford.

New River Valley Medical Center chaplain Jonathan Webster was attending a conference meeting at Mountain Lake in nearby Giles County when he got the news of the killings and word from the hospital that he needed to get there as soon as possible. He and his wife, "Donna," jumped in their car and rushed back to Radford.

Jonathan Webster, hospital chaplain: I've been a hospital chaplain for seventeen years, four different hospitals, twelve at this one. By far, April 16 was the worst professional day of my life. This one was difficult because normally I'm alone here at the hospital. If it's at night and I get paged, normally Donna's asleep. I wake her up and say, "Hey, something's going on, I'll be home in a few hours." This one, Donna was with me, so I cried some driving down Mountain Lake, which would be unusual for me. So how do I control my emotions? I'm not sure I did this time.

Caught off guard by the event, Virginia Tech had no immediate number that families could phone to check on their children. The tide of desperate cell phone calls soon overwhelmed service capacity for the region, which meant that many parents who were unable to get in touch with their children decided to get on the road to Blacksburg to get answers in person. Many who arrived found the campus blocked off and instead made their way to area hospitals. With numbers of people converging on the hospitals, authorities realized a need for more security. In August, a hospital security guard had been shot and killed by an escaped prisoner, an incident that would later spill over onto the Tech campus and result in the killing of a Montgomery County sheriff's deputy near the school. That incident was clearly on the minds of local officials as police moved in to secure the Radford hospital.

Jonathan Webster: When I got there, all security was at the end of the parking lot stopping folks. Within twenty to thirty minutes after I got there, the SWAT team from the Pulaski Sheriff's Department got there. At that point, they did not know that the shooter was dead. They didn't know who the shooter was at that point. . . . The security and police were wanding folks as they came in to make sure there weren't any weapons on anybody. There was some fear. Not just a deep concern and compassion for folks, but there was a real fear at that point that this was just the beginning.

Derek O'Dell, shot in Jamie Bishop's Introductory German class, was among the injured sent to Montgomery Regional Hospital in

Blacksburg. Montgomery Regional is the smallest of the hospitals used that day, but it is the closest to Virginia Tech.

Derek O'Dell: I arrived at the hospital and they were well prepared for us in their small emergency area. The doctors were fast, calm, and efficient in their diagnoses and treatments. I was transferred to a hospital room with a bed after a few portable radiographs were taken. I was only in the emergency area of the hospital for ten minutes before they moved me to make space for the more critically injured who were coming in. It took a while until a doctor was able to look at my radiographs, so I sat there in my bed watching the breaking news of the tragedy that I had just experienced. I was still in shock, so the bullet wound never really hurt until about a half hour after arriving at Montgomery Regional Hospital. It was driving me crazy not being able to talk to anyone besides the occasional nurse. I couldn't get up because they were running IV fluids into me. I started to try and call all of my family and my girlfriend who is a freshman at Virginia Tech. I couldn't get through to a lot of them and you're not supposed to use a cellular phone in the hospital. I resorted to text messaging them all. My aunt got through to me and she lived in Roanoke and told me that she and my uncle were on their way up. One of my girlfriend's friends finally got through to me, and I could let her know that I was relatively okay. She had my class schedule, and saw that I was in Norris Hall at that time, so she was already on her way to the hospital after hearing that the injured were transported there initially.

Jonathan Webster: One of the first ladies I ran into was a mother of one of the victims looking for her child. She had been to the other hospitals in the community. I'm not sure I realized the extent of it yet. So often as a hospital chaplain, somebody sees an accident on the interstate, they think they recognized your car and they come to the hospital thinking it's their husband or someone they know. We take that seriously, of course. But we think, obviously, it's not that person. I assumed at that point the person who was looking for the child, the student, had just not been able to get through to the cell phone, that thirty minutes later they'd be able to and everything would be fine. We couldn't get any information for that woman. So I gave her some support. I had a prayer for the safety of her child. She asked me to have a second prayer for the safety of all the students. I did that. She left to meet her husband. Later on, the next day, she found her child was one of the victims that was killed.

Tommy McDearis, Blacksburg police chaplain: The hospital environment was controlled chaos. The hospital did a wonderful job. They had a disaster plan, and they activated that plan. They had all of their surgeons and everybody in place. As a chaplain, it was my job to minister to anybody that was awake and alert and needed someone to talk to. I did that, and I've spent a lot of time doing that. Once all of the patients were treated, and we were also out there unloading the ambulances as they were coming in as part of the police department, we started setting up hospitality areas for families that were coming in. We set up a big hospitality area for the students to come into, friends of the injured. When friends would come in, as their friends who were shot were taken to rooms, we would escort them up to see their friends and spend time with them there. It was very busy. It was a high-emotion time. There was a lot of security around the hospital just to make sure that they felt safe. That would startle them at first, and then they'd start to feel more comfortable with it. My job was just to spend a lot of time with those individuals, give them the opportunity to try to settle down. A lot of tears. A lot of emotion then. A lot of uncertainty, but it was our job to try to make things a little more certain, to try to calm things down a little bit as well.

Derek O'Dell: Watching the news on the television in the hospital was frustrating. It seemed like they had so many things wrong. That's when I learned of the first shooting earlier that morning in West Ambler Johnston. The estimated casualties began to come in at four or five. I knew that number would unfortunately jump much higher. Somehow the media had found out I was among those injured, and my number flowed across "the wire." The media calls started to come in. I unknowingly answered the first "Unknown #." It turned out to be MSNBC on the phone wanting an eyewitness account. I willingly gave them an interview as I had not heard back from my mom, who was at a pharmacy conference at Colorado Springs, Colorado.

Jonathan Webster: I went to the emergency room. At that point we had three of the students here at the hospital. I spent some brief time with two of them. One of them was already in surgery. I helped contact the parents of one of them, trying to make arrangements for the parents to get here. Then I spent some time with him, waiting for his parents. I went out and waited for his parents and brought them back to the room. Their was a joyous union of them coming together with their injured child. Then I kind of backed off from the situation for a while, to let the medical people do what they needed to do, to help the folks get settled.

Ishwar Puri and Scott Case, the two men who headed up the Department of Engineering Science and Mechanics, realized they had to get to the local hospitals to try to find out more information about the department's students and faculty who were missing. But when Puri arrived at Montgomery Regional he quickly discovered that other families wanted answers.

Ishwar Puri: I was the first one at the hospital from Virginia Tech, as a professional administrator or faculty member or staff member, there. And, boy, they were just the best people. The hospital's CEO was there helping out. There were many other people who were there. They were just fantastic. There was a police presence and they weren't letting people into the emergency room. So I went down to the emergency room and said, "I am the department head of engineering science and mechanics." They put us in this sort of family room. I remember meeting so many people there because I was the only one from Virginia Tech. Juan Ortiz's widow was there with a few friends, and her husband was in G. V. Loganathan's class. She came to me and she said, "Are you from Virginia Tech? Do you know where Juan is?" And I said, "No, but I'll ask." And so there were a lot of sort of family and friends who wrote one name for me to find out about. I remember writing about twenty names down, because these were the kids in Liviu's class. And slowly, Scott Case would call me and said, "Okay, we located this person."

In Radford, hospital officials finally realized they had absorbed the worst of the day.

Jonathan Webster: We have a "code green," which means a disaster. We also implemented a system that we have called "incident command," where there is a very definite system of who is in charge and what roles different folks have. We set up the command center to do that. I guess at about 2:30, 3:00 maybe, we realized we weren't going to get any more victims. We realized we could get back to normal hospital operations. . . . Stuff I normally don't do, when they called off the code green, I was standing at the edge of the command center and said, "We need to pray." Twenty to thirty of us held hands and prayed. It was just a sense of overwhelming pain, overwhelming sense that these things are not supposed to happen here. Nothing felt normal that day. Nothing felt normal.

Ishwar Puri: I met a couple of the students who'd been shot; I went upstairs and met them and tried to comfort them. They were in very good spirits considering. One of them had broken his leg, and one had been shot two times. But they were in good spirits, very good spirits. They were under anesthesia. And one of the questions one of them asked me was, "You know, I think I left my backpack when I jumped out. When can I get that back? Because that has my notes which I will need for the next class next year." And then the other guy said, "Well, you know, I think I left my scientific calculator in the classroom. Can I get that back?" It's amazing how focused people are on what they have to do. ESM is not an elitist program, but it is an elite program in a sense that we have some very special students. Over half of our students graduate with distinction: cum laude, summa cum laude, magna cum laude. These are very dedicated students.

Soon, though, the mood at the hospital turned darker.

Ishwar Puri: Before I left campus, I found out that Liviu Librescu had been shot in the face. So I was dreading that, because Montgomery Regional had no record of Liviu.

Puri asked his assistant department head, Scott Case, and Case's wife, Carrie, to help with another phone tree that would call around to all the other area hospitals looking for missing faculty and students. Puri also phoned his wife, Beth Levinson, who remained locked down at Blacksburg Middle School, to enlist her help in the phone tree effort.

Ishwar Puri: That's the kind of support network you need. Things need to get done. And I didn't have cell phone numbers handy. I just had what I had on my cell phone in my directory. Then a student came in. And he said, "Have you heard about G. V. Loganathan?" And I said, "No." We put Loganathan's name down. Then there were the friends of Minal Panchal. She was shot in Liviu's class. Her name went on my list.

The list was not a good place to be. Your name remained on it only if no one had heard from you and no hospital had you listed as a patient.

Ishwar Puri: Later in the afternoon there were just a few names left. I heard around three that there was a command center being set up at the Inn at Virginia Tech. And I was having a bad feeling about Liviu. I was having a pretty bad feeling about G.V. Because none of the hospitals had their names. G. V. Loganathan's friends came, and one of them knew some physicians. We called those physicians, we got into the Carilion network and found out that some of the names I had on my list were not at any of the Carilion hospitals. That's when things started to get really bad.

Even though they hadn't been officially told, Puri and Case realized that colleagues and students had died. It would be a long day of bad news at Montgomery Regional, interspersed with joyful reunions.

Loressa Cole, chief nursing officer, Montgomery Regional Hospital: This tragedy affected our hospital in many ways. Those of us who cared for the injured will never forget the strength and courage we saw in each patient and family. The visits from Virginia Tech students and staff were respectful of the work we do, and never interfered with the rest and healing that each patient needed. Our staff is here to care for the community, and have dedicated their lives to helping the sick or injured. This event has reminded us of why we do what we do, and given us the opportunity to rededicate ourselves to our health-care professions.

As the afternoon wore on, Ishwar Puri realized that the mystery of the names still on his list wouldn't be resolved at the hospital. He would have to go to the Inn at Virginia Tech, where Tech officials were preparing to tell families news of the worst kind.

The Inn at Virginia Tech

Observers may have thought it odd that the university chose to house the victims' families at the Inn at Virginia Tech, the same place it also selected as the base for the dozens of media organizations and hundreds of reporters who converged on campus. It may not have been ideal, one university media official explained, but the Inn and its Skelton Conference Center offered the only facilities on campus that could house either group adequately.

Jenna Lazenby Nelson, news bureau manager, Office of University Relations: The next several hours Monday afternoon are honestly a blur. Phone calls were pouring in, media and reporters from across the United States were calling. Like the rest of us they wanted to know what was going on. It was close to two that afternoon when I received orders from Burruss Hall to head over to the Inn at Virginia Tech. With its vast amount of conference space and its attachment with the Holtzman Alumni Center, the Inn became the location for families to meet up with their students and the alumni center became the location for press conferences and media to work. When I arrived at the Inn, the media satellite trucks were starting to engulf the parking lot and there were reporters and cameramen everywhere. As I first entered the upper portion of the Inn and made my way toward the alumni center, I passed by a few rooms of parents and family members looking for their lost students. Chills went through my body as I saw the worry and fear on their faces.

Tommy McDearis, Blacksburg police chaplain: I was at the Inn round the clock. It was a very similar feeling to the hospital, very intense emotion. You had all of those families that were coming in. A lot of people who had been killed had not been identified at that point. So there were people anxious to hear the news. They were hoping to be told, "No, you're loved ones are not in this group." But in reality, most of them knew that they were going to hear different news. I was just trying to keep them calm and as settled as they can be before the news got to them. That was a big portion of the job at the time. A lot of the friends came over there wanting to know and were looking for their friends but couldn't find them. They were afraid that they were dead. So I was trying to deal with those students and to say, "We'll tell you as soon as we can, but we can't tell you before we can tell the families." Most of them would understand that. All they needed was somebody to spend some time telling them that. Usually, within a day when they were initially told, they would start with going through the denial stage of grief, where they just couldn't believe it. They just needed somebody to assure them that this had happened and that this is real. Some of them very quickly got to the anger stage. You would be there to give them somebody to yell at. If people are experiencing an anger stage of grief and they don't have a way to vent that in a managed way, then somebody who they may pass on the sidewalk who says the wrong things to them will get hit. So what we try to do is give them somebody to yell at. They would take it out on us without actually taking it out on us; they vented to us and at us without actually getting angry with us. So that was very important to get someone to do that with for them, to where they had permission to be as mad as they wanted to be about what had happened without actually doing something with that anger that would not be healthy. We spent a lot of time doing that. I haven't had a day yet where I hadn't thought about this. I ended up working with twenty sets of families and friends who had been told that their loved ones and friends were dead. You don't spend time listening to those cries and screams and not live with that for a while.

Megan Meadows, Virginia Tech student: I was with my friends waiting at the Inn to hear any sort of news about our close friend Reema Samaha. Thinking about being at that Inn literally makes me feel sick to my stomach. It was a virtual hell on earth. Every few minutes you could hear spontaneous cries and screams from families and friends of the victims finding out devastating news about their loved ones. Knowing that every one of those cries and screams was a representation of a lost life is something I will never forget. I felt sympathy for those criers and screamers, but also prayed to God that I would not have to become one of them.

Jenna Lazenby Nelson: Once I reached the alumni center I started to look for familiar faces in a sea of the unfamiliar and found a few coworkers from our audiovisual team in University Relations. I wanted to know how I could help, what I could do. It didn't take long to figure out what my role would become. There were hundreds of media representatives, newspaper and TV reporters, cameramen, photographers, producers, editors, and they all had questions and needs. I did my job as best I could, I worked to assist them, to answer their questions, although I had very few answers myself.

Megan Meadows: Even with all of the vivid and now blurred sense memories I have from that day, one of the ones that is the most powerful in my mind is an interaction I observed at the Inn between a police officer and a stranger. Part of the Inn was sectioned off for family members of the deceased or missing, and the police were guarding the entrance to this part of the building; primarily to keep out the media. As we were standing at the entrance, a sickly pale man coming from outside walked up next to us. His eyes were glazed over and he was in such a trance. He looked at one of the police officers guarding the restricted area, and in the most unsettling voice I have ever heard muttered, "My daughter is dead." He went on to explain with very abrupt sentences that his daughter was missing and how some policemen had come to his home and told him of his daughter's death. His words sounded like they were coming from an insanely distressed movie character, not a real human being. When he first started speaking the dark-haired woman he was with was telling the police officer how he didn't know if she was dead, she was just missing. But after he told the part about the other policeman's confirmation she just started screaming and crying, "You didn't tell me that! *No! She is just missing!*" Everyone around us was speechless and the police officer barely knew how to respond, but moments later we saw the man and woman being escorted back into the restricted area.

John Chermak, Virginia Tech faculty: The first reports I believe were twenty people were killed. I went home, and as I pulled in the driveway I remembered that my next-door neighbor worked in Norris Hall, which is Kevin Granata. And I went directly over to their house to ask them if they'd heard from Kevin, and Linda's sister answered the door. She said, no, they hadn't heard from him yet. But with all the phone lines were tied up, people not getting to the phone. There was concern, but there wasn't. I guess I was more worried than they were at that time. Unfortunately they continued not to hear from him and went over to the Inn at VT at three o'clock. They went over there to try and find out something and they still couldn't find out anything.

Ishwar Puri: Then I went to the Inn, and Linda Granata called as I was on the way and said, "Where's Kevin?" And I said, "Gee, you know, I don't know. But let me find out." And I was really worried. I was worried sick. But I thought, "You know Kevin. Maybe he went to Wake Forest," because he's part of the school of biomedical engineering and sciences as well. He's an appointment at that school, and so, it's a Wake Forest/Virginia Tech school. No Kevin. I'm at the Inn. There's no news. We're sitting around in this room where they're streaming news conferences and CNN. It's very stressful, because all the families start to sort of converge there. They needed like a private space or something.

John Chermak: The toughest moment was when I had a feeling; I was starting to deal with it before it was officially known that Kevin was a victim.

Ishwar Puri: They had one of the rooms set up for private rooms, and the families were converging. And I knew, I got a call at some point. I won't name names, but someone had seen Kevin get shot and it didn't look good. He was at Roanoke Memorial, and I pretty much knew that he wasn't going to make it, judging from the call that I got on my cell phone. So it was time then to get Marlena Librescu and Linda Granata to the Inn because they'd be told there at some point. And I didn't want to be there alone, so I called my wife, and I called Mike Hyer and his wife to come there. And, I mean, these are all senior professors. Gloria Henneke was there, she's Ed Henneke's wife. Ed's a professor and also the associate dean in the college of engineering. We wanted to have a support system.

Unfortunately, "knowing" and getting official word were two different things. In some ways, that wasn't entirely bad, because it gave friends and family a small amount of time to brace themselves for the hardest messages.

Ishwar Puri: I asked Chief Flinchum, I gave him the names of Liviu Librescu and Kevin Granata and another student, whom I won't name because I thought at that time he was missing. He surfaced later, thank God. I found out that he surfaced later because somebody forwarded me a media report where he had been interviewed. So, I thought, "All right, well, fine. You know, he's alive."

The chief said, "Liviu Librescu, no, I don't have any record of him. No. Kevin Granata." And then the police chief said, "Are you a family member?" I said, "No, I'm his department head." And he said, "Well, we only give information to family members." And I thought, "Okay, red flag. He didn't say that when I gave him the first two names. He said that when I gave him Kevin's name."

That's when Puri began to accept that Granata and Librescu were gone.

Ishwar Puri: And the hardest part was that I pretty much suspected that we'd lost them, but I didn't know. And I recall Marlena Librescu coming into the Inn and saying, "Tell me, Ishwar." And I said, "I don't know, Marlena." And she said, "You know." And I said, "I don't know." I guess I did, but I really didn't. And I just couldn't tell her. Linda was in shock, and she came with her sister.

John Chermak: At five o'clock at night my wife went over there and Linda, Kevin's wife, was a total wreck, as you can imagine. She was trying to decide what to do, where to go and then eventually they went over to the Inn at VT and found out about 7:30 that evening. We were hoping that Kevin was just hurt badly enough that he couldn't contact his wife or family and was in a hospital somewhere because we had heard there were lots of people in hospitals around.

Puri watched university officials deliver the news to families and realized that the next of kin needed privacy and a room with furniture more suited to absorbing extremely difficult information.

Ishwar Puri: G.V.'s wife was there with a support system with a lot of friends. But the way the families were being told was that Mark McNamee, the provost, was there in one of the last ballrooms with the police chief, Chief Flinchum. He had a list and you would go and give him a name, and he'd tell you something or the other. G.V.'s family went there. I was in the room when they said, "G. V. Loganathan," and Flinchum looked at the list. And I think either he or Mark told G.V.'s wife, "Sorry. Your husband . . . we've lost your husband." And she collapsed in grief and so did some other people with her. And I remember going to Karen DePauw and saying, "Karen, we can't do this this way. You can't have like a podium and banquet room furniture." And then Karen said, "Okay, we'll do something." And in very short order they brought a lot of counselors in, they set up private rooms at the Inn where the families would be told, and you know, I think they handled it really, really well. We all learned as we went along what needed to be done. I don't regret being pushy because I think that the families needed all the dignity that they required. So they opened up one of the ballrooms. Karen was there with John Dooley, the vice provost. Terrific people. They got all the rooms open.

Even the presence of counselors in a private room couldn't remove the darkness. One counselor recalled helping the families fill out coroner's forms. What shape are your child's fingernails? How long are your child's eyelashes? The counselor went home that night, looked at her children and asked, "Do I know the shape of their fingernails? The length of their eyelashes?"

Puri knew that Professor Wally Grant's wounds were being treated at Lewis Gale Hospital in Salem. At the Inn, Puri encountered professors Brian and Nancy Love, who had come to the Inn to help out. He asked them to go to Salem to be with Grant, and they readily agreed.

Ishwar Puri: At some point Linda and Marlena were told. We had a support system there. Quite a few of us were there after they were told. My wife rode back with Linda and Linda's sister back to Linda's home. Gloria Henneke was with Marlena, and Marlena had another additional support system. It was tough, it was tough. At that point I didn't know about Liviu's bravery and at that point I didn't know about Kevin's bravery. It was just us getting through the day.

Gaurav Bansal, Tech graduate student; friend of Jeremy Herbstritt: I was at home when I heard classes were canceled because of the shootings in the morning. I didn't know anyone I knew would be involved. I didn't think that was going to be the case with twenty-six thousand students. But then his girlfriend called me. She said he was one of the ones in building. So we started calling him and some of the people we knew. Word got out, later on in the day, we went around to the hospitals, to the Inn at Virginia Tech trying to get information. Hospitals had lists of everyone who was admitted. But for people that weren't there, they didn't have any information. Throughout the day, we had heard some good news. Some people who were in the department that knew others had mentioned that they saw Jeremy come out of there. So we weren't in touch with him, we were thinking he was lost or in shock himself and not talking to anyone. Maybe he was out somewhere. Late that night, maybe about 11 p.m. or so, we found out about him and some others. I was shocked and surprised. You don't expect this to happen. You see it on the news and what not, but you never think it's going to be yourself. Again, with twenty-six thousand students at Tech, you don't think it's going to be any of your friends. I was really shocked to find him and so many others I knew went down. That was my initial thought—disbelief, shock. At the Inn we were just waiting for results from police. We went to the Inn. There was a lot of people there because everyone was sad, calling people they knew. I got calls from people I haven't talked to in years and it was really touching, but at the same time it was a shocker. So when we finally got the news, it was heartbreaking. All the good hope that you had is now gone. Sadness came in later, but really it was amazing shock.

Meanwhile, the growing media presence had created another sort of chaos in another part of the facility throughout the afternoon and evening.

Jenna Lazenby Nelson: President Charles Steger had already held a brief press conference at noon and shared with the world a glimpse of the tragedy Virginia Tech had endured. He confirmed that at least twenty-two were dead, canceled classes for the following day, and announced plans for a convocation ceremony to honor the fallen. Another press conference was to follow at 5 p.m. to discuss more details of the incident.

Omar Maglalang: Kevin Tosh and I were watching the press conference in the TV lounge at the Inn. I saw two police officers guarding a door. I overheard two women saying that the officers were guarding a room where the victims' families were watching the press conference.

Jenna Lazenby Nelson: As the five o'clock press conference neared, many of the major network and primetime reporters arrived along with their entourage. Katie Couric and her group was one of the first to appear. They set up a large production area in the Holtzman Alumni Center and the producers went to work trying to line up key interviews for the evening news and the CBS morning show. Other groups quickly followed, including Brian Williams and others from NBC, ABC, and CNN.

Neal Turnage, Planet Blacksburg sports editor: I hightailed it across campus to the Inn to find it teeming with satellite trucks from every imaginable television station. I'd never seen anything like it. There were trucks from all the major networks as well as representatives from small, local stations. There were reporters and their crews set up just a few feet apart doing stand-ups on the lawn of the Inn.

Jenna Lazenby Nelson: The room was filled for the five o'clock press conference. President Steger and chief of Virginia Tech Police Wendell Flinchum entered and took their place at the podium. At this time there was little additional information. The count of the dead was now at thirty-two and police and investigators were working hard to identify victims and the killer; however, until proper tests were run, and identities were one hundred percent confirmed, names would not be officially released.

Neal Turnage: Left and right the reporters were asking ridiculous questions. It had been less than six hours since the shootings ended and already they were trying to assign blame. Even a monkey could tell you it was too soon for those types of questions.

Jenna Lazenby Nelson: A question-and-answer session was held after the press conference and it became clear that there were going to be many tough questions for Virginia Tech. Of course media wanted the details of the events, how they occurred, who was responsible, and why. However, many also wanted to know if the university had responded efficiently after the first incident and if any of deaths could have been prevented. Finally the questions were cut off and another press conference for later that evening was announced.

Neal Turnage: I lost respect for the entire profession that day. It was obvious that the majority of the people there were not trying to help the public, they were trying to break the big story about who was responsible. I'm all for asking the tough questions, but those questions need to have a basis in helping the public.

Jenna Lazenby Nelson: Following the press conference, the major television network news stations fought to be the first to interview President Steger. CBS got him first. They were also the first to interview injured student Derek O'Dell, one of the students from Jamie Bishop's German class in Norris Hall. O'Dell, whose injured arm was in a sling, recounted to Katie Couric and the rest of the world the terror he had endured that morning.

Neal Turnage: We saw a story in the process of how Katie and her show managed to score an interview with Derek O'Dell so soon after he had been shot. When asked, Katie indicated that they had bookers who took care of that sort of thing for her. She didn't speak much on the appropriateness of doing a television interview with a shooting survivor so quickly after the incident, but did say that O'Dell seemed to still be in shock when she interviewed him.

> **Jenna Lazenby Nelson:** As the night went on, the alumni center continued to fill with media representatives. The international press was beginning to arrive and as the numbers increased so did the questions and requests. At one point I overheard one of the student leaders mention that he wanted to get word out about a candlelight vigil that would be held the next evening. I grabbed him, got the information, and began recounting it to the media. It took only minutes for the news of the vigil to be sent to the community and the world. Never in my life had I witnessed this level of media coverage. Had I actually had the time to take it in I would have been completely overwhelmed, but I was too busy to consider what I was dealing with.

One source indicated the *Washington Post* had responded to the news by putting dozens of reporters on the Tech story. Other major news organizations followed suit.

> **Jenna Lazenby Nelson:** Problems began to arise about twenty minutes before the final press conference for that evening. We had police officers and university staff at the door checking media credentials and signing in. However, it soon became evident that there were many more media than the room could accommodate. Police announced that we were at capacity and without warning closed off the entrance. There was an overflow spot where media could watch the press conference, but they would not be in the room and therefore unable to ask questions. Panic filled many who were unable to get in. Several had computers inside the room that they couldn't get to and others were irate that they would not be able to ask the important questions they had for university and state police representatives.

With many of the top university representatives busy trying to understand the situation and craft response messages, it left only a few of us to try and handle the situation in and around the conference center. Our staff was even more of a skeleton crew because many of the college communicators had gone home when the university closed earlier that afternoon. There were only a few of us to answer questions and calm the media who were unable to get in the conference room. I myself missed the last press conference of the evening and spent the remaining hours recounting all of the information I had regarding the situation. There was still no new information about the victims or the killer. However, many of the media who were just arriving needed questions answered to catch up on what they had missed. The university also released a time line about the morning's events and announced a press conference would be held at nine the next morning in hopes of having more details to release.

Neal Turnage: At a later press conference the crowd was too large and we got shut out. We ended up in the lobby with some other members of the media. Andy Mager and I looked over and who was sitting across the way but Katie Couric. I'm sure that over the course of my journalistic career I'd get to meet and rub elbows with big names of news, but doing so under these circumstances could not have been foretold. Andy leaned in and whispered, "Hey, that's Katie Couric. I've got to meet her." In between us and Katie was one of her assistants or "handlers" as I like to call them. Andy blew right past her and walked up to Katie to introduce himself. I followed right along and we had a brief conversation. She was pleasant enough, though I expected nothing less. She was short and cute; not a knockout, but that's part of her appeal. As we chatted she was snacking on a bag of M&M's. She poured a handful into her palm and offered them up to us. Such a simple gesture from a big-time celeb just added to the surreal feeling of the day.

Jenna Lazenby Nelson: It was a little after eleven when I finally left the alumni center. The parking lot was now filled with media satellite trucks and many stations were still reporting live. As I headed out I passed back by the rooms filled with families, many of whom were still there. However, at this time, many of the faces had changed from worry and fear to utter heartache. I shed a tear as I considered the nightmare they must be experiencing, I couldn't imagine, I didn't want to.

Ishwar Puri: I remember just going to bed; it was really late at night. I think that first week I had two or three hours of sleep a night because there's so much to do and so much to process. I remember I started shivering, and saying, "Oh my God. I can't believe this is happening." I don't question that it happened. It's just a sense of disbelief that it happened. You know, bad things happen, but it's just a . . . Because you're so used to these things happening, you read about it in the media, right? But it's always somewhat far away.

Kristina Ticknor, Virginia Tech student: The rest of the afternoon was spent sitting in front of a television screen, watching news stories of what had occurred right outside our doors hours before. It was horrifying to watch and yet I couldn't peel my eyes away. We literally watched scenes of the campus that were being filmed right outside our window. The cell phone circuits were busy, and it became harder and harder to keep in touch. My mother made it clear that she wanted me to come home, without specifically telling me to do so, knowing that I was now an adult and had to make the decision for myself. By five my hall-mate informed me that we could return to our rooms to get any necessary belongings, but that we were not allowed to sleep in our dorm rooms. I then made a second terrifying walk across the Drillfield toward West Ambler Johnston with my roommate and her cadet boyfriend escorting us. It was as if the three of us were walking through a ghost town, with no one to be seen aside from the police officers standing guard. Finally we reached our dormitory, and reluctantly entered. Taped to the fourth-floor entrance was a sign from our residential adviser that urged us to find somewhere else to stay, and to be safe. As we walked down the hallway we could see the yellow tape blocking the entrance to the elevators. Again, not a soul was to be seen. Once inside our rooms, we each packed up a small backpack of essentials and headed back out. After finishing my meal, I decided where I needed to be: home. The three of us walked to my car, where we were stopped by a policeman who informed us that if we left campus, we would be unable to return. We got in the car and I took my roommate and her boyfriend to an area off campus that was closer to his dormitory. Throughout the entire day I had been in shock, so bewildered that such an event could happen to me, my school, my dormitory, my floor, my Hokies. It wasn't until I was alone in my car with two hundred miles between me and home when I finally broke down into tears. I cried the entire way home, listening to the news on the radio and talking to my boyfriend about the fear I still held within me.

Fear also gripped Karan Grewal and two of his suitemates on the second floor of Tech's Harper Hall that Monday night. At 7:30, someone started banging on their door.

Karan Grewal, Virginia Tech senior: The FBI, ATF, and state police were knocking on our door. We suitemates were inside. I don't know if you've seen the suites, but there's a main door, and three rooms. All the doors were locked so none of us opened when they were knocking. They said "Police," but we didn't open the door because we weren't sure if it was them. I guess they got the key from the RA and they got in, and then they were knocking on my door. I still didn't want to open the door, but finally I opened the door and there were three cops with guns drawn and everything and they took us out, all the suitemates. They handcuffed us so I knew something was going on. I had no idea what. I had heard reports on TV about some person who was in some other college who had a dispute with his girlfriend or something. Until that time I thought it was not a student.

Grewal and his suitemates had not considered that their missing suitemate might be involved.

Karan Grewal: They took us out and separated all of us to question us, and they kept asking questions about Cho again and again. "What did he look like?" They didn't tell us exactly who it was; they just kept asking questions. So I guess that's the first time I thought it was him. Then they left us alone while they searched our rooms, and then one of the ATF agents came out and he told me your roommate actually did the murders today, so don't hide anything from us. I told them the same thing. I didn't know him that well.

The scenario seemed too fantastic to believe.

Karan Grewal: I guess we didn't have time to process it then. It was still shocking. I didn't believe it until everybody left. Even the next morning when they actually showed his picture on TV, I was like "Oh my God." I thought that maybe they made a mistake. He didn't seem like the person that would do anything like that. I mean, living with him, he wasn't an aggressive person or he wasn't even the kind of person I could think could hold two guns and shoot people. I mean he wasn't big or anything. I've never held a gun myself, but I'm sure it's very heavy and to fire 170 shots in nine minutes, they said, requires a lot of stamina.

PART II
AFTERMATH

CHAPTER 4

The Shadow Figure

That Tuesday morning of April 17, a stunned and horrified Virginia Tech community awakened to find that the dreamlike events of the day before were no dream. They were brutally real, even though that reality remained quite elusive. Worst of all, the incident made no sense whatsoever.

The deep confusion that settled on Blacksburg and the world demanded answers. Who had committed such an unfathomable act? And why?

The first question was answered publicly in a packed press conference at the Inn at Virginia Tech Tuesday morning.

The killer was Seung-Hui Cho, a twenty-three-year-old senior English major of Korean heritage from the Washington, D.C., suburbs of northern Virginia.

As for why, the Virginia State Police would spend thousands of hours investigating the incident only to discover that the answers were just that, unfathomable, lost in the deep, silent confusion of a madman, who among the few communications in his life left these last words: "I died—like Jesus Christ."

In all likelihood, just about everything related to Seung-Hui Cho will remain forever mysterious, because he was a shadow figure, locked in a world of willful silence.

Since August 2006, Karan Grewal had shared a suite with Cho on the second floor of Harper Hall. Yet the first time Grewal heard his suitemate's voice was on the video aired by NBC in the days after the killings.

Karan Grewal, Cho's suitemate: I thought he was the shyest person I ever knew, that's what I would think of him. I would think he was lonely a lot, too. He used to sit sometimes and stare out the window. I didn't see any pain. That's just how I felt about him, that he was really lonely. But there was no way for me to help him, since he never even looked you in the eye. So I didn't feel responsible that I didn't do anything. But I never saw any kind of anger with him, like he was pissed off at something. Never displayed any happiness either. He was really, really shy. I mean, some people don't even remember him living here. The people next door to us don't remember him being here at all.

The suitemates made attempts to converse with Cho, but he had developed a means of rebuffing them without acknowledging them.

Karan Grewal: He would just pretend that he didn't hear you. Just keep on sitting there. If he was staring one way, and you came down and sat there he'd just look the other way. One of our suitemates, Joseph Aust, talked to him once. He said it was like a one-word conversation that time. He just asked him what major he was, and in like one word he just said "business," which wasn't even true. I was still surprised he'd been in the United States since third grade. I just thought it was something to do with the culture, maybe with him not making eye contact with people. I thought he just needed time to open up. More recently he was in the common area more. He was there reading, typing on his laptop. There's no Internet in the common area so he had to be working on something. The only time I

> saw him was in the bathroom, the common area, typing on his laptop or sitting, staring out the window, or there's a TV lounge downstairs. He'd be there sometimes on the weekends, late at night around midnight or so.

One place that Cho did indulge in communication with others was in English classes, with disastrous results. Five different English teachers had complained about Cho's strange, sometimes threatening behavior, Lucinda Roy, then the English department chair, told reporters who swarmed in and around the academic department in Shanks Hall on April 17.

In class, Cho often wore sunglasses and a hat pulled down over his eyes. He took photos of other students with his cell phone and acted generally strange. "The threats seemed to be underneath the surface," Roy told reporters. "They were not explicit, and that was the difficulty the police had. My argument was that he seemed so disturbed that we needed to do something about this."

To calm her fears as well as those of students and other faculty, Roy began teaching Cho one-on-one, an arrangement that would last through the semester. "I had my assistant ready, ready to call for help if I needed it," Roy told reporters, acknowledging her own fear.

"I just felt I was between a rock and a hard place," Roy said. "It seemed the only alternative was to send him back to the classroom, and I wouldn't do it."

The individual instruction helped open Cho up to limited conversation during which Roy began asking him about his circumstances. "He said, 'I am so lonely,' and I knew that that was true and I felt terrible for him," she told the *Roanoke Times*. "I was always so worried that he was suicidal."

In the wake of the April 16 shootings, police acknowledged that two female Virginia Tech students had filed complaints about Cho's harassing behavior in 2005. In late November 2005, Cho made comments in person and also through phone calls that so disturbed a female student she called the campus police. The student decided not to file charges and Cho was referred to the university's disciplinary system. About two weeks later, on December 12, Cho sent an "annoying" instant message to a second female student that prompted her to file a second complaint against him.

Police contacted Cho and asked him not to bother the student again.

That December, a Montgomery County magistrate ordered Cho to be mentally evaluated. General District Court records document that the magistrate found probable cause that Cho was "mentally ill" and an "imminent danger to self and others" and was so seriously mentally ill as to be substantially unable to care for himself.

He was placed in a mental health facility for a brief time. A counselor familiar with his records said that Cho learned much from the forced hospitalization. Mainly he learned what to say when questioned by mental health authorities so that he could avoid future commitments to a mental health facility.

Reporters immediately questioned whether authorities or the university had properly responded to Cho's erratic and disturbing behavior.

Roy had also talked to Tech police about her concerns about Cho. While he made no overt threats, his behavior had been clearly threatening to faculty and students alike. The behavior just wasn't serious enough, or of a criminal nature, to warrant his detention.

"He seemed to be crying behind his sunglasses," Roy later told reporters.

Clearly, the killer presented a substantial mystery for the public and authorities. In search of clues about his issues, news organizations turned immediately to his native Korea. They found a picture of a life locked in strange silence.

Kim Yang-Soon, Cho's eighty-four-year-old great-aunt, recalled for the *New York Times* that she talked about his silence with his mother: "When I told his mother that he was a good boy, quiet but well behaved, she said she would rather have him respond to her when talked to than be good and meek."

Other relatives wondered if the strange little boy wasn't a mute or possessed by some mental illness.

His mother told her relatives that she prayed in church for God to help her son to open up, to find a way to break out of his silence. For much of Cho's early life, the family lived in Seoul, South Korea, in a two-room basement apartment, paid for by the meager earnings his father pulled from owning a used bookstore. Prior to that, his father, Seung-Tae Cho, had worked in construction in Saudi Arabia. The parents had come together in an arranged union. His mother, Kim Hwang-Im, was a North Korean farm girl until her family had been forced to flee south during the Korean War.

In 1984, some family members in America had suggested Cho and his parents and sister come join them in the United States. The family applied for a visa, then waited almost a decade. Finally, the visa came through in 1992. Cho was eight. His parents hoped a change of culture and scenery would help. First they went to Detroit, then to Centreville, Virginia, where the dry-cleaning industry offered employment for Cho's father. The suburbs of D.C. also offered a thriving Korean community, based in part on ownership of hundreds of dry-cleaning businesses. Cho's father, though, never managed to own his own laundry. Instead he has worked for years as a dry-cleaning presser in an industry that is perfect for assimilation because it requires few language skills for the limited interaction with customers.

Cho's mother eventually found a job working in a school cafeteria, which helped pay for the family's row house in Centreville. They attended church and kept to themselves for the most part, although over time they formed a friendship with their neighbors, including a Virginia Tech family next door.

Their son, however, clung to his silence. One relative said you could get a "yes, sir" as a reply but little more. As staff writers for planetblacksburg.com discovered, Cho was soley distinguished by his alienation, which seemed almost self-imposed. In his manifesto mailed to NBC, he seemed to rail against schoolmates, an implication that his personality may have made him a target for teasing in a school system that fed into Virginia's largest high school.

Killer Came from Virginia High School That Has Produced Many Fine Members of Tech Community

by Tricia Sangalang
News Staff Writer
April 18, 2007

Just seven years old, Westfield High in Chantilly is the state's largest high school with a student body that has just over 3,200 students.

Among its grads are some of Virginia Tech's best-known faces, specifically the Hokies' quarterback and receiver tandem of Sean Glennon and Eddie Royal.

Sadly, perversely, there's a new name to add to that Westfield list, a name that forever forward will strike dread in hearts everywhere.

Seung-Hui Cho.

Students who knew him at Westfield said he preferred to be called Seung Cho.

Tech students from Westfield describe him as a quiet person who would have "no expression on his face" during interactions. In these cases, students more so knew of him as a peer who rarely participated in class discussions and often refused to take part in social outings.

"He was very odd [and] didn't like to interact with anyone," said Patrick Song, a senior Marketing major who also attended Westfield. "He always had a blank stare on his face, but looked puzzled and even serious."

Song and Cho had calculus class together during their senior year at Westfield.

Song said Cho would pass him in the halls every once in a while but Cho was alone each time.

"I don't think he had friends," Song said.

Cho, twenty-three, was a senior English major at Tech and native of South Korea. He and his family lived in Centreville, Virginia, and he graduated from Westfield in 2003.

Jessica Bowen, a senior Aerospace Engineering major and high school classmate, shared similar memories.

"The only images of him that I remember are of him alone and with no expression on his face," she said. "I never got a chance to talk to him because he was really hard to even talk to, but I did know of him."

Cho's reticent nature defined his interactions in Blacksburg as well. His former suitemate, junior Business Management major Andy Koch, recalled: "He was quiet, shy. We tried to do stuff with him in the beginning of the year, but things just got weirder and weirder."

By "weirder," Koch explained that he and his friends took Cho to a party during the first month of school. He kept telling them he had "an imaginary girlfriend."

In addition, there were incidents of Cho "stalking girls," Koch said. Authorities had to step in during those occurrences, although it's not entirely clear how they were dealt with.

Koch recalled most interaction with him was in the suite's common room.

"He spent time in the common room. There was one time he wrote 'dark' lyrics to a Nirvana song on the walls and we reported that because we didn't want to get in trouble for that."

Koch declined to reveal those lyrics.

He said he and his friends saw him around campus a few times after they moved out of Cochrane; the most recent encounter was this past Sunday, and Cho did not say a word.

"There was one instance he said he was going to commit suicide and we reported that and they took him away. It was at that point he shut down," Koch said.

Cho then ignored all attempts Koch made to talk to him, and Koch and his friends, in turn, began ignoring him, too.

"After I heard I knew him, I was in shock," Koch said. "I didn't think he'd do something like that."

Katie Dolan, a Virginia Tech senior Marketing major who graduated from Centreville High School in 2003, was shocked to discover that Cho lived in her hometown.

"I felt sick to my stomach knowing the shooter was from Centreville," she said. "I was scared and confused. I didn't really know what to think, but I didn't want people thinking that Centreville is a bad place."

Dolan did not know Cho personally. Westfield and Centreville are approximately seven miles from each other.

"It made me mad because he lives so close to me," she said. "It's pretty scary because he could have done something like this a long time ago. I just want to know what his motive was for doing it now."

Like Dolan, Sean Glennon, the quarterback of Tech's football team, expressed dismay at learning that the killer was from his hometown.

Asked what he thought when he realized he had gone to high

school with the man who killed so many of his fellow Hokies, Glennon told the *Roanoke Times*: "The whole Virginia Tech thing here hits so close to home because it's my college. And then to find out that the person involved is from my other home is just unbelievable."

Terrance Steffens, a Tech senior Building Construction major and another 2003 graduate of Westfield, found himself and his family fielding calls from the media in the wake of Monday's killing spree simply because he was a high school classmate of the shooter.

"I didn't know him," Steffens said, "but I would feel badly for him. Clearly he was a troubled kid. Maybe all he needed was someone to talk to. I'd hate to think that someone I knew wouldn't be able to count on me as a friend or a helping hand."

All the students interviewed expressed the intention of moving on the best way they can, both personally and academically. All acknowledged the sense of community and togetherness they have felt in the past few days within this "Hokie family," as Bowen referred to it.

Others have put the situation in another perspective.

"Last night, I was trying to think about the number thirty-three, and how it has been thrown around as a measure of how tragic [Monday] was," Steffens said. "Each of our stories is different, but they converge on one day. Monday, April 16, 2007, was the day that the number thirty-three made twenty-six thousand people become one."

Ultimately, journalistic investigations yielded few clues to the killer's motives.

The only answers for a stunned and curious public would be the bare facts pinned down by detectives, and they would be scant. Grewal, Cho's suitemate, saw him in the restroom early that Monday morning. About an hour later, another student would see the killer waiting outside of West Ambler Johnston dorm at about 6:45. Sometime after seven Cho's gun fired the shots that killed Ryan Clark and Emily Hilscher. Cho had returned to his dorm in Harper Hall by 7:17 a.m., according to the card swipe that granted him access.

At 7:20, campus police were called to West Ambler Johnston, where they found the two shooting victims in Room 4040.

Five minutes later, Cho checked his email. Between 8:10 and 8:20, a witness saw Cho near the Duck Pond on campus.

At 9:01 he was in the post office on North Main Street in downtown Blacksburg, where he mailed his manifesto and video information to NBC.

At 9:15, the first eyewitnesses placed him in Norris Hall. At 9:42, authorities received the first 911 call from Norris. At 9:51, police heard the last gunshot, the one Cho used to take his own life.

At 10:08, officers conducting a search of the building found his body near those of his victims. He had killed himself with a shot to the head. His two handguns lay nearby, along with a backpack that contained two knives, a hammer, and additional ammunition for his weapons.

Karan Grewal: I just saw him that Monday at 5:30 in the morning. I was up all the night, so I was in the bathroom at 5:30. He just walked in like every morning, just a little bit earlier than usual. We'd pass each other without any kind of eye contact or anything. So it was routine. I just thought it was a little earlier than usual. I have an 8 a.m. class on Tuesdays and Thursdays and he's usually up by then. None of us saw anything. Joseph [another suitemate] never saw any guns either. We were thinking, could he have hidden the guns? Because it's just not easy to hide something in the room. I think the cops were talking about it, too, because the cops kept asking us if we saw any ammunition ever in the room. When we didn't, they were talking about maybe he hid it somewhere else. Then they started asking about what kind of bags did he carry.

Rosanna Brown, Harper Hall resident: I was not even acquainted with Cho. I may have seen him on a few occasions eating alone in a study lounge, but that would be the extent of our relationship. No one really knew him; he was a bona fide social pariah. Unfortunately someone as disturbed as he never took it upon himself to become sociable with those he lived with. His most recent suitemates even gave up asking him out to dinner after they extended many invitations. Little could be done to convince him that he could be a part of reality and I believe his own self-induced loneliness is what drove him to his depressed state.

Jenna Lazenby Nelson, Virginia Tech news bureau manager: According to Virginia Tech police records, Cho had two runins with police in the fall of 2005, stemming from contact Cho had initiated with two different female students. Although both students had made complaints to the Virginia Tech police, neither had pressed charges. The same day the second student made a complaint about several text messages Cho had sent her, police received a call from Cho's roommate that Cho might have been suicidal. Police met with Cho and he agreed to speak to a counselor, which resulted in him being taken to Carilion Saint Albans Behavioral Health Center.

Tricia Sangalang: I arrived on campus Tuesday morning fairly early. The morning press conference revealed the identity of the killer—I could put a name and a face to the callous and merciless shootings: Seung-Hui Cho. Later, I would discover he Americanized his name to Seung Cho, but introduced himself to others as "question mark." He is a question, indeed.

In the end, investigators would know little more than they offered the public that morning after the event. Times, places, minor details. Ballistics tests confirmed that one of the guns used in Norris Hall was also used to shoot Emily Hilscher and Ryan Clark at West Ambler Johnston Hall. Authorities also revealed that Cho was probably the author of a bomb-threat note for engineering school department buildings found Monday at the scene in Norris Hall.

As for the weapons, authorities determined that Cho had purchased the two handguns—a 9mm and a .22-caliber—over a period of about five weeks. He tried to remove the serial numbers on both weapons, but police were able to trace them through sales receipts. Cho purchased the Walther P22 on February 9 from a pawn shop in Blacksburg. The pawn shop owner told authorities he collected a processing fee from Cho that allowed him to purchase the gun out of state.

The killer apparently bought the Glock and a box of fifty bullets on or about March 12 at Roanoke Firearms by charging $571 on a credit card.

The *Roanoke Times* interviewed the gunstore owner and quoted him as saying, "It's bad enough watching the news to find out what he did. But to find out he bought it here makes it so much worse."

There was nothing about Cho that would have caused the state to prevent the purchase.

"The sale was so straightforward," the firearms seller told the newspaper. "There's nothing that stood out."

After the shooting, Virginia State Police searched Room 2121 in Harper Hall and seized a number of Cho's personal effects, none of which offered any more than slightly ironic details.

If anything, the mystery only deepened the public's grief and anger that Tuesday.

At Montgomery Regional Hospital, some parents expressed frustration that they had not heard from Virginia Tech concerning their injured children. One parent even showed up at Squires Student Center looking for financial help for medical bills. The parent explained she had come to Squires because she didn't know where else to turn.

Sensing a problem, Ishwar Puri, head of Engineering Science and Mechanics, had asked faculty spouses, including his own wife, Beth Levinson, to get to the hospital Tuesday morning to help get information for injured students and their families from his department. The spouses arrived to find that no Tech official had made it to the hospital to discuss the situation with parents.

> **Ishwar Puri:** I remember at one point, there was a parent who lost it with Beth. The parent said to Beth, "I've got to talk to someone [from Virginia Tech]." Beth said she would try to arrange that. I gave the phone over to Dick Benson, the dean, who was sitting two steps away. He talked to Beth, and then I said, "Dick, I'm sorry. I apologize for being pushy, but somebody needs to step up. You need to sort of tell the provost or somebody to get some people over to the hospital." And Dick did that. He's just been a great guy with this whole thing. Dick had a better chance of getting the message to the provost, who had a better chance of getting the message to Charles, to the president. So Dick gave it to Mark McNamee [the provost], and Mark gave it to Charles [Steger]. And I think things sort of came together. There was a lot of frustration on Tuesday morning, but it subsided. I think Virginia Tech finally instituted things.

Authorities also began releasing the first names of the victims Tuesday morning, as their identities were confirmed by their families and coroners. For other victims, their names became known to their friends and schoolmates well in advance of official notification.

Melissa Croushorn, Virginia Tech student: What do you say when you wake up to the sound of your friend crying because she just got a call confirming the death of her friend? What do you do when you can't get ahold of your brother who lives in WAJ? What do you do when you realize that your former French teacher who played French techno music videos on Fridays [Couture] and peers [Austin, Caitlin, Daniel, Erin, and Matt] are dead? What do you think about when you realize that you could have been in that class had you not dropped your French minor because of academic difficulties? What do you think about when you realize that the reason you weren't in adjoining Holden Hall was because you overslept and your professor canceled class because his daughter was sick? What do you do when the U.S. president issues a national statement regarding your school and the hell that left so many dead? What do you tell your brother when he can't find his study partner Lauren that you met at a football game? You think *why*. You scream in anger and hurt. You watch TV for eight hours to hear the same news. You hug your friend till she doesn't have any tears left. You choke on your own tears. You check Facebook profiles. You reflect. You stare. You try to keep busy. You try to pray and fail. And then you think of the words in Esther in the Old Testament when Mordecai tells her, "Who knows but that you were spared for such a time as this?" And you think, what is there left for me to accomplish? What was left for beautiful Caitlin, freshman Austin, easygoing (and good-smelling) Daniel, my conversation partner Matt? What was left for Ms. Couture to do with her daughter and husband? What songs were left for Erin to mix? And you feel responsible to make your life meaningful and purposeful enough on behalf of the people whose lives are done. And you remember every stupid, selfish, careless thing you've done and see that time has slipped through your hands like sand. And you frantically try to figure out how to make your time be real, all the time. You regret giving your teacher a hard time. You remember laughing with Austin at the pool. You remember Erin and Austin joking around in class. You remember giving Daniel a hard time for falling asleep in class. You remember being impressed by Matt's deeply personal essays in class. You remember Caitlin's beautiful, always available smile. You remember comparing Christmas break plans. You check the wounded and dead list every two seconds but not wanting to look at the screen. You cry every time CNN comes on so you watch *The Cosby Show* instead and realize that laughter only makes you feel worse. You remember thinking your senior year would be pretty boring and remember the shootings in August, the bomb threats, and now this. You are angry at the newscasters for calling it a massacre over and over again. Nikki Giovanni tells you Tech will prevail. And you avoid being alone until you're so tired you can't even brush your teeth.

CHAPTER 5
Candlelight

Mere hours after the shootings, students began planning a community gathering in memory of the victims. It would be the first of many of the community's expressions of grief.

Jenna Lazenby Nelson: At one point I overheard one of the student leaders mention that he wanted to get word out about a candlelight vigil that would be held the next evening. I grabbed him, got the information, and began recounting it to the media. It took only minutes for the news of the vigil to be sent to the community and the world. Never in my life had I witnessed this level of media coverage. Had I actually had the time to take it in I would have been completely overwhelmed, but I was too busy to consider what I was dealing with.

Within hours after the incident, Virginia Tech had posted a news release announcing the cancellation of classes for the remainder of the week, as well as the scheduling of the convocation at Cassell Coliseum at two on Tuesday. Students and faculty, community residents, families and friends, alumni, and many others awakened early to line up to get a seat inside the basketball stadium.

Justin Cates, editor/writer, Planet Blacksburg: Tuesday was more of the surreal. My friends and I arrived outside Cassell Coliseum at 11 a.m. for the 2 p.m. convocation, and found thousands clad in orange and maroon already waiting. While in the crowd an F-16 rocketed overhead, surveying the area in preparation for the arrival of the president.

The seats inside quickly filled, and the crowd outside stood in line under the warm April sun. The "spillover" could watch the convocation on the HokieVision screen in Lane Stadium. The scene on Washington Street and Spring Road was chaotic, with state police directing traffic, the SWAT team blockading the road, and people wondering when they could file in to Lane Stadium.

Ezra "Bud" Brown: I do remember seeing dozens—maybe over a hundred—police cars and the now-ubiquitous TV satellite trucks at the Tech Airport, ready and waiting for the president of the United States and the governor of Virginia to arrive and to be escorted to Cassell Coliseum for the 2 p.m. convocation. My wife expressed the thoughts of many thousands when she said, "This can't be happening in Little Old Blacksburg, in our safe little town where the number of murders over the past thirty-eight years suddenly doubled in as many minutes. No, this can't be happening." Can't be, can't be.

Ishwar Puri: I remember walking to the convocation with Scott Case, my associate head, and there was a huge line, and it struck me, the enormity of the response. People were so generous.

Tricia Sangalang: Minutes before the convocation was to start, police allowed the crowd to enter Lane Stadium. Inside, it was even more a sea of maroon and orange. The bleachers were filled, and students who sat on Worsham Field faced the HokieVision screen. I walked down the sideline, and the jumbotron just seemed so far away. At one point, I stopped just to get a feel of how many people were actually there. I looked around and sighed. The only word I can use to describe my reaction: *Wow*. I didn't expect this turnout, and I certainly didn't expect for Cassell to fill so quickly. Omar and I decided we wanted to write a story on the scene outside and about watching the convocation from Lane.

Community Watched Convocation in Lane Stadium

by Omar Maglalang and Tricia Sangalang
Planet Blacksburg Staff Writers
April 17, 2007

The crowd standing on the sidewalk was silent early Tuesday afternoon. Many looked down Spring Road, which was blockaded by two motorcycles and an armored state police car, and wondered what was happening. Muffled whispers circulated in the crowd that President Bush was on his way, but a few minutes later police directed the waiting crowd to enter Lane Stadium to proceed to gate six.

At that moment, people from both sides of the street flocked towards the gates. Inside, it was a sea of orange and maroon. Many students, parents, administrators, and people from all over the state, country, and even the world sat on the bleachers, while others sat on the dirt ground of Worsham Field.

Many had somber faces. Many were filled with hope, and others seemed afraid and helpless after the massacre of thirty-two people the day before.

"The events yesterday were just unpredictable," said Rebecca Greer, an Interdisciplinary Studies major at Virginia Tech. "It was tragic, but I was very happy that so many people went to the convocation. I thought people might be afraid after what happened, but I think we've come out as a community to support each other in this tragic time."

Anna Rizzo, a freshman in University Studies, also felt that the response by the community showed how much everyone had been affected by the shootings.

"It's going to take a lot of time, and it's going to take a while to understand why something like this has happened," she said. "It's shocking, and it hasn't set in, really."

Like many people who attended the convocation, Greer felt helpless and came to the convocation because she felt that she could do something to show support for the Hokie community.

"I was really hoping for a lot of people to come together when I decided to come here to the convocation," said Greer. "From being here at Virginia Tech for a while, people here have this sense of community and they just come together during tragic times like these, like, for example, with sporting events, or even the Morva situation last year."

As thousands watched in Lane Stadium, the atmosphere inside Cassell, where the actual convocation took place, gave the world a greater sense of the community spirit that exists among the Virginia Tech family.

Justin Cates: Everyone felt a need to be there, to heal, to be together, and to bask in the amazing events that followed. Of course we all know what happened during the ceremony. The world began to see what we already knew: the Hokie Nation is real, and its bond is incredibly strong. We came together to cry, to hope, and to heal as only Hokies can do. Orange and maroon never looked so good.

The ceremony began a little after 2 p.m.

Tricia Sangalang: The presentation of the colors was underway, I stood on the same side stairs I came up minutes before, and looked out onto the crowd again. Three girls in the front row hooked arms, gripping each other tightly. With their hands over their hearts, these students held their chins high.

Cassell Convocation Starts Healing Process for VT Community

by Anthony Della Calce
Planet Blacksburg Executive Editor
April 17, 2007

A basketball arena was turned into a place of prayer and healing for the Virginia Tech community Tuesday afternoon. A convocation held at Cassell Coliseum, Virginia Tech's on-campus basketball venue, brought together thousands of maroon- and orange-clad students seeking to find comfort and support in the wake of Monday's shootings.

Family, friends, teachers, Blacksburg residents, and other members of the Virginia Tech community joined the students. In fact, Cassell Coliseum could not fit all the thousands of people who turned out, so many were sent to Lane Stadium to view the convocation on the scoreboard's big screen.

Inside Cassell, the atmosphere was understandably somber. Many people sought comfort in conversations with those around them. But the voices were hushed as a sense of silence seemed to prevail over the dimmed noise. Indeed, many people sat silent, letting their facial expressions speak for them as they waited for the convocation to begin.

"It was really important for me to come here," said junior Molly Reed, an Animal and Poultry Sciences major from Boyds, Maryland. "Hopefully this event will bring us together and we can all show our Hokie pride."

As Reed and others looked on, the somber sounds of the Highty-Tighties, the Virginia Tech Corps of Cadets band, echoed throughout Cassell. In between songs, no one spoke. The hum of an air conditioner and the occasional cries of a baby were all that could be heard.

At about 2:15 p.m., the ceremony finally began with the presentation of the colors by the Corps of Cadets and the playing of the national anthem by the Highty-Tighties.

When the convocation began, Zenobia L. Hikes, Vice President of Student Affairs, offered opening remarks. Hikes moderated the convocation and was one of several distinguished guests who spoke to a grieving audience in an attempt to reach out to the Virginia Tech community and begin the healing process.

We have gathered here to "share in our sorrow," Hikes said.

"[The victims] will never be replaced in our hallways or in our hearts."

"With the help and support of each other and our brothers and sisters all over the world, we will eventually recover, but we will never forget," Hikes said.

Virginia Tech president Charles Steger followed Hikes's opening remarks. As he walked to the podium, he received an extended standing ovation, which was no doubt a sign of support from the Virginia Tech community.

"We have come together to mourn and grieve all the while hoping to awake from the horrible nightmare," Steger said. "Words are very weak symbols in times like this."

Steger thanked law enforcement for their ongoing hard work and dedication in dealing with the shootings and their aftermath. He emphasized the counseling available to students, faculty, and staff. "[We are] grateful we do not have to travel this path alone."

Virginia governor Timothy Kaine spoke next and also received a standing ovation. He stepped to the podium, looked around and began: "What an amazing community this is."

Kaine, who was in Japan at the time of the shootings, quickly canceled the remainder of his scheduled two-week trip to Asia. He and the first lady of Virginia, Anne Holton, flew back to Virginia to be in Blacksburg for the convocation. "There is nowhere else we'd rather be than with you here today," Kaine said of himself and his wife.

Kaine said students, faculty, friends, and family should be grieving. He said anger and despair were natural emotions to have in response to this tragedy. But, "as you wrestle with your sadness," he added, "do not lose hold of unity and community. The world needs you; they were watching you [yesterday]. They saw you respond in a way that built community. This is a remarkable place; do not let go of that sense of community."

President George W. Bush followed. Like Kaine and Steger before him, he, too, received a standing ovation. First Lady Laura Bush made the trip with the president and she sat and watched with the rest of the crowd as Bush delivered his speech.

"[You have] a passionate and resilient community at Virginia Tech," he said during his remarks. "Reach out to those who ache for sons and daughters who will never come home."

"People who have never met you are praying for you," he said.

"Although it does not seem possible right now, such a day will come when Virginia Tech will return to normal."

Indeed, that day seemed very much unimaginable given the current cloud of grief hovering above the campus and the entire Virginia Tech community. But before the convocation was over, it would seem within reach.

As several other speakers followed—community religious leaders and other Virginia Tech leaders, including members of the university support and counseling programs—members of the audience leaned on one another, wiped each other's tears, and shared embraces.

The anguish was still clearly expressed on the faces of students as Nikki Giovanni, an alumna and distinguished English professor at Virginia Tech, came to the podium for closing remarks. They were brief, but they were powerful.

"We are sad today, and we will be sad for quite a while," she said. "We are not moving on. We are embracing our mourning. We are Virginia Tech."

Giovanni ended her emotionally charged speech with the words, "We will prevail. We will prevail. We will prevail. We are Virginia Tech."

The audience immediately rose and clapped as Giovanni stepped away from the podium. In a time when words seem so inadequate, it was Giovanni's words that lifted a grieving community.

The crowd eventually began to cheer as Giovanni urged them on. Near the end of the event, a chant of "Let's Go Hokies" broke out. It was a chant that had been uttered many times within the walls of Cassell Coliseum. But now it took on new meaning. The repetition of those three simple words took on the task of starting the healing process for students and everyone within in the Virginia Tech community. The cheer was a much-needed emotional release.

"Let's Go Hokies" reminded the entire Hokie Nation that it can and will recover in due time. Someday soon, maroon- and orange-clad fans will pile into Cassell Coliseum for a Virginia Tech basketball game. And unified Hokies will cheer not as a grieving community but as fans: "Let's Go Hokies."

Brittney Asbury: As I sat through the convocation, I was trying to make myself understand how big of a deal this was. The president of the United States was twenty-five yards from me telling me my school was going to be okay. But no matter who spoke or what they said, I was still in denial, not really comprehending what had happened. Just as my eyes were begging to dry, our closing speaker, Nikki Giovanni, stood up to speak. Her speech was the most powerful and moving speech I have ever heard, and as long as I live, I will never forget what happened next. In the midst of the most trying times, I stood with eleven thousand of my fellow Hokies and with tears streaming down my face chanted, "Lets Go Hokies." I didn't know whether to smile or cry.

Ishwar Puri: I thought that Nikki's poem was the turning point, at least for me. I suppose it gave us a few phrases to hang on to. "We are Virginia Tech. We will prevail." I can't overemphasize the importance of that moment.

Kevin Cupp: At the end of Nikki Giovanni's speech, I remember saying, "Wow, we really needed that." All of the speeches before hers were more about how we had lost fellow Hokies and how we'd always remember them. While those words were necessary to say, Nikki Giovanni's speech was the perfect closing speech to really show what the Hokie spirit was all about. I couldn't help but start laughing during the "Let's Go Hokies" chant; not that it was funny, but it was just such an overwhelming change of mood and sense of Hokie spirit. With that kind of spirit, we can get through anything.

Jenna Lazenby Nelson: After grabbing a cup of coffee, I made it in front of the TV in time to catch the last half of the convocation ceremony. I listened to President Bush talk about his experience as a father and how a child was never far from a parent's heart. I stole a moment and thought about my son and somehow managed to smile. I was a bit dazed for much of the rest of the ceremony and it wasn't until Nikki Giovanni came forward that I refocused. In a little more than 250 words, Nikki delivered a speech of truth and comfort that conveyed to the rest of the world the spirit of Virginia Tech. As the speech ended, a crowd of students began to chant "Let's Go Hokies." It was a proud moment to be a Hokie.

Furthering that same spirit and support for the Hokie community, students were inspired to take action to honor their fallen peers. Facebook became one medium to communicate. In addition to using the social network to inform peers of their whereabouts and well-being, students all over the country used Facebook to form tribute groups and send invitations for vigils and other commemorations.

Students Use Facebook to Organize Vigils

by Tricia Sangalang
Planet Blacksburg Staff Writer
April 18, 2007

In addition to the convocation at Cassell Coliseum, students across the country are organizing their own vigils to honor those involved in Monday's shootings. For many of these students, Facebook is their main means of communicating the event or group to others.

"I sent out invitations to the group at about six p.m. [Monday] to eighty to one hundred people. About forty-five to fifty people actually attended," freshman Thomas Lane said. "I'm impressed by the universities all over the country. Schools from all over have sent me things. There is even a JMU Facebook group for Tech, which is great."

Lane created the event "PY Prayer Vigil," which took place in the downstairs lobby of Peddrew-Yates Residence Hall at 9 p.m., April 16.

"There were a lot of tears," Lane said. "It was encouraging and sad at the same time. We bonded a lot and just wanted to send the message that we're there for each other."

A simple "vigil Virginia Tech" search will bring up a number of hits for groups or events created by students. Some are for candlelit gatherings at a public location, like War Memorial Chapel, or a personal reflection open to "everyone, everywhere."

A search conducted today would bring up many events encouraging students at any university to wear maroon and orange.

An event called “Remembrance Day” features a tagline stating, “Forget any and all college affiliations today. For today we are all Hokies.” Jose Torres, a student at New River Valley Community College who plans to attend Virginia Tech next semester, created an event called “Student Gathering at the Drillfield.” Over one thousand students were invited to attend, and 176 confirmed, to gather on the Drillfield near War Memorial Chapel, beginning at 8:30 p.m. that Monday evening.

“We got together and made a big VT sign and tied it to a tree. Students came, talked to others, and signed. We want to show everyone we’re going to stick together,” Torres said. “We can go and see there are other people who share how we feel. I’ve had many people I don’t know come up to me and say, ‘Thank you for making this event.’ ”

Just before midnight, Torres returned to his apartment to get more paper for the guest sign-in binder. He estimated over two hundred people had attended by that point. The event was scheduled to continue until 2:30 Tuesday.

Students at the University of Virginia, in California, in Canada, in Denver, at the University of Florida, and Cabrini are among the many who have used Facebook as the main communication medium for vigils, moments of silences, and just simple remembrances.

“I’m planning a vigil for [Friday, April 20] at our ‘spirit rock.’ I remember when Columbine happened and I just felt it was needed to give support,” said Lauren Yono, Advertising and Public Relations major at Michigan State University. “I spread the word through Facebook hoping hundreds of people will come. Facebook has become easier than email and I felt it was the best way to contact people.”

Yono created a group called “Spartans Memorializing Virginia Tech Tragedy,” where, in the description, she encouraged her fellow students that "it is of character to come together and show support for the Virginia Tech Hokies and all those suffering from such a tragic incident."

Brandon Hayes, a sophomore and Management major, is an admin for the event "Evening Vigil," and is friends with the creator, Rebecca Spilman.

Students are encouraged to light a candle outside their room or window to remember those who died. In the description, Spilman suggests participants should "ask [themselves] how many more will it take until we realize our generation needs to make a change."

"I invited a few of my Facebook friends because you can communicate to a mass amount of people in a little amount of time," Hayes said. "[Spilman] created the event because she is wonderful and cares about everyone. With it not having a location or a time, it shows that people should remember those affected all the time."

In each event or group, the common theme is a sense of camaraderie, encouraging students everywhere to "come together" or to "rally behind the Hokies."

In the wake of the events, students have shown they want to "get to the next stage," as Torres said. "No one wants to be alone. We lost friends. We lost our Hokies. Many of us are afraid that it could have been us."

Hours after the convocation, thousands gathered on the Drillfield for the candlelight vigil. On that starry night, the winds had calmed, and the candles could finally burn. Volunteers unloaded boxes of thousands of candles donated by various groups.

Ezra "Bud" Brown: Someone, apparently from Charlottesville, found out that there would be a candlelight ceremony Tuesday night, called up the university and said, "I am donating forty thousand candles and paper cups to protect the flames from the wind. They will arrive in a truck on Tuesday afternoon. This is a donation and you cannot refuse." Whoever you are, we thank you.

Courtney Thomas: On the evening of the 17th, a candlelight vigil was held on the Drillfield. I walked from Shanks with Andy Mager to attend. We stopped because the Corps of Cadets, or some part of them, were walking in front of us. It took at least ten minutes for all of them to pass and then we fell in behind them. From the Upper Quad we could see a long snaking line of uniformed cadets disappearing into a growing mass of people gathering on the Drillfield. Andy took pictures. Members of the German Club and Hokies United handed out large candles inserted into holes in the bottoms of cups. We each took one and wandered into the mass.

Tables were set up at the beginning of each of the pathways, with students handing out those candles. As many slowly made their way to the center of the greens, standing facing Burruss Hall, a noticeable orange glow, a bright Hokie orange, illuminated the Drillfield.

By 8 p.m., the silence in the crowd was interrupted as speeches from various members of the community began.

"We're here tonight to remember the members of our Hokie family we've lost," SGA president Adeel Khan said.

Boasting Hokie colors of maroon and orange, the crowd stood in silence, listening to the words of the speakers. The mood was somber. Students and others stood in groups with friends and family, some even embraced each other warmly.

Vice President of Student Affairs, Zenobia Hikes, took to the microphone after Khan, and said, "I want America and the world to see this outpouring on the Drillfield this evening. This is love, and we appreciate it. We will move on from this, but it will take the strength of each other to do that. We want the world to know we will recover, we will survive with your prayers."

Ezra "Bud" Brown: Some said ten thousand, others said twenty thousand. There was a brief procession of a detachment from the Virginia Tech Corps of Cadets, the SGA president said a few words . . . and then one person lit one candle with one match, lit two other candles with his candle, and so it proceeded across all the thousands of candles.

Laura Schamus: As the world came together around us, we as Hokies united in a bond strong enough to impress onlookers in every corner of the earth. As I stood in the presence of thousands on the Drillfield, nothing else existed. My world froze.

Courtney Thomas: The vigil began with speeches. I don't remember who spoke or what was said. When it came time to light the candles, the speaker kind of laughed and commented that it seemed we had already taken care of that. She mentioned that someone up front would be lighting theirs at that time.

Tricia Sangalang: The speeches lasted for maybe fifteen minutes, and afterwards the crowd stood in silence, few moved. I wasn't ready to go home, and my roommate stood beside me, not ready to move either. In the distance, students started singing "Amazing Grace." I let myself cry for the first time. I had held my tears back many times over the two days. Many times my eyes only watered, and when I felt that desire to cry, I fought back the feeling. I wanted to stay strong and poised. I thought that letting my emotions take hold was a form of weakness. But I soon realized that I needed to let go.

Ezra "Bud" Brown: At various times we heard the singing of various melodies, including the VT alma mater, "Amazing Grace," and the national anthem. Someone began the Lord's Prayer and soon we were all saying it together. When all candles were lit, the SGA president said, "We will now have the playing of Echo Taps." One trumpeter near the public-address system would play a phrase from Taps, which was echoed by another trumpeter at the far end of the drill field . . . then another phrase, and its echo . . . and so on until the end of Taps. The playing of Echo Taps at the candlelight vigil was one of the most chilling things I have ever heard.

Courtney Thomas: When the vigil was over they invited everyone to stay as long as they liked and no one moved. The crowd was a mix of students and others from the community. Somewhere near the center a group of priests stood together. Small groups began to sing songs that would slowly spread throughout the crowd, until we reached a verse that few people knew the words to and the song would die out. Soon another would start. "Amazing Grace," "Lean on Me," a few Hokie cheers. The crowd began to dissipate a little while later. Groups gathered to sing or pray. One group with several priests held hands and recited the Lord's Prayer. I was standing nearby and recited it with them.

Laura Massey: Toward the end [of the vigil], we caught the sound of a woman singing the national anthem. Being musicians ourselves, we were moved by the music, and decided to sing the anthem ourselves. The CNN camera had finally moved away to focus on someone else, and we sang. Instantly, cameras swarmed around us. The media, in their attempt to cover the story, intruded on what we were trying to do and perverted any kind of meaning we could pull from performing that song. The focus was now on the fact that we had three camera lenses up our noses. I mean, really, would it have been so terrible to stand two feet back and use a zoom?

Tricia Sangalang: Students yelled, "Let's Go!" Just like at the convocation hours before, a thunderous sound echoed through the crowd in response: "Ho-kies!" With each response, the crowd lifted their candles high.

Suzanne Higgs: I held it together the whole time until everyone started chanting "Let's Go Hokies!" It was just the spirit of the moment and it showed who the Hokie Nation really was. At that moment, I knew we would endure this, I knew we would make it.

Laura Massey: The vigil played a role in allowing everyone to come together to mourn. Everyone mourns in different ways, and I think it's important to be able to see that even though someone might not mourn the same way you do, he or she is, in fact, mourning. The vigil gave the community the opportunity to mourn in their own ways but together, and together was and is the best way to be.

Adeel Khan mentioned to the crowd that thirty-two Hokie stones, lined in a semicircle, would remain on the Drillfield as a memorial. Each one, in honor of each victim, originally only had a single orange flower with a Virginia Tech flag tied to the stem laying on top.

Soon, each stone was designated for each victim—more flowers were placed from local florists, addressing a note to each victim and his or her family. Friends, family, and others followed the florists' gestures by leaving pictures, notes, poems, and other items honoring the students and faculty members.

CHAPTER 6
Darkness Again

What would prove to be an unbearable Wednesday began with rumors of a possible threat to university president Charles W. Steger.

The *Chronicle of Higher Education* reported, "Virginia Tech police officers raced to a main administration building with their guns drawn this morning in response to a threat. . . . The building, Burruss Hall, is located near the Drillfield in the center of the campus."

Ishwar Puri: The morning of Wednesday, the dean's office and the dean, and some of his staff, my associate head and I, we met in a conference room in Durham because, of course, we didn't have any offices. . . . That was the first time I saw TV. I found it very distracting, but I didn't pay very much attention to it until there was a threat. There was a threat or scare to Burruss Hall. And I remember that everyone was on edge, and the custodian in Durham simply ran to all the doors and locked them, yelling, "Lock down! Lock down!" And then Dean Benson and I said, "All right, we need to help the custodians." And I took one of the floors, and he took one of the floors, and we ran door to door. There weren't very many people in the building. The people who were there were very cooperative, which shows you their resilience. It also showed us that there was a feeling that lightning can strike twice, and I really hope that's not true. I don't think we want to go through this again.

Jenna Lazenby Nelson: I looked up and noticed several of the media leaving the building. I grabbed the police officer who was manning the door to the press room and asked him what all the commotion was about. Discretely he told me that there had been a threat against President Steger and somebody suspicious was seen in the building. Police were responding to the situation and Burruss Hall was being evacuated. I felt sick to my stomach. Hasn't our university been through enough? I quickly dialed numbers to see if I could get additional information. Media were approaching to find out what was going on before they rushed to Burruss.

As word spread quickly through the media, Mark Owczarski, director of news and information for University Relations, assured his employees that there was nothing to worry about.

Jenna Lazenby Nelson: Due to the heightened level of security, the police took necessary precautions and responded to the situation appropriately. The reports of suspicious activity were unfounded.

The morning press conference was delayed while police searched Burruss Hall. Commencing shortly after 9 a.m., the public address began with Tech police chief Wendell Flinchum addressing the incident at Burruss some short time before.

He confirmed that a threat had been called in on President Steger and emphasized that reports of this kind weren't uncommon after a tragedy.

Just prior to the press conference scheduled for 4 p.m., more news surfaced to the university about the killer.

Jenna Lazenby Nelson: I hadn't been there long on Wednesday when Corrine Gellar, spokesman for the Virginia State Police, entered the room and walked directly toward Larry Hincker. "It gets worse," she said with a bit of exasperation. Pausing for only a moment, Larry responded, "How could it possibly be any worse?"

The university learned about a package sent to NBC. The disclosure of information delayed the afternoon press conference.

State police and university officials were still meeting to discuss their new dilemma and weren't ready to address the media. As a school official made the announcement that the press conference would be postponed there were a few grumbles in the room, but not much else was said. There was no choice but to wait.

The conference began with the disclosure of more victims' names. Following that, Colonel Flaherty announced to the public that a package had been sent to the NBC headquarters in New York City.

He commended NBC for immediately notifying authorities and handing the package over to the FBI for investigation. No further questions about the package were allowed following Flaherty's announcement. Flaherty and the rest of the group left the room promptly as a room full of reporters shouted questions at them.

This, the shortest press conference in regards to the April 16 events, aggravated media and viewers alike. The disclosure of what the package contained would be aired on *NBC Nightly News* two and a half hours later.

Jenna Lazenby Nelson: Larry Hincker was sitting alone in a chair near the back of the room. The distraught look on his face almost deterred me from approaching him, but I pushed my fears aside. "Larry, I have spent a lot of time over the past few days in the alumni center working with the media, answering their questions and taking their requests," I said speedily, not wanting to waste any more of his time than necessary. "I think you should know that many of them are upset with how that press conference was handled and that questions weren't answered. They feel that their time was wasted."

Botched Press Conference Leaves Tech Apologizing

by Courtney Thomas
News Editor
April 18, 2007

An announcement by Colonel W. Steven Flaherty of the Virginia State Police at a 4:30 p.m. press conference Wednesday revealed that Monday's shooter, Seung-Hui Cho, mailed a package to NBC News in the two hours between shootings.

Flaherty offered very little information about the contents of the package. He said that police were working with NBC and did not allow reporters to ask questions, then abruptly, some said arrogantly, strode out of the interview room at the Inn at Virginia Tech.

The move angered many in the room and left Virginia Tech's chief spokesperson, Larry Hincker, apologizing. "I'm sorry," Hincker said, adding that he, too, was upset at how the event was handled.

Flaherty's abrupt departure left reporters stunned and complaining.

"I was upset that they didn't take more questions," said Beth Gorham, a reporter for the Canadian Press Wire Service. "So much of this is still up in the air and unexplained. It's our duty, as somebody here said, to ask questions and we're not getting good responses."

Frustration is focused on the situation, though, not individuals. Hincker's apology in an interview after the press conference eased the media's reaction.

"He's got to do his job and we have to do ours, so I'm quite understanding of that. And it's nothing against any of them on a personal level at all," Gorham said.

Information released to reporters is limited because of the ongoing criminal investigation. Dorry Gundy-Rice, an editor for BBC News, deals with this often.

"I get frustrated every day by the way authorities withhold information. Not just this, but all the time. They say it's for criminal investigations and you have to trust that and respect that," Gundy-Rice said.

Sean Tinnelly, a reporter for WVU News, agreed.

"As far as the information they're not giving, maybe it's better for their investigation that they're not giving it," Tinnelly said. "This is a hard time for them. I would say they're doing whatever is best for them."

The number of media organizations on campus seems to increase by the hour and students are growing tired of their presence.

Still, reporters say Virginia Tech has welcomed them.

"I have found the people here to be nothing but absolutely amazing and gracious in the face of such a devastating tragedy," Gorham said. "I can't believe it. I cannot believe how wonderful the students and the faculty and the staff are here. I think you guys are setting an incredible example for the rest of the world."

Reporters continue to contact students and local officials for information, many of whom are already overwhelmed with interview requests.

"People are busy," Gundy-Rice said. "They're overwhelmed with requests. We're trying to respect that, but everyone here on campus has been as accommodating as they can be.

"No one's been grumpy or mean or anything. Today, we wanted to talk to one of Cho's roommates or friends or something and he said, 'I just can't do it.' And we totally understand. Totally and completely. We're just trying to do our jobs, too, with some level of respect."

The Inn, where press conferences are held and satellite trucks fill every available space (paved or not), has served as a homebase for news media. Gundy-Rice said the amenities Virginia Tech is providing exceed her expectations.

"It's such a heartbreaking story," Gundy-Rice said. "It's just so hard not to feel this grief. I have been to stories where there's immense sadness and grief like this, but usually there's not running water, there's not hot coffee, there's no muffins, no toilet paper . . . and it's such a beautiful campus."

The airing of the tapes later that evening added to the feelings of frustration and anger stemming from the press conference a few hours earlier. Moments after the show aired, nearly every news station and website reported the disclosure of the package, blasting the images of Cho across TV and computer screens. Such images would resonate in the minds of viewers for days, igniting even greater feelings of outrage within the already grieving Hokie community.

Killer Sent Package to NBC Between Killings

by Planet Blacksburg Staff

April 18, 2007

According to *NBC Nightly News*, the package contained an eight-page, single-spaced document with twenty-three embedded videos and twenty-nine photos of himself, many with weapons including a hammer, knife, and the guns believed to be used in the shootings.

MSNBC.com reports that they have received a package from

Seung-Hui Cho timestamped 9:01 a.m. on the morning of the shootings.

According to NBC, the package contained numerous photos, information, and over twenty videos.

In the documents, Cho is quoted as saying, "This didn't have to happen," said NBC. No images of the first shooting were contained in the package.

Suzanne Higgs: I watched the tapes that night when NBC aired them. I was glad they did, because I wanted to know what his reasons were. They made me see that he was really disturbed, but didn't really clarify anything for me.

Roland Lazenby: Watching that newscast with the student reporters was really painful. We were all so angry we decided to quit using Cho's name on Planet Blacksburg. Some readers got upset with us. It probably wasn't a great decision journalistically. But it was an important symbolic statement to our community.

Theresa Walsh: You know, I've never really thought of him as a person. To me he doesn't even have a name. He's always been just "the shooter" or "the killer" in my mind. It's really too bad that the media have been keeping him alive by giving him all this publicity. That is exactly what he wanted when he set out to do this. To me he's just an unfortunate person who didn't have love in his life who made a bad decision and a really, really bad mistake. And that's all I'll say about him.

Karan Grewal, Cho's suitemate: He kind of got what he wanted exactly, to be on TV, I guess. I guess he talked to more people on TV than he ever talked to in his life. I guess that was his way of communicating. I wasn't angry at all; I was kind of happy that they released them, personally, because I wanted to know what kind of person he was. I think the more I know about him it helps me maybe forgive him a little bit and just forget about him a little bit. Because if I didn't know about him I'd keep thinking about why he did it. Now that I know what he was thinking it just helps me. It helps me understand he was disturbed. I was really glad that I got to see the videos. I actually wanted to see more of the whole story. I mean, I still want to find out more about him if I could in any way. Did he go to class? I don't know; I want to know that. I guess what I really want to know is was he doing it the entire year? While living with us? That's disturbing to me; was he doing it the entire year since he moved in with us, or was it recently?

Neal Turnage: All the anger and pain I had suppressed up to that point came out within four seconds of the video's airing. Seeing this gutless punk lay blame on society for his mental anguish made me sick. He had the audacity to record all of his ramblings and plan out this attack with the intent of the entire world hearing his "message" on the six o'clock news? He was a college student in the United States of America. His parents worked to provide as good a life as they thought they could for him. What atrocities could possibly have befallen him as he grew up on the mean streets of northern Virginia? HE KILLED A HOLOCAUST SURVIVOR!! I don't care how "unstable" he was. It was evil. Pure. Unadulterated.

Jenna Lazenby Nelson: By Thursday morning I was starting to wear out from mental fatigue and lack of sleep. Wednesday's events had been troublesome and I couldn't erase the disturbing images of Cho from my head. It made me sick to think about how the families must feel. To deal with the inconsolable grief of losing a child or loved one and then to see those images and hear reporters make statements like, "this is how many of the victims saw their killer in their final minutes" made me question the type of society we live in.

A catalyst for the growing disgust of the media's presence in Blacksburg, the NBC tapes heightened sickening emotions in the wake of the venerated candlelight vigil and the convocation. The tapes raised concern about the agenda of the media at Virginia Tech. Are the media here to inform their constituencies about stories of Virginia Tech's quest to move forward or are they here to indulge in a killer whose sole purpose was to gain personal attention? The media made their presence on campus well-known, not only at the Inn at Virginia Tech, but also throughout campus on the Drillfield, in academic buildings and dining halls and along sidewalks, waiting for a student or faculty member to be willing to comment on their next story. Yet, apart from such feelings of annoyance and irritation, questions arose about the approach of reporters and how the stories were aired, questions about journalism ethics.

On Monday, April 16, until Monday, April 23, the media became a staple on the Virginia Tech campus. While local media were on the site first, filtering out the main images and videos that would be used for days to come, the word quickly spread and the big networks flooded the campus. Soon after hearing casualties and injuries, big news organizations began to contact students immediately.

> **Karan Grewal, Cho's suitemate:** It was helping me really to talk about it on TV, and keep myself busy with that also, keep my mind off of other disturbing things. I was pretty tired but it was really helping a lot not to have any time to think about anything else. So that's why I agreed to do everything. I had my voicemails full and I was like, I'll do whatever I can. I think that it was a lot of personal coping. If this had happened somewhere else and somebody knew anything and wasn't talking I'd be kind of mad, so I just thought I should give any kind of information I had to. I don't know if it helped anyone. I can't say personally about the

families how they felt about all this news coverage, but it helped me a lot.

Laura Spaventa, Virginia Tech student: My friend Jon instant messaged me, telling me he had a friend who worked for CNN. CNN was looking to talk to students who were on campus and he asked if he could give her my number. I said yes, not knowing what I was getting into. I was released from Shanks Hall after being on lockdown for about three hours. CNN called me as I was weaving in and out of countless cop cars, ambulances, police with bulletproof vests, etcetera CNN grilled me with questions and I stupidly fell into their trap of placing blame on our administration. I told them I questioned going six and a half hours from home when I wasn't safe. Looking back at this idiotic statement I shudder, but at the time I was ignorant of what had happened and CNN had no problem taking advantage of that.

Chelsea Benincasa, Virginia Tech senior: I decided to go to the Drillfield alone to sit at the memorials and think. I held a tea light in my hand, and the wax burned me, but I didn't notice. Tears streamed down my cheeks as I sat in front of the podium at Burruss. A photographer hung over the side of the podium snapping pictures of me, but I hardly noticed. My knees shook as I walked toward Norris. A police officer stood in the doorway. The windows were still open on the second floor. I could barely stand it. I laid flowers by a tree and walked down the street with tears stinging my eyes. I tried to find a bus stop, but didn't know where to go since the buses were running on strange schedules. Suddenly, three reporters surrounded me. They wanted to ask me some questions. I felt trapped and vulnerable. I didn't see a camera, so maybe they wouldn't ask my name, I thought. As soon as I had let out a weak "okay," one guy was throwing a microphone down my sweatshirt, and before I knew it, I was being directed where to walk and answering harsh questions about gun policy. I felt out of control. Finally, after what seemed like forever, the interview was over, but NBC was right behind me, waiting. I told the new reporter that I didn't want to discuss gun issues. So she asked me a couple of questions about the package that had been sent to the media and I gave a blurry response. My head was swimming, and I ran off to the nearest parking lot. Frustrated by my media attack, I cried all the way to Roanoke Regional Airport.

Theresa Walsh: I only spoke to the ones that were really nice. Some of them just got on my nerves. My classmate Lisa [Kaiser] had asked me to do an interview with her because she didn't want to do it alone. I said, "Definitely, I'll go with you. I don't mind." Everyone at that point was telling me that I needed to get it out anyway and to not hold it in. That ended up being *ABC Primetime* or whatever. A lot of people tried getting at me, radio and talk shows and whatnot, but I didn't do many. I felt that I didn't want to get singled out within my classroom because all of us survived in my class and everyone should have the chance to tell their side of it.

Ezra "Bud" Brown: In the time since April 16, the students have been simply sensational. In their dealings with the media, and with the huge numbers of visitors, they have conducted themselves with dignity and their responses to interviewers of every kind have been uniformly positive. They saw every trap set for them by interviewers, and without heat or anger, cleverly avoided those traps. They reached out to each other and to the entire university community, and because of the 24/7 media coverage of this tragic event, the world knows what a classy bunch of students we have here, and we faculty are tremendously proud of them.

The Inn at Virginia Tech served as the command center for the media. From the press briefings there, they spread out across Blacksburg looking for stories and students to interview.

Jenna Lazenby Nelson: Somehow the parking lot at the Inn appeared more packed with media trucks that morning than it had been Monday night. When I arrived inside, many media were bustling about, writing and filing stories and consuming the urns of coffee and breakfast pastries the Inn had graciously supplied. It was decided to check media credentials more rigorously and limit the number of media from each organization that were granted access into the press briefings. Although some of the media were annoyed by the additional hassle, most cooperated.

Suzanne Higgs: My parents and I drove back to campus and we passed the Inn. I looked out the window and couldn't believe the number of satellite trucks and media persons. Our campus had been overrun.

Courtney Thomas: Andy Mager and I walked around the lot behind the Inn after I interviewed with the BBC. I remember commenting that this place really was a journalism student's playground, if only they'd come for some other reason. We had joked before that the interview that the BBC was a pretty big deal. Ha, maybe they'll hire us. I felt sick to my stomach as I said it.

After they became settled, reporters and cameramen seemed to be everywhere. Speaking with students from Squires to the Drillfield, during the convocation and the candlelight vigil. Many students linked the intrusion with bad experiences, while others did not mind them as much.

Ashley Hall, Virginia Tech alum: I watched as the media, for lack of a better word, raped my school. Everywhere I turned, I saw my Drillfield where I used to walk every day for four years. Except now, there were no Frisbees, no dogs, no cadets, no one reading in between classes—just hindsight, horrible descriptions, and accusations. I saw Matt Lauer framed by my Duck Pond. Every new camera angle was filled with a wonderful memory that was now stained with blood.

Laura Massey: Standing in Cassell Coliseum lot, we were approached by a woman who asked us for directions. The next words out of her mouth were, "I'd just like to apologize for the media as a whole. We know there's no good way for us to approach this." Instantaneously I was willing to talk to her. She showed me an understanding consistent with the Hokie Nation and appropriate to the situation, unlike several others, one of which I actually saw break into a prayer circle to get the camera angle they wanted.

Jenna Lazenby Nelson: It was a few minutes before two when I started to head to the Joint Information Center to take a breather and watch the ceremony [convocation]. As I walked up the stairs a CBS staffer grabbed me and asked for my assistance. I followed her outside to a trailer and makeshift production studio where Katie Couric was giving live commentary for the convocation. In between breaks Katie would ask me questions about the university and campus. Small things including graduation date, how to spell Cassell, and how many students attended Virginia Tech. Typically these were questions I could spout out, but lack of sleep and a bit of nervousness caused me to hesitate with each response.

Kevin Cupp: Tuesday, the day of the convocation, is where they started being disrespectful. I was waiting in line to get into Cassell Coliseum for the convocation when CBS called saying they wanted to talk to me about Facebook. I told them that if they could get to Cassell before I went in, I would talk to them. They did not make it in time and I had to go in and sit down. The reporter called me to tell me he was there, I told him I could not come back out because we were already in there. I tried to explain this to the reporter, but he kept saying, "C'mon, you'll be doing people a service, it'll only take five minutes," and anything else he could say to try to "sell" me. I eventually caved and went out to talk to him and hoped to be back in the five minutes he promised; I felt bad walking out on my friends in the coliseum. I get out there and he's on the phone, not ready to start. I try to tell him I'm short on time and that I need to get back in there, he finally gets off a few minutes later. CBS stopped calling me after that. I then learned of more stories much worse about the media being on campus; that's when I decided not to talk to any more media. I actually had a friend who works for one of the local news stations say that he was seriously considering leaving the business because he was so ashamed about how the media had been treating us. This is a guy whose lifelong dream it's been to be in this business, all changed because of what he saw them do.

Suzanne Higgs: While my parents wanted me to drive home Tuesday afternoon, I really wanted to stay for the vigil that night. My boyfriend, Collin Greiser, is in the Corps of Cadets and he had to march in with his company to the candlelight vigil, but he eventually found me in the crowd. I needed him to stand with me. During the moment of silence, I had my arm in his and my head on his shoulder. Four photographers lined up in front of us and took continuous pictures. I got angry after a while and we finally moved so they would stop. I could deal with that but I had to say something when Jamie Farnsworth, my roommate, and I tried to go up to the memorial, two cameramen were there. Granted, as a media person, I understand getting the shot, but blocking the way the entire time is rude and unnecessary. I finally said something, I told him to move because this was for us. The memorial was for students, not the media.

Courtney Thomas: The first time I visited the memorials I went with Melissa, Katie, and Jen. The Drillfield was filled with people. The walls had been placed under a couple of tents. We walked through the tent and I was reading them, not paying much attention to the people around me, when I looked up and a reporter was speaking to me. I looked around and Melissa and Katie had disappeared. She said something about being sorry for my loss and asked me to come and be on camera. I said no and went to find my friends. I told them what had happened and they laughed a little, saying they had ditched me when they saw her. Can't blame them for that. A little while later I saw her approach a guy who was kneeling in front of a wall, crying. She said something to him and he pulled her down to kneel with him. They prayed together for a few minutes and he refused the interview.

Carol Bishop, Virginia Tech staff member: I watched them; I eagle-eyed them. We could not tell them, "No, you are not allowed in the building," but we did try to keep them on the first floor so the second and third floors were still sacred because the counseling centers were there, for one thing, and we wanted them to stay away from that. We did set up a room, the Cardinal Room, for the media. We put refreshments in it so that if they needed a place to go and work on their stories, plug in their laptops, whatever the case may be to accommodate them. And yet try to watch them so our students and our community were not harassed because some of them were relentless, quite relentless.

Dr. Yannis Stivachtis, university faculty: Media perform a particular function in our society. Sometimes they do better than others, they have to pose the right questions, but of course I expect them to bring forward some answers, too. Sometimes I was disappointed. You have people telling you how things are who have never been here.

While some media professionals understood the situation of the students and were respectful and polite, many were rude and relentless. Some even challenged the limits of good taste.

Karan Grewal: Yeah, I remember the first night when I agreed to do *Good Morning America* the next morning, I was told—I thought this was really disturbing—that they had someone outside Harper just to see that I didn't leave that night so I'd be there the next morning. A lot of reporters were trying to get into [Cho's] room to take pictures, but the room had been locked. I think somebody did get in and put a marker on the window over here; they put a little plastic cup. The plastic cup on the window was on the news.

Carol Bishop: And actually one day we had an altercation between a gentleman in the building and a reporter from, I believe, CNN. The man was sitting on one of the sofas, the reporter came up to a student and at first the student seemed to welcome his questions. Then she just quickly became distraught and, I mean, he didn't let up. And this man saw it happening, he was the father of a student here, and he got really angry, went over and there was a shoving match. I had to come out from behind the desk and say, "Whoa! Gentlemen, what's going on here?" It did get ugly. That wasn't the only [incident]; I think that was about the ugliest one we had in Squires, but I witnessed many incidents where reporters were trying to stick microphones in the faces of people who didn't want it.

Gary Schroeder, Lutheran minister: The Saturday before Sunday the 22nd of April, which was the first Sunday after the 16th, we received ten separate requests from media who wanted to film our service on Sunday. In any case, I indicated to them that I would never, ever refuse to allow somebody to worship with us. And if they wanted to worship with us, they were welcome to come. They could sit and take notes if they wanted to, but they would not have their cameras in our sanctuary. I said, on the 22nd of April, our sanctuary is going to be precisely that, a sanctuary for our people. After I said that, no one showed up. So they were clearly out for the sensational. Let's get pictures of people crying. Let's milk this for all it's worth. I think at that point, it just got way out of hand.

However, not all were without heart. Neal Turnage, sports editor of Planet Blacksburg, recalls reading a press pass that was left at a memorial that said: "My heart breaks that we were brought here. News is often showing people in pain and grief . . . know we here this week cried tears when we went home at night."

John Chermak: The media was all over me. I had *People* magazine wanting to talk about Kevin Granata and I declined. My brother is a professor at Michigan State; he does media, victims, and crimes in the Sociology department and his advice to me was, "Don't talk to the media." I talked to *Fort Collins Media* because it was a more personal experience piece. It wasn't more like, "Did the administration do their job?" I had no interest in talking about that.

Laura Spaventa: The media made this experience ten times harder than it already was. It amazes me how heartless these people were when it came to getting their stories. I understand it is their job and their livelihood, but where did their conscience and human side go? It was disgusting how the reporters were suddenly so concerned once the camera lens was focused on their faces.

Suzanne Higgs: The media annoyed me when they couldn't get names of people and places correct. They mispronounced Steger, and they kept calling AJ something else that none of us understood. If you come here, and you want to be sensitive, do your research.

Jessica Ross, executive producer at WSLS in Roanoke: The seriousness of the situation crushed me to the point where I felt like I couldn't breathe. For what was probably only five seconds, but felt like an eternity, I sat in silence and swallowed back tears. But then I remembered. This is my job. I have to get this information on air. I have to let my news director know and all the reporters on their way to the New River Valley. And above all, I have to stay calm. I cannot freak out. I will not freak out. I am the executive producer. This is my job.

CHAPTER 7

Hokie Stone

As the week wore on, thousands of Virginia Tech alums and residents from around the state made a pilgrimage to Blacksburg. Once there, they found a campus dominated by makeshift memorials—Hokie stones, wooden message boards, flowers, orange and maroon ribbons, shreds of emotion as tribute, an outpouring of grief. Central to this outpouring was a collection of thirty-three Hokie stones on the Drillfield, one for each victim, even the killer, although most Hokies preferred to think of that stone as placed to acknowledge the grief of the Cho family. His sister had issued a statement apologizing on behalf of the family.

"He has made the world weep. We are living a nightmare," said the statement prepared by the killer's sister, Sun-Kyung Cho.

The statement was issued Friday, April 20, as mourners across the state of Virginia wore orange and maroon for the commonwealth's official day of mourning, a day marked by pealing church bells and services honoring the fallen.

"We are humbled by this darkness. We feel hopeless, helpless, and lost. This is someone that I grew up with and loved. Now I feel like I didn't know this person," the sister said. "We have always been a close, peaceful, and loving family. My brother was quiet and re-

NEAL TURNAGE

View from the sidewalk of Norris Hall taken the day after the shooting.

President Bush makes a rare visit to Blacksburg to give his condolences and words of encouragement.

KEVIN CUPP

KEVIN CUPP

Thousands of students and community members come together to remember those lost or injured during a candlelight vigil on the Drillfield.

Two cadets stand in memory during the candlelight vigil on the Drillfield.

KEVIN CUPP

The first day the Hokie stone memorials were placed in front of Burruss Hall. Each was adorned with a flower and a flag and was not labeled with any particular name.

NEAL TURNAGE

NEAL TURNAGE

A cameraman films a student as she grieves.

Several media outlets happened to be at the hospital and wanted to talk to the drum major, Stephen Shelburne, and several band members about what they hoped their performance would do for the injured victims.

KEVIN CUPP

KEVIN CUPP

Virginia Tech's marching band played outside the hospital for those injured to listen in through their windows. Will Petersen, assistant director to the MVs, gives the band thanks for volunteering to give the people inside joy as they heal.

KEVIN CUPP

By mid-week, Virginia Tech made the front page of every local and national newpaper with words such as "tragedy" and "massacre."

KEVIN CUPP

News organizations from as far away as Chile and the United Kingdom came to interview students who worked on Planet Blacksburg. Pictured is Courtney Thomas, Planet Blacksburg's news editor at the time.

KEVIN CUPP

Complaints about media invasion on campus led to the creation of these signs to be hung on virtually every door on the campus.

KEVIN CUPP

Neal Turnage, Planet Blacksburg's executive editor, had a lot to say to reporters about the way Planet Blacksburg covered the events.

KEVIN CUPP

Students and community members write messages on large walls on the Drillfield for those who were lost.

KEVIN CUPP

Friends and family of those lost left items of memorial around the walls on the Drillfield. A Hokie-colored shirt is left for Dr. G. V. Loganathan, a professor of engineering.

A student signs a poster of support for the university administration.

NEAL TURNAGE

KEVIN CUPP

Students arrive back at Dr. Cintia Easterwood's accounting class to discuss how the rest of the semester will be handled.

NEAL TURNAGE

A memorial poster featuring an excerpt from Nikki Giovanni's convocation speech.

NEAL TURNAGE

A message of support from a student in Lane Stadium during the convocation.

served, yet struggled to fit in. We never could have envisioned that he was capable of so much violence."

As a symbolic statement, Planet Blacksburg had made an editorial decision not to publish the killer's name. This decision was not an expression of hatred for the killer, but a refusal to give him what he desired in killing thirty-two Virginia Tech students and faculty and wounding nearly a dozen more people in a shooting rampage that Monday morning.

"Our family is so very sorry for my brother's unspeakable actions. It is a terrible tragedy for all of us," said Sun-Kyung Cho. The sister is a 2004 Princeton University graduate who at the time of the shooting was working as a contractor for the federal government, handling American aid for Iraq.

"We pray for their families and loved ones who are experiencing so much excruciating grief. And we pray for those who were injured and for those whose lives are changed forever because of what they witnessed and experienced," the killer's sister said. "Each of these people had so much love, talent, and gifts to offer, and their lives were cut short by a horrible and senseless act."

The sister said the killer's family "will do whatever we can to help authorities understand why these senseless acts happened. We have many unanswered questions as well."

According to various press reports, the family remained in seclusion in the days after the shootings, guarded by the Virginia State Police.

Jeff Wood, alum and former member of the Marching Virginians: I made my way to the memorial stones and slowly moved from one to the next. When I arrived at Ryan Clark's, it was hard to not break down entirely. As I looked at the mementos on the stone, I saw one that stood out. It was an image of the band in the shape of Virginia, one of our band's favorite formations. Each time we take the field, we're announced as "330 Strong," indicating that we field 330 musicians. The photo had only two words on it: "329 Strong." I don't think I'll ever be able to forget that, how personally it touched me.

Suzanne Higgs: I began to cry when I got to Ryan Clark's stone, which is about halfway through all of them. All I could think of was how much of a waste of life it was. He had almost completed a triple major, and in two weeks would be walking across that stage. He had so much going for him, as did all the victims.

Tricia Sangalang: One stone particularly caught my attention: the one addressed to Cho and his family. Someone had placed the stone there days after the others were placed. Like the others, flowers, flags, notes, and candles lay before it. Many wrote notes sending their prayers to his family. Others, on the other hand, directly addressed Cho. To my surprise, none of the notes I read expressed hatred, animosity, or condemnation. The ones I read explained how they did not understand why he chose to shoot his peers and some even said they wish they would have known him so they could have tried to help in any way. One note simply stated on an index card, "I forgive you."

Courtney Thomas: When I reached the memorials, I bent down to look at each one and read the notes that had been placed there. I had seen them briefly at the picnic the following Saturday, but people were crowded around and the mood of the picnic seemed to contrast with viewing the memorials. As I neared the end of the stones, something shocked me. I saw the shooter's name. I learned later that someone had placed a stone there for his family. But it was placed in between stones of two of his victims. I didn't like it and quickly moved on.

Tricia Sangalang: I went to the Hokie stones memorial and passed Norris each day, partly because every day there'd be a new sign, something new that someone left, but also because it was therapeutic. I took that time to read the messages people left for the victims, the messages addressed to President Steger, to the Hokie community, and to law enforcement. It made me feel better to see that outpouring of support and know that there was good that came out of that horrible day.

Amy Stanford, alum: The message boards and Hokie stone memorial on the Drillfield have been wonderful, and I hope they are in some way tied into some type of permanent memorial. The first time I saw the Hokie stone memorial, I had to choke back tears, it was the first time I had such a visual that represented each victim. It was chilling seeing just how many stones were lying there on the ground.

Theresa Walsh: My favorite memorial was the one in front of all the science buildings that said, "WE ARE VIRGINIA TECH" in lights. It was just shocking that so many people from around the country have given their condolences.

In addition to Norris Hall, the Hokie stones, lights, banners, and signed boards alike, the scene of two deaths in West Ambler Johnston prompted residents and visitors to remember the lives of Ryan Clark and Emily Hilscher with memorials as well.

Tricia Sangalang: Once I made that second right turn after getting off the elevator to the fourth floor, I saw a white wall with a picture of Snoopy in the middle and messages from residents written in black permanent marker. "Ryan, 4030 misses you," one message read. A bouquet of flowers also lay on the brown tile before the wall. My friend explained that, for some time, police had extended yellow and black crime scene tape there. She also explained how she and a few others were asked to move Ryan's belongings out of his room. Emily's roommate had to take out her possessions from her room before police took Emily's out. With a despondent look on her face, my friend said, "I woke up one morning and a wall was there." She's not sure who put up the wall or who decided a wall should be there. "With it up," she said, "they are acting as if they never lived there." People talk about turning Norris Hall into a memorial, and then they put up a wall around Ryan and Emily's room almost pretending like nothing happened there? It's ridiculous. That frustrates me.

Squires Student Center also became a collection site for memorial items such as signed banners, paper cranes, quilts, cards, and other creative forms of remembrance. A hub for many of the organizations on campus, as well as several classes, Squires Student Center became the place for the collection of items that the university received. Schools and other organizations from around the world immediately wanted a place to send their condolences and gifts for the Virginia Tech community. Squires quickly turned into a shrine of support.

Carol Bishop, manager, Squires Student Center: Even beginning on the 17th, banners, posters, cookies, goodie bags, just everything started pouring into the student center. Even other places on campus that were receiving items were sending them to Squires. Squires became the campus museum and memorial for the incident. The week after, there were no classes, so the students went home. There were no students to have their organization meetings and so forth; all we did was put up posters, take and document what was coming in so we had accurate records. We wanted to make sure everyone that sent anything got a personal thank you, and we were so busy handling all the stuff that we didn't have time to sit and grieve. I don't feel any of us really had a chance to deal with it because we were so busy dealing with everything that was being sent in to the university. All those origami birds are just amazing—literally, thousands and thousands of origami birds.

Tricia Sangalang: If you walk through Squires Student Center, the foyer is filled with messages hanging from the banisters on the second floor, along the walls, up the railings of the stairs, and on every bulletin in the building. It's overwhelming, yet also comforting to know that all these people care enough to send a message.

Brittney Asbury: I was speechless to see the banners and posters that filled our student center from schools and organizations across the nation. It was unbelievable to see the messages from some of our biggest rivals, like UVA.

Carol Bishop: We are at the point where we have taken down the items and have archived and worked through the Library of Congress. Jewelry. Oh, the car hood, that's a good one. The hood off of the race car, that was quite unique. It's hanging in the rafters, you can see it out in the atrium. And the little handmade cards, by the really young kids, elementary schools and kindergartners are unique. We have just received, and we couldn't begin to count all the cards from corporations, schools, colleges, universities, middle schools, grade schools, daycares. We have one adorable quilt that was made by, I think, five-year-olds, and they put everything that they love individually into little quilt patches; it's really cute. The crisis dogs that came in were just amazing, seeing there were two or three different groups, or organizations, that brought in healing dogs. We had them in the building, which typically we do not allow animals in the facility, however, this was an incredibly special time. It was a wonderful need that was met because pets have a remarkable way to heal and help take your mind off things, and to bring comfort in their own way to show love. Then there was one gentleman who travels around in his truck with a piano in the back with his dog, and they were here, too. Just the look on the students' faces when they'd walk into Squires where they'd see the dogs in the building, it was great to see them piled up all over the floor playing with the dogs.

Theresa Walsh: I don't think there's ever a good time to take the memorials down. Some people are going to think it's too soon while others don't want to dwell on it and think we should move on. A lot of people are not here in the summertime so it might feel like you're just keeping a horrible memory alive. But I think there are things the school can do to help heal that don't have to be big and drastic and by taking things down maybe we can start healing from it. I know it was difficult for me to come into Squires because of all the tributes that were in there.

Larry Hincker, Virginia Tech's vice president for university relations, had taken the full brunt of the media effort, and he had done so under immense duress. His many years of experience as the university's chief spokesperson served him well in this regard. Over his long tenure at the school, Hincker had established a level of trust with the state's media.

Jenna Lazenby Nelson: The Thursday press conference after the Wednesday night airing of Cho's manifesto was important. There was still a police officer at the door and several university employees checking media credentials; however, the media numbers had dwindled considerably. This time Virginia Tech spokesperson Larry Hincker and Colonel Steve Flaherty were accompanied by an entourage of university officials to answer questions and to help provide understanding into how the university handles police issues, counseling, and student affairs. After the frustration from Wednesday's events and press briefings, it was obvious that Larry wanted to pull all of the university's resources together to help get the media any answers they could provide. The press briefing began with Larry reading the list of newly released identities who had been positively identified and their next of kin notified. Brian Roy Bluhm. Ryan Christopher Clark. Austin Michelle Cloyd. Caitlin Millar Hammaren. Jeremy Michael Herbstritt. Jarrett Lee Lane. Partahi Mamora Halomoan Lumbantoruan. Daniel Patrick O'Neil. Juan Ramon Ortiz-Ortiz. Daniel Alegandro Perez Cueva. Michael Steven Pohle Jr. Julia Kathleen Pryde. Mary Karen Read. Reema Joseph Samaha. The room was silent as each name, hometown, and major was read. I listened carefully and tried hard to commit the names to memory. It was the victims I wanted to remember, not the killer. Colonel Flaherty stepped to the podium and announced that the state police had closed their on-scene phase of the Virginia Tech investigation and were moving on to the task of evaluating, reviewing, and building a case to explain what, and, as much as possible, why the April 16 tragedy occurred. The question-and-answer session that ensued was long. The media asked many questions and it felt at times as if the same questions were asked repeatedly. There was a myriad of questions regarding Cho's mental health and his history of stalking students. Other questions focused on how he obtained gun permits, or on possible connections Cho may have had with Emily Hilscher, the female victim from West Ambler Johnston. After the press conference concluded, Larry stayed back to answer a few additional questions. He asked the media if they thought this press conference had been helpful and if they would like to have another one. The afternoon press conference was up in the air for sometime. Larry was exhausted, the state police were finished with press briefings, and there was not a whole lot more information. But, by midafternoon, it was decided that there would be another press conference at 4 p.m. This time, Larry walked to the podium alone. He took a deep breath and began to read the final group of victim names. His voice cracked several times as he spoke, and although I was behind him and couldn't see his face, I knew he had tears in his eyes. Exhausted, he looked around the room and asked the media, "How do we do it, folks? How do we go on from here?" Although it was all over his face and in his body language, he shared with the group, which he addressed as his colleagues and friends, that he was totally exhausted and running on six hours of sleep since Monday. "We cannot begin to let this horror define Virginia Tech, and our university needs time to heal," he continued. As he looked around for a response the room was quiet. But it was only a moment until a pair of hands began to clap and then quickly others joined and the room broke out into applause. Maybe the applause was for his honesty, maybe the applause was out of respect for him, maybe the applause was out of sympathy. Whatever it was, it felt good, and I too stood up and put my hands together.

The university had announced its plans for students to complete the remainder of the spring semester. The university offered students individual options as to how they wished to proceed: to take their grade prior to April 16, to take that grade plus any other additional work the student chose to submit, or to complete the course as outlined by the original syllabus.

The news release explained that options were given due to the general concern by the faculty "for the education of our students, as well as their physical and mental well-being. We realize that various students will react differently to [the] events."

The idea of going back to class delighted some, yet others felt a sense of nervousness and hesitation.

Students, Faculty Anticipate Holding Class Again

by Omar Maglalang and Tricia Sangalang
Planet Blacksburg Staff Writers
April 20, 2007

Virginia Tech students have questions and some apprehension about the resumption of classes Monday. Others are eager to re-join their groups and meet again.

Like many Virginia Tech students, Ryan Anthony, a junior majoring in wood science and forestry products, will attend his classes on Monday. He has four classes, including Engineering Economy: the class where he learned about the Norris Hall and West Ambler Johnston shootings Monday. He also takes wood chemistry, wood science and forestry products, and also, packaging.

"I don't think I'll be uneasy about going to class on Monday," Anthony said. "I've always thought of [Tech] as probably the safest campus in the world for me."

Gail Senatore, Agricultural Science major, said some students might feel perturbed to go back to their class for the first time after the horrific events. This would be especially true for students who knew any of the deceased victims.

"It's going to be hard to adjust for some," she said. "They're not going to see some of their classmates in class anymore."

According to Senatore, the first day is going to be awkward

for a lot of students, but she noted that it was a better decision to start on Monday than later on in the month or week. She felt that it would allow for a better transition back to academic life and a return to a sense of normalcy for the community.

"Teachers have to understand that people aren't going to be the same as they were before," Anthony said. "It's going to be a lot quieter now."

In light of students' concerns, however, several faculty and staff have prepared for Monday's classes. But even with planning, some faculty members discussed that "flexibility" will be the key theme of most classes: flexibility in assigning grades, flexibility in determining class schedules, and flexibility in implementing course work.

Faculty members took a class-based approach in implementing these policies. They want to cater to the needs of individuals first. Then, collectively, they will act according to the needs of the students, whether these are emotional needs or academic needs.

One such example is Patricia Lavender, professor in the theatre arts department, who sent an email to her arts marketing students Wednesday morning informing them of her plans for class on Monday. Even prior to the university's announcement of how the remainder of the semester will unravel, Lavender proposed an open discussion and provided students the opportunity to decide for themselves how they wanted to finish the class.

In her email, she stated, "We will make whatever adjustments are necessary and reasonable . . . [I am] more concerned to be fair to each of you in what you need at this difficult time."

She reiterated this outlook in response to McNamee's statement.

"[Our] primary concern is for students and students' needs," she said. "This requires flexibility. Some will feel better if they complete the course as scheduled. Others will find it difficult to focus."

Donald Wood, a communications instructor, also voiced similar concerns for his Media Institutions students in an email, encouraging each student to "touch base" with him.

"I am prepared to do business as usual if the students want to," he said. "There is no attempt to be evasive, but we are being counseled to be considerate of the need of all to grieve. I have not revealed a plan because, to be honest, no one was completely sure of how to wrap up the semester."

Derek O'Dell: As Monday neared I became more and more anxious. I wanted to get back to class again and have things return to some sense of a regular routine.

Jerome Copulsky, assistant professor and director in Judaic Studies: Classes at Virginia Tech resume this week, and the cacophonous presence of the media that had settled upon the campus has begun to dissipate. Students clad in orange and maroon mull about the Drillfield; some toss Frisbees, kick soccer balls, fly kites. Others gather by the newly placed memorials, inscribing their thoughts and prayers on huge placards, leaving flowers and candles, VT memorabilia and Bibles, before heading off to class. But classes this week will not be as they were before, and like many other professors here, I have been thinking about what I should do when I enter the classroom. In the face of such horror, what can we possibly teach our students? But with my students I can go no further. When I step into the classroom this week I reach my limits as a teacher. I know that many students are struggling with how to reconcile the events of April 16th with their own beliefs and commitments.

Jenna Lazenby Nelson: Finally it was Friday. A good portion of the media had left. Those who remained would more than likely stay through Monday when classes resumed. Governor Kaine had declared Friday a day of mourning for victims of the tragedy. At noon, church bells would chime statewide and a moment of silence to remember the victims would follow. The Alumni Association had also declared Friday Maroon and Orange day and asked all of those in support of Virginia Tech to wear Hokie colors. Dressed in a maroon sweater and HokieBird earrings, I spent most of the morning wrapping up things at the JIC [Joint Information Center]. Plans were to move the JIC over to Burruss Hall that afternoon and to run it with a skeleton staff through the weekend. My boss [Mark Owczarski] wanted me to return to my office in the Media Building and spend the next week working to get things back to normal at the news bureau—or as normal as could be expected. Shortly before noon, I gathered up my stuff at the JIC and said goodbye to many of my coworkers and staff who I had worked alongside for the past week. It was a beautiful spring morning and I decided to walk across campus, something I had not had the chance to do that week. I arrived on the Drillfield just minutes before twelve and joined the hundreds clad in maroon and orange who had gathered to pause for a moment of silence in honor of the lives lost. No bells rang, but the moment of silence lasted not sixty seconds, but six hundred seconds, until a single voice started to shout "Let's Go" and another responded "Hokies." Although others joined the ritualistic chant, the attempt was only halfhearted, and the air on the Drillfield remained somber. As the crowd started to disband, I walked by the Hokie stones that had been placed on the ground for each of the victims. I read the numerous notes, poems, and tributes that rested on each. I said my prayers for the lives lost and the families that remained. What a week it had been.

Getting back to this "regular routine" would also mean the resumption of sporting events. An Atlantic Coast Conference baseball game was scheduled for Blacksburg that Friday.

Justin Cates: Friday rolled around and the first athletic event since the events of that fateful Monday were held at English Field as the baseball team took on the Miami Hurricanes. . . . We made it into the crowd on the hill and settled in just in time for the pregame ceremonies. The teams lined up and Miami presented the university with a check for ten thousand dollars. This was one of the many generous acts Virginia Tech saw from other institutions. It's safe to say that, for a while at least, the Hokies won't have many rivals after the compassion shown by even our fiercest competition.

Amy Stanford, alum: During the seventh inning stretch, instead of playing the traditional "Take Me Out to the Ballgame," a new, original song, "Forever Changed VT" by The Season was played. I listened closely to the lyrics, which are incredibly moving. What a beautiful song that so accurately reflected the events of that week.

Justin Cates: An amazing play kept these valiant Hokies from tying the game, but despite the 11–9 Miami victory, Virginia Tech also won. A baseball game has never held so much importance in Blacksburg. It was a step toward normalcy, and on that Friday night the sound of aluminum bats and cheering fans signaled a very real beginning to the healing process of a thousand Hokie hearts.

While crowds cheered for the Hokies on English Field, another event a few yards away on the Johnson Track and Field, Relay for Life, was taking place. Always an emotional event, Relay took on added meaning on April 20, 2007.

Derek O'Dell: When Friday came I knew that I was going to walk in the relay, although my mom didn't want me to. I would be staying the whole night out in the middle of the track at the relay event, and in the same week that it had snowed earlier, this was becoming more and more hazardous for the process of my healthy recovery.

But against my mom's wishes, I traveled back to Blacksburg after the memorial service at my church in Roanoke. I got to the event to find my team captain from the Pre-Veterinary Club at Virginia Tech, her boyfriend, and another officer as the only representatives from my team. With no classes all week and an uneasy feeling around campus, practically everyone had gone home to be with their families. Nearly everyone left from campus that came to the relay. I'd say there were easily over five hundred people there. My night started with speeches of cancer survivors and their messages of hope. I then realized that the toughest part of the tragedy that had occurred only four days earlier had passed, and relative to these people's stories of survival, my battle was easy and short. This helped me comprehend that I was and would be okay and that there was hope for me and everyone else at Virginia Tech. These survivors' messages of hope were just what our community of battered and shocked Hokies needed. As the night began with everyone walking around the track, it became clear that this would be like a diversion from everything that had happened earlier that week. There were simple reminders of what happened on April 16, like a touching memorial of luminaries with the thirty-two victims' names on them. The candles burned brightly as everyone walked past the bleachers beside the track that they were placed on. There was also another student who was running thirty-two miles, 128 laps around the track, in honor and in memory of those who had fallen. I went up to him and thanked him for doing that and asked him how he found the strength to run thirty-two miles in the short amount of time that he did (around six hours, I think). He replied with something that I will never forget. He said, "There were thirty-two angels running with me."

Despite his injuries, O'Dell wanted to make a statement with his participation that night.

Derek O'Dell: I knew running thirty-two miles for me was not very likely, even in good health. So I started walking with my girlfriend, Laura, by my side every step of the way. I had finished about fifteen laps when I decided I needed a little break. I went to my tent and took a nap for about two or three hours. By this time it was 2 a.m. when I woke again. I decided to try and walk another seventeen laps and do eight miles, a total of thirty-two laps, to try and honor and memorialize those who had died. I walked another nine laps to bring my total to twenty-four. Then I went back to my tent again and fell asleep. I awoke again to find that it was already 5:30 a.m. and I had only another hour to finish my last nine laps. I started walking again, more hurriedly this time. An hour to do a little more than two miles normally for me would be a piece of cake. I played soccer for my high school and was in excellent shape prior to college. But now it seemed like I was exhausted, and the week's events had taken their toll on me mentally and physically. It was like the track was becoming like quicksand, each step becoming heavier and harder to take. And then the announcement came that only thirty minutes were left and I had only finished two of the nine laps. I needed to make the goal of thirty-two. I started fast walking and by the time I reached the last five laps only about fifteen minutes were left before the 6:30 ending time. I started to run; it didn't make much sense to many people watching me at the time, I'm sure. To see this guy in jeans and a jacket with one sleeve waving free in the wind because my arm lay in a sling bound close to my body, I'm sure it was a peculiar sight, to say the least. But none of that was on my mind. All I could think about were the numbers five and thirty-two. Five was made by the four classmates and one professor who were killed in my room. I had each of their pictures taped around my sling strap and they had gone everywhere with me that week. As I started on my final five laps, I was determined

to run a lap for each of them. I wasn't t
my arm hurt, how odd I looked, or eve
smelled at that point. All I could think abo
run as quickly as I could for them. I started
Maxine. As I went past the luminaries by the sid
could smell the collection of scented candles th been placed around each bag to help light their names. Next was Nicole's lap, followed by Lauren's, and Mike's. Finally I got to Jamie Bishop's lap, my professor. That final lap around that track will be one of the most memorable points in my life. Not just because I reached my goal of thirty-two and had run a mile and a quarter with a gunshot wound in my arm, but also because Herr Bishop had a profound impact on my life that I hadn't realized until I started to really think about everything on that last lap. My mind had never been clearer. Now the tough decision of going back to classes that following Monday became not even an option. I would continue for Herr Bishop and my four classmates who were killed. I would finish for them. Five amazing people whose high aspirations in life were stopped short. Although I felt a sense of relief when finishing the last few steps of lap thirty-two, I knew it was just the beginning of a series of final few steps that would be significantly harder to take than those I took on the track. Like the final few steps of walking to Henh Ly's memorial service in my hometown; like the final few steps of walking to campus to my 8 a.m. lecture on Monday, April 23; like the final few steps of walking into my new German class with a new teacher and a smaller class; or like the final few steps of taking my things out of my apartment in Blacksburg and heading home for the summer, not being able to visit on a daily basis the memorial stones placed on the Drillfield for all of the victims who were killed. A series of final steps that would be more challenging than most any test or exam I've taken to this point. It was my own tragically formed personal test to see if I could continue

on at Virginia Tech, and return to a campus where so many good memories were now clouded and convoluted with this awful massacre that had occurred. I had passed maybe not with flying colors, but nonetheless a passing grade here was warranted by a worthy effort. Now there was hope for me and for the others who were there. I could feel this resounding sensation that everyone who had been at Relay for Life that night would be able to spread this message of hope to the next week's classes. It was our job to welcome back the frightened and anxious students, and calm their fears and help them just as the thirty-two angels had helped the man running the thirty-two miles. It was time to move on, but at the same time not forgetting the memories we have of the thirty-two classmates and professors who were killed.

In another attempt to get back to normal, the university told the media to move from the Inn at Virginia Tech by the time classes resumed on Monday.

As the weekend approached, reporters weren't as visible. They soon returned, yet again stirring up feelings of hostility and animosity as they attempted to cover classes resuming and moments of silences scheduled to honor the victims.

Media Presence Annoys Mourners Gathered to Honor Victims Monday

by Tricia Sangalang
Planet Blacksburg Staff Writer
April 20, 2007

Rise early at Virginia Tech and you can discover true quiet at, say, 7 a.m. Few students or faculty can be seen, except for the occasional early bird eager to snare a hot breakfast.

That seemed to be the point of "A Moment in Time," another remembrance event from a week of events that occurred Monday morning to mark the 7:15 a.m. incident at West Ambler Johnston, April 16, which left two people dead and ignited the ensuing rampage in Norris Hall two hours later.

This Monday the idea seemed simple enough: Have students and other members of the Tech community gather on Dietrick Lawn to mark last week's event.

This time, however, a few Virginia Tech police officers, students, and various members of campus ministry found themselves accompanied by a bevy of reporters, with their cameras and microphones in hand.

Media stationed themselves on the sidewalk in front of East Ambler Johnston, pointing their cameras toward about twenty marching members of the National Association for the Prevention of Starvation (NAPS), a nonprofit volunteer relief organization started in Alabama that was on hand to mark the occasion.

Dressed in dark blue sweatshirts, these members, who represent several colleges and states, played music just before the remembrance event began.

As the NAPS members continued down the sidewalk, one cameraman walked backward in front of them, capturing their march on camera. Other media scurried down the sidewalk in hopes of catching a good shot of the seemingly impromptu performance.

Meanwhile, students and campus ministry members walked toward the center of the lawn to honor Ryan Clark and Emily Hilscher, who were shot in West Ambler Johnston last Monday.

"I had English class with Emily," freshman August Sarrol said. "I came to show support. Everyone seems to know about the other [victims in Norris], but these students are just as important."

While walking to join the group, a reporter stopped a student and asked, "What do you think about all the media that are here right now?"

When he responded, "I'm part of student media," the reporter backed away and continued to observe.

At about 7:10 a.m., two campus ministry members called for the crowd's attention.

At that moment, the media bustled, without hesitation, toward the group, eager to catch the opening of the remembrance on camera.

In a piqued tone, one of the leaders asked the media to step away, encouraging students to come and join the circle.

"Please respect us," the group leader said to the media. "This is for the students."

Although some listened and stayed a few feet back, one reporter knelt down, holding a microphone toward the two leaders. She was the only person in the middle of the circle.

It seemed the number of media personnel in attendance outnumbered the number of students and community members present.

A few minutes later, the two ministry members led the group in a Buddhist chant. Many sang along, others hummed.

At 7:15, they rang a bell for each victim, followed by one minute of silence.

As students bowed their heads, one cameraman made his way through the crowd, and stuck his camera in a mourner's face; the reporter, with a microphone in her left hand, followed close behind.

On the other side of the circle, a cameraman stood in front of students in order to capture the moment. A Red Cross representative, perturbed by his insistency, covered the camera lens with her hand. He responded in an equally annoyed tone: "Don't touch my camera."

"I guess it's their job to put this on air," Sarrol said. "It's not good. One guy was pushing over students."

One minute later, three more bells rang. One minute of silence for the other victim.

By that time, at least one hundred people stood on Dietrick Lawn, including the members of NAPS, who, according to their website, came to Virginia Tech to "remind the nation that even in the midst of tragedy, small acts of kindness may leave a greater impression than many kind words."

The camera operators persisted, however.

The same Red Cross representative who had covered a cameraman's lens earlier walked over to a crying student during the second moment of silence.

"I'm blocking you from cameras," she said.

"I'm just so angry," the student said. "Why are they here?"

The Red Cross representative put her hand on her shoulder, and guided her in the direction the group was moving.

One of the members of NAPS began playing the violin. Media gathered around him. After the song was finished, the crowd proceeded to the Drillfield, led by members carrying "prayer flags." The media followed, taking pictures, filming, or holding their microphones within conversations among students.

This "problem," this "intrusion," as some have called it, again was in evidence at the university-wide moment of silence on the Drillfield later Monday morning.

The ceremony, which was organized by Hokies United, was marked by the toll of one bell from the tower of Burruss Hall at 9:45 a.m. Monday, April 23, 2007.

Media positioned themselves near the Hokie stone memorial, on the steps of Burruss Hall and elsewhere within the crowd.

Ezra "Bud" Brown: A huge brass bell was placed on the platform on the Drillfield right in front of Burruss Hall, and thirty-two blocks of Hokie stone had been placed in a semicircle downhill and directly in front of that platform. Sumeet Bagai of Hokies United made a few remarks, and thirty-two students, faculty, and staff members walked in and arranged themselves in the semicircle, each behind one of the thirty-two blocks of Hokie stone.

As volunteers walked out of Burruss, each carrying one white balloon, photographers hurried up the stairs to capture them walking. Their clicking cameras echoed.

One minute later, a bell tolled. At each toll, one white balloon was released.

At each toll, more clicks of cameras could be heard in the stillness.

Neal Turnage: The only thing that broke the silence was the clickety-click of dozens of professional-grade cameras. Thousands of students and hundreds of faculty and staff members honoring the victims in silence, yet here come the cameras.

The bell rang a total of thirty-two times, one time in memory of each victim.

Laura Massey: The feeling of loss didn't really hit me until the return to campus. At the ceremony with the releasing of balloons, I really felt the number thirty-two. Thirty-two is just a number until you stand and listen to thirty-two tolls of a bell and watch a balloon float away for each life lost. The amount of time that that took was astonishing and heartbreaking.

About midway through, a photographer quietly walked up the Burruss steps and aimed his camera. A student, who was standing behind him, said, "Can you please move? You're in my way."

A release of one thousand maroon and orange balloons concluded the ceremony. As the crowd looked up to the clear, blue sky to watch the balloons drift away, the zoom lenses of photographers' cameras were pointed in the same direction.

Laura Schamus: As we marked one week, with moments of silence and the releasing of balloons, I was once again brought to an understanding of what mattered in those times. There was no place I would have rather been than at Virginia Tech, drowning in strength and unity, melding into bonds I never knew could exist.

Thousands of students, faculty, and community members attended the ceremony, and to many students' dismay, hundreds of media were present as well.

"There are so many photographers right here," a student said on the phone while walking to her class after the ceremony. "They're in my way."

Ezra "Bud" Brown: When the sound of the bell faded for the last time, a vast number of orange and maroon balloons were released from in front of Burruss Hall, and they rose and traveled east. Twenty seconds later, a second huge crowd of balloons were launched from another point in front of Burruss Hall, and they rose. Twenty seconds later, a third and last collection of balloons went up in the air. And the ceremony was over. There was, however, one very striking thing about the launch of those maroon and orange balloons. Although the three bunches were launched at different times, they joined up together and traveled out of sight together, almost as if the earlier launch waited for its comrades to join it . . . and then they disappeared as one.

Traffic around the Drillfield had been at a standstill, and as students attempted to meander their way through the streets to their 10:10 a.m. class, some students still found the events a little all too surreal.

Laura Massey: What really drove it home was walking around campus. In a community of tens of thousands of students, it's impossible to know everyone. But as the semester wears on, I walk the same paths to class everyday and begin to recognize people as they pass. Returning to classes and realizing that someone's not there, or seeing them, but being able to see in their demeanor a destroyed but defiant air, really made this real for me.

Ashley Brohawn: My teacher went through a complete transformation, and he was always kind of the hard-ass, kind of sarcastic, trying to get us to talk and speak up, he'd always try to egg us on and after that he was a very mellow, very calm guy. It was sad seeing that.

Derek O'Dell: I woke up the morning of the 23rd and proceeded to make my way to campus. My girlfriend came and picked me up at my apartment and we walked to our 8 a.m. classes together that morning, which were in the same building, McBryde Hall. It was about a quarter-mile walk from where I parked my car in the commuter lot. A camera crew from Katie Couric's news team had contacted me about following me around campus to my first class since the shootings. Since they had me on the show on the 16th, they said that America was anxiously waiting to see me again returning to class. I had agreed, so there was a cameraman along with dozens of other news stations around campus, this one just was following my every step. I awkwardly made my way out of the car, trying not to hit my [injured] arm. My girlfriend and I started to make our way to McBryde. I slowly made my way up the steps and down the sidewalk, then we came to a point of no return for me. It was a temporary sidewalk (displaced by construction) made of gravel that was leading up to McBryde Hall. At this point halfway up the sidewalk I could see the back of Norris Hall, where the shootings had happened. I practically froze. Everything had flashed back into my mind from the previous Monday, and it was horrifying. I fought just to keep myself standing in place and not running back to my car. I thought if I turned around now, how many people I would be failing. I'd let myself down, all thirty-two people who died, especially the five who were in my class that I could look down and see their pictures on my sling, and I'd be letting down all of the people watching on the national news that night. I was supposed to provide all of these people with hope that Virginia Tech was healing and recovering from tragedy. So I fought to put one foot in front of the other. I squeezed my girlfriend's hand harder and step-by-step, I made my way to class. The cameras stopped filming and a routine animal physiology lecture was waiting for me. Never did I think when I signed up for an 8 a.m. class it would be this hard to make it to class once I got out of bed. When I looked for a seat to sit in, it was immensely alarming what went through my head. Instead of sitting in my regular seat halfway back in the class, close enough where I could see and hear everything clearly, but far enough away where I wouldn't be called on, a new criterion ran through my mind for selecting a seat. I wanted to be as far away from all the doors as possible. It was ridiculous. If another gunman came into the room I wanted more time to be able to react and to be as far away from the gunman as possible. This was far from the normal logic that a student exercises when selecting a seat. This happened in all of my classes that I wasn't already sitting somewhere far away from the doors. The first few minutes of class we discussed the numerous resources that were available to us as students. Counselors were there in the rooms and were more than willing to spend the entire class helping us cope, but it felt like the best way to cope with everything was to return to a somewhat normal lecture. I had asked a friend of Jamie Bishop's who worked at the university in the political science department to accompany me to my classes that morning. He had offered his help to me, and for the first time in a long while my stubborn self accepted it. His name was Craig, and without his help I might have left my classes that morning. He was a retired police officer who was hurt in the line of duty, so he knew some of what I was going through. I didn't want to ask an armed police officer to come to class, as this might alarm the students and the professor and do more harm than good. Craig showed up about five minutes into class, and I was the most anxious person prior to his arrival. I was jittery and could hardly focus on getting out my laptop to take notes. Somehow when he arrived, it just seemed to comfort me enough knowing someone was there for me and that I could continue and focus in class. The class was uneventful other than the occasional loud noise from the doors outside our room slamming shut. This would send me into an abbreviated survival mode, until the sound side of my mind could suppress my fears. The class ended, and I walked with Craig to my new German class location in Major Williams Hall. My German class began with the head of the German department as our new temporary professor. I think four people came to that class on Monday, including myself. Trey and Erin were the only other people who had come to class on the 16th who returned to class besides me. I was the only injured person from Norris 207 who was able to return to class because the others were still in the hospital, I think. I was hopeful that I would be able to see the others who were shot in my class later on that week in the new German class, but unfortunately none came back. I almost felt isolated in that aspect, but on occasion I would see someone else who was injured on the 16th walking across campus. Craig and I arrived at the new German classroom. For fear that an actual classroom resembling that of Norris 207 would evoke unwanted memories, the new classroom was more of a boardroom with one single long table and chairs around it. This was suitable for the small elementary German class that now was even smaller. We generally had three to five students who came back to the German class, some of whom were absent on the 16th.

Ezra "Bud" Brown: I welcomed my students back and said, "We can talk about mathematics or we can talk about important things. It's up to you." They did talk for about fifteen minutes about the events of the previous week. I told them that they could only improve their grade by continuing in the course and taking the third midterm and the final exam. They said, "Let's review for the third test," and so we did. It turned out to be a lively class, of all things, and apparently they made an effort to cheer me up.

Derek O'Dell: Other than the occasional discussion of something involving April 16, our learning of German continued with our consent on the first day back to classes. We continued learning about the German grammar that we had begun on the 16th. It was the process of quoting someone in the media and using the correct format of conjugating a verb to the subject. We didn't get into much new material as there were only five classes between when classes resumed and when exams began. I thought the effort that our new professor made was motivational for me. I figured as long as she could keep coming to class and preparing lesson plans, then the least I could do would be to come to class. I wasn't one to disappoint a lot of people, and I sure wasn't going to start then.

University officials said that about eighty percent of the student body returned to class April 23. Both faculty and students alike battled their emotions during such an attempt to move forward and feel a sense of "normalcy." However, the usually quite peaceful Blacksburg setting on a Monday morning was inundated with media personnel and also with more than two hundred volunteers marked with yellow and purple armbands to provide counseling to those who asked.

Tommy McDearis, pastor, Blacksburg Baptist Church: When the students got back about a week after, I looked out my window, and there's about thirty to forty college students just walking across the street. I didn't know what they were doing. They just walked across the street, and walked straight to our sanctuary. They went in there, sat down, and just started praying. One of the students got up and did a short devotional, led them in a group prayer, and then, they all just got up and left. That happened all week long. Students we had never seen before because our church was just across the street from campus. They'd just walk in our sanctuary to sit and pray. We had our sanctuary open all day until about midnight every day that week for people to just go in there and do that.

In the wake of the events on Monday, emotions ran high, and fear and doubt were close behind. Students, faculty, and the community all mourned together for Virginia Tech and all that were involved. The university soon established grief counselors on a phone line that the public could call for guidance and help. Cook Counseling Center responded to the call for counselors, as did churches in the area. While many turned to these sources for counseling, many relied on friendship to help cope.

Gary Schroeder, Lutheran minister: The more profound injuries, the things that we'll be dealing with for a long time to come, are with friends that were killed. I think one person lost a roommate, and the faculty lost colleagues. One member of our congregation is the department head, so he lost one faculty member and eight of his students. So, those are the kinds of things that we just now are starting to deal with because in the immediate aftermath of the killings, I think everybody was in shock. And then, the collective mood was, "Okay, let's keep it together through commencement." We have this goal that we want to reach, and I'm thinking now, from what I'm hearing, that people are allowing themselves permission to deal with the grief, the loss, and in some cases, there are issues of survivor guilt. "I should've been in the building, but I wasn't." That sort of thing. So a lot of different emotions.

Joanna Stallings, Lutheran youth pastor: The kids in the group were feeling some guilt, some anger, some just a profound kind of sadness. And for some, I think it stirred up other issues like undealt-with grief, with family members that had died a few years before. That kind of thing. And just a general malaise, discomfort with how our world had just been turned upside down. And some kids that are graduating. One of our kids said, "You know, I'm set to leave. I have a job and an apartment. I'm ready to go, but I don't want to go." I think one of the ways that we've dealt with students is to provide some resources for parents, just letting them know, because their kids are away from their support network. And to perhaps hint to those who are outside of our community who really don't know what everybody's been experiencing, telling them you just can't assume things by CNN's coverage, the way it had kind of a narrowed, false scope of things. And we tried to communicate that with the Lutheran students and their pastors, so that their pastors are alert to the fact that, like a dandelion, everybody's kind of blown out of town, and there are folks really hurting and grieving from everywhere. And they need to attend to them.

Chelsea Benincasa: Going to class didn't help. It made it worse. Because in each class, I learned more details from my classmates.

I heard more stories, many which I wish I hadn't heard. Nicole and I sat together in our new classroom in Litton Reaves instead of Norris, and I couldn't bring myself to meet eyes with my graduate student instructor. It was just too hard. Some students whispered, "I am so glad I am not graduating right now. Thank God we have the summer—things will be okay when we come back." My stomach had tightened into a ball by the end of the second day, and I didn't know what else to do. Suddenly I found myself stumbling toward Squires at 4:30 p.m. I paced back and forth in front of the room where the counselors were sitting, wondering if it was too late to speak with someone. I decided it was, and started to leave the building. But it was the first time I had been in Squires since it happened, and the building was filled with memorials. I was walking really slowly, running my hand along a poster on the banister, when I noticed the woman beside me. She said, "Excuse me, miss, I saw that you were looking at the counseling room and I just wanted you to know that it's not too late if you need to speak with someone." I couldn't look at her. I started bawling my eyes out. I couldn't catch my breath or speak, so she put her hand on my back and steered me to a counselor. For the next twenty minutes, I talked about the fears I had been having about graduating and moving to NYC, and how now I didn't want to leave, and how I couldn't remember what had happened before Monday the 16th, and about the nightmares I kept having about Norris and my sister. It was so much. The counselor gave me two teddy bears—one for me and one for Nicole. We named them Counselor One and Counselor Two. Then I took Nicole to my yoga class and tried to relax. I wondered if I would ever smile again at Tech. A couple days later, I looked at Burruss. It was shining in the sunlight. And I smiled. I realized that it was okay. It is okay to leave. Graduation will be a celebration—and I finally believed that. I cannot let what happened define my time at Tech. Even though the buzz is saying, "Those tragic events of 4/16," I cannot let my birthday date not be a happy and special occasion anymore. I am graduating from Virginia Tech next week and I am proud to be a Hokie. We lost a huge part of our world and our school on April 16, 2007, but we also grew as a community and a people. Those tragic events changed my life, and while I am still struggling to heal, I will never forget what happened. Sure, I might freak out on the subway or cry because no one in NYC will ever really know what I went through, but my school will be in my heart forever. I am a proud member of the graduating class of 2007. As Nikki said, no one asks for a tragedy—no one deserves a tragedy—but we will prevail and can grow together, and that is exactly what I intend to do, despite whatever happens in the future. Sometimes life cannot be lived by a schedule, and that's the biggest lesson my college experience has taught me. It's time to live for the moment.

Theresa Walsh: I keep a lot of things on the inside. I had a lot of nightmares. They say that you get nightmares and that you have a lot of twitching, like your body can't control itself. Within the first week I had gone to Kabuki with my old teammates and old coaches who had invited me and my family to dinner. Somebody dropped a plate and I immediately started crying. I didn't know what came over me. It was like I was a kid again hearing a loud noise and bawling my eyes out. Then after two minutes I was back to normal. It was weird to me. At that point I started to realize that I needed to start dealing with this and really start letting it out. I had several nightmares so we started sleeping in the living room as a "family" in our apartment. It's tough to be alone. I can't be in complete silence because it bothers me. My ears still hurt so it brings back memories. My friends have gotten me through a lot of this, but I still have moments where I'm like, "Did this really happen?" It's still so surreal to me. It's only when I see my classmates or hear people talk about it that I can believe that it really did happen. A lot of it still hasn't hit me and I'm sure it will. I guess it just has to settle.

Suzanne Higgs: People kept calling to speak with me, but I finally just said I'm tired of talking about it. And I was kind of mean about it, I think, but I just didn't want to tell my story anymore. If they knew I was okay and at home, I didn't feel I needed or could explain any more than that.

Jeff Wood: After visiting the memorials, I met with old friends. They had lived in my "pod" in Slusher freshman year and we had become friends, but we'd had a few disagreements and had gone our separate ways around the end of my junior year. Seeing them again, recounting old stories, it was like none of that had ever happened, and I remember thinking that this is exactly the kind of thing that needed to happen, we needed to take this tragedy and use it to bring us closer together, we needed to make something positive come from this, no matter how big or small, to honor those we had lost.

Rosanna Brown, *Collegiate Times* reporter: I chose to work extra hours and continue writing for the student newspaper. The *Collegiate Times* wanted to put out an issue that would include extended obituaries for all of the victims. It was our job to interview family and friends to compile these stories. My initial reaction in my mind was, "I can never do this, this will be way too hard." I knew that even if I did attempt these stories, that every word I placed on the page would be accompanied by tears and sorrow. I also knew that these stories had to be written and my student body would rely on these articles to receive some closure on the loss of their friends. I chose to write the stories. After speaking with countless friends and select family members, I felt like I was a close friend to those I wrote about—Daniel O'Neil and Mora Lumbantoruan. Talking with those who were so close to them in the midst of their grief is a very humbling experience. Neither is it easy nor comfortable; but, during my efforts I was able to see how much these people were loved and realize that the significance of a single life is so much broader than what it seems on the surface. Daniel O'Neil's father graciously gave me a few moments of his time. In hearing the pain in his voice throughout our short interview I was forever changed. I had never heard someone so sad and so confused that their son, who was intelligent, motivated, and for all intents and purposes a normal kid, would be taken away from him in this way. No one understood why these people had to leave us; but we all understood that the world would be missing out on many extraordinary lives.

Sarah Walker, public relations officer, Blacksburg Rescue Squad: People cope in different ways, and for some that means being back behind an ambulance. We're a big family here. We ask each other, "Are you doing okay?" Those that needed to disappear, disappeared for a few days. We all know we can talk to each other. If we need help, it's available.

Melanie Harris: It hits you. It hits you that the saying really is true, the good all too often die young, and while it is so terrible and so sad, everything happens for a reason. But when you hear stories, and share memories, it hits you that life is so valuable and that the lives lost were so incredible. And yes, it hits you when you see the stuff being moved out of your friend's room directly across the hall, but being hit is how you begin to cope, and coping is how you press forward.

Carol Bishop: The week or two afterward, we took all of Commonwealth Ballroom and set it up for various types of counseling. There were ministers; the Student Affairs Division had all kinds of information on where you could go if you needed help—any kind of counseling, legal advice, whatever it may be. So there were various services set up for the students. Anyone who wanted to come and talk. There were two separate counseling rooms. One was for students particularly and the other for faculty and staff. So we did offer that. We extended the hours of the building so we could be open more if anyone just needed to come and hang out, be with friends, partake in any of the services offered.

The commencement ceremony on May 11 was a highly anticipated date for many seniors. The event marks not only an individual's accomplishment in completing his or her degree, but also the first step into the real world. This commencement was different. It came nearly one month after the shootings that devastated a Hokie Nation. Celebration in achievement would come with lingering feelings of grief and loss.

Dr. Yannis Stivachtis, Virginia Tech faculty: We knew what could happen, we knew we'd be very emotional, but the question was, could we handle it well?

The university anticipated twenty-five thousand to thirty-five thousand students, family, and other guests to campus over that weekend, and even prepared for the media by posting a news release four days prior, outlining how to obtain media credentials.

The commencement ceremony began at 7:30 p.m., with graduates filing in, adorning their black robes and motarboards. Some even uniquely decorated theirs in memory of April 16 and in honor of the slain Hokies.

More than 3,500 students received their bachelor's degrees, more than 1,100 received graduate degrees, thirty-two received associate degrees, and eighty-eight received Doctor of Veterinary Medicine degrees.

General John Abizaid and university president Steger offered words of comfort, encouragement for the future, and a genuine admiration for their poise and resilience over the course of time following the shootings.

"As your class moves forward into this complicated twenty-first century of ours, you have been burdened by an inexplicable act of cruel violence. . . . But because you have experienced this burden you know that character in crisis matters, that honoring those lost and caring for those most affected are duties all of us share," Abizaid said. "This twenty-first century of ours will challenge us in many unexpected ways, yet for all of the complications and difficulties it will bring, you will have the ability to make a difference, to show strength of character, and to lead with the firm knowledge that you have been given the tools to shape a better world."

To honor the victims, President Steger and Provost Mark McNamee handed out class rings to the families.

"Revel in the joy of this day, celebrate your accomplishments," Steger said. "Celebrate all those lives that have touched yours and helped bring you to this point. Reach out and hug them if you can. . . . You have united, and you have shown the world the meaning of *Ut prosim,* that I may serve. I love you all."

Ezra "Bud" Brown: Eventually, we all got underway and a huge procession of honored guests, pipe band, faculty members, Honors Flags carried by Sam Abboud and Kristin Brugh, and five hundred members of University Honors and graduates with distinction snaked its way from Hillcrest past Wallace Hall, across West Campus Drive, down Washington Street and across by Cassell Coliseum and through the Merryman Center to line up in the Tunnel, where we'd enter the field. Soon enough, the ceremony began and it took quite a while to seat the thousands of students, followed by the stage party. We on the Commencement Committee had wondered about the ceremony and hoped that it would strike a proper balance between the joy of the day and the sorrow of the previous month. We needn't have worried. The ceremony was perfect.

Amidst the applause and standing ovations, graduates cheered, "Let's Go Hokies!" Like the other times before, following April 16, the cheer so commonly used to emit school spirit at sporting events epitomized a true sense of camaraderie and strong desire to move forward as one united Hokie Nation.

Carol Bishop: Graduation was very bittersweet. There was one ceremony that had eleven families, in political science. At one point I had gone outside to do a perimeter check and see what all's going on on the outside of the building. And that [ceremony] was just letting out. I didn't know it and I just walked right into it. A lot of families were coming out and they had the very nice diplomas that they had been awarded. Seeing them cry, and over here you have this family that's just jubilant. And they should be, I mean, they've invested a lot of time and money and the student has invested X number of years to get to this point. It's what they've been working toward their whole life. Huge, joyous occasion and then you have this other family within ten feet of them that's looking at a diploma that their child will never see, and crying. It's tough.

On North Main Street to greet the graduation crowds was a lineup of international flags flying high from poles ringing the parking lot of Blacksburg Baptist Church.

Tommy McDearis, pastor, Blacksburg Baptist Church: It was a joint idea. The chief of police called me, and there was a company that offered to donate flagpoles and flags to use as a memorial to all these people who passed away if somebody wanted them. The chief of police initially contacted the university, but the university didn't know quite what to do with them or where to put them. I got a call saying, "You've got that front yard outside of your church out there. Is that a good place we could use all this?" I got together with my deacons and called back and said, "I'd be happy to put them up, but there's got to be one condition on this. All of these people weren't Americans. I don't want to put up American flags for people who are other nationalities." We got together with the Cranwell International Center and met to find out what nationalities we have there. Let them contact the families and make sure it's okay for us to put up a flag out there for them. The Cranwell Center called all of the international families, and four of the international families truthfully asked to have American flags because their families had fallen in love with America and they wanted to have those. The rest of them wanted to have the flags that you see out there. So the Cranwell Center got the international flags for us, and then we erected the poles. This company that donated them brought them to the police department, and we transported them up here, dug the holes, and got the flags up. Since we didn't have a thirty-third flagpole, we wanted to do something that recognizes the Cho family. They can't help what happened over there. I said, "We need to recognize mental illness," so we made signs to put out there with it and be able to recognize that. The sign reads, "While only 32 flag poles were donated to the town and ultimately to our church for this project, it is important to also remember the Cho family in their grief. Our prayer is for the healing of everyone touched by the tragedy of April 16, 2007, and for every family on earth touched by the struggle of profound mental illness." We thought putting up the flags would be a nice gesture. We never imagined that it would capture the emotions and imaginations of the community. I had a guy stop me downtown. "I want to tell you right up front. Aren't you the pastor of the church across the street?" And I said, "Yeah." He said, "I want to tell you right up front that I'm an atheist, but I want to tell you that that is one of the most moving things I have ever seen. Thank you for doing that. That's just been a very special thing for all of us." That was my hope of what we would get out of that. So it's just been that way all over the community. We've been contacted by people from the university, by faculty and staff, and students. During graduation week, I [presided over] the funeral of the Indonesian PhD student. We called him "Mora." I did his funeral and his family was Christian. When the family came here for graduation, they wanted to meet me. When they came over here and saw these flags, they wanted a picture under their son's flag, and they were just moved to tears by that flag memorial that was out there. That's been the feeling of many people around to see these flags. Those flags have been a huge ministry, particularly during graduation week. It's amazing how many people were touched by it.

PART III
IN MEMORY

IN MEMORY

CHAPTER 8

Mary Read Speaks to Us All

Editor's note: Over the days following April 16, authorities moved through the excruciating process of identifying those killed by Seung-Hui Cho. Virginia Tech released a partial list of the victims each day, as their identities became available. The staff of the *Collegiate Times* worked to write profiles of each person that would show the huge loss of uniquely talented scholars and students. Many of those profiles are included in this section. This first story is Virginia Tech student journalist David Covucci's remembrance of writing about a very special Tech freshman, Mary Read.

It was the only fair way to write about her. I'd go to her funeral at noon the next day and then set about on my interviews. I'd gotten in touch with several of her old teachers, setting up some interviews. Those would be fine; I wasn't worried about any interview save one: Mary's parents.

But even before I could interview them, I had to get in touch with them. I started out with the safest path, calling the university first. Every victim's family had a personal grief counselor. I figured that would be the most tactful way to reach her parents. But the school didn't seem to want to help, giving me the bureaucratic runaround.

Arriving in northern Virginia, I stopped at some strip mall to change. I threw on a black suit, red tie, and my badly scuffed Kenneth Coles. A few miles away was St. Mary of Sorrows, Mary's Catholic church. Police were directing traffic outside. The family expected a crowd and got one, more than nine hundred people.

I sat in the very last row, on the aisle.

Before the opening procession, an usher pulled up a casket, right next to me. There was Mary. The casket was bright white. It would have been austere, but friends of Mary's signed it in bright Sharpies. Pink and green and blue messages dotted the casket. The ceremony was simple. No eulogy was delivered. Instead, her father, Peter, came up near the end and read from a quote book he found in Mary's dorm. Most came from her last entry, a few months before the shooting. They were about forgiveness.

He didn't say exactly why he read them, but it seemed obvious. Just a week ago, he'd been told his daughter was shot to death. But when he came down to Blacksburg and emptied out her room, he found her still there, telling him about forgiveness. I'm sure he'd been filled with rage and hatred toward that sinister kid. So Mary's last act as his daughter was to tell him to forgive, not to hate, to put her dad at peace. His daughter taught him the greatest lesson of all, days after her death.

Afterward, six pallbearers carried Mary away. Peter carried his three-year-old son, Brendan, who bawled the length of the procession. And with him, so did we all.

After the funeral, I ran into a friend's mother.

"My other daughter knew Mary," she said, scribbling down a number. "Call her later."

As much as I didn't want to, I knew that to do the story the right way, I'd have to call Mary's parents myself. I said a little prayer as I looked up the Reads' number, hoping it was listed. If it wasn't, my last resort was to go knock on her front door, which I really didn't want to do. It was listed. I couldn't call now, though. They had probably just gotten home from the reception. I'll call later, I said, knowing full well I might never do so.

At that point, I'd been working for six hours straight. I was exhausted, tired, miserable. So, to fix that, I did what any college student playing journalist would do. I called my mom and asked her to make me dinner.

I drove the ten miles around the D.C. beltway to my mom's new condo. There, some kind of Mexican casserole waited. It looked like slop but tasted phenomenal; I ate three plates of it, washing it down with a Belgian wheat beer. The combination worked, flipping my mood.

Refreshed, I called Emily, the girl whose mother I met at the funeral. Twenty minutes with her, and I started to understand Mary. She gave me a perfect summary in a quote: "She was what you think of when you think of the girl in band: cute, smiley, but still a band nerd. But she was the first band nerd to ever be elected to homecoming court. She was the only one of us that fit in anywhere."

Those forty-six words were so simple, but they captured Mary's essence. It would be simplistic to say that three sentences could explain a person, but those words are still the best description I got of her. They revealed the most important quality of Mary, that she was never bothered by arbitrarily delineated lines; she breezed through cliques and groups with ease.

I finished with Emily. It was time to call Mary's father. I picked up my Samsung, flipped it open, and punched in the number I'd scribbled on my hand an hour or so earlier.

"Hello," a woman answered.

"Hi, I'd like to speak with Peter Read."

"Who is this?" She was terse. She'd heard that statement way too many times.

"My name's David Covucci. I went to Annandale with Mary Read and I'm a Virginia Tech student."

"Oh, hold on, let me get him," she said, her mood seemingly improved.

"Wait, wait, wait," I shouted before she got off the line, needing to tell her who I was. I had no desire to ambush her father. "Let him know I work for the *Collegiate Times,* the student paper down here, and I want to do a profile on Mary."

"It's okay, he wants to talk to you," she said, as though he was expecting my call.

I heard her relay my information to her husband.

"Hello."

It was the weariest greeting I'd ever heard.

I repeated my Annandale/Tech connection, finishing with a stupid "How are you doing?"

"About as well as can be." His voice had a definitive resoluteness to it.

"I'd like to talk to you about Mary. When could you do it?"

"Tomorrow would be better."

That relieved me; I'd had no intention of interviewing a man the same day he buried his daughter.

We agreed on eleven.

I hung up and passed out.

Nine a.m. came quickly.

I reached Mary's neighborhood twenty minutes before eleven. I pensively drove around, running words of encouragement through my head. I finally pulled onto her street. The family lived in a sandy-colored house at the end of a short cul-de-sac. Theirs was impossible to miss; candles and flowers covered the lawn. Several people milled about out front. Brendan was crying again. He'd been running around and scraped up his knee, and he bawled just as he had yesterday.

Peter came up and introduced himself. We took a seat on a

wooden bench that sat in the shade of a broad-leafed tree. The sun shone, but not nearly bright enough to mask the family's collective dreariness. Peter wore an Annandale polo, jeans, and Teva sandals. He held a mug of coffee but rarely sipped it.

The first few moments were awkward; Brendan ran around crying, his mother, Cathy (Mary's stepmother), tried to coddle him. Peter sat there, taking in the scene. He seemed to cherish it, the relative normalcy and routine of family life, something the last week had sorely lacked. Eventually Cathy herded the child inside. She came back out for the interview, but had to excuse herself several minutes in. She began sobbing uncontrollably. She walked away, came back, and the scene replayed itself. She left for good. It was a painful contrast, Cathy bawling as Peter spoke. Peter struggled at times, too, but he never lost control of himself. It was actually harder to watch him try and stay strong than to watch Cathy cry. I knew he wanted to break down, I could see it, but he wouldn't allow himself to. I don't know if it was because he was in front of me or because it's how he always held himself. Either way, I wanted to tell him: Let yourself go, it's okay to cry.

I wanted to ask him about Mary's faith. From what I had so far culled, she was devoutly religious. I first asked if it was okay to broach the subject. He said yes.

Well, what did you know about it?

"That's really something we are learning along the way, too."

When he said that, I realized we were more alike than different. This wasn't reporter-subject, but rather two people who both wanted to find out as much as we could about a girl. It wasn't a forty-five-minute Q&A, but rather an intertwined quest. I offered up all the information I had so far gathered. He enjoyed listening to the stories her friends had told me. He tried to give me as much as he knew. He was honest and open, hoping that I could find out more about who his daughter was, and then, in turn, tell him.

There was frequent silence, as he'd often end on a poignant

note, which I struggled to digest. I missed many follow-up questions because I was too choked up to speak. He held his composure better than I did, and it made me feel terrible.

After the interview, he brought me into the house, showing me picture after picture of his daughter, several of which were from the day before she died. We sat in his office, which held a small, makeshift memorial. Newspapers, photos, and letters littered a white tableclothed desk. I silently wondered if he shouldn't put it away, so he wouldn't have to be constantly reminded of Mary. I guess it didn't matter; nothing could make him forget, so why try?

He walked me outside to my car. I don't remember what prompted what happened next. I certainly didn't coerce this story out of him; I guess he just wanted to tell me. While the Reads are devout Catholics, the most comforting words Peter heard came from outside his faith. A Jewish friend had called him several days before. From the way he said it, it didn't sound like the person was a close friend. This friend, though, offered up an old Jewish proverb: If a funeral procession and wedding procession ever meet on a road, the funeral yields to the wedding party, because life goes on. He said those last words—"life goes on"—with a shrug and a sort of laugh, the kind that's mostly just an exhale. It seemed he really could someday believe those words, just not yet.

I left him to grieve. My ordeal was over. His would never be.

Editor's note: Mary Read is one of the thirty-two members of the Tech community who lost their lives. They came from all over the world, arriving in Blacksburg to study, to teach, to grow, to build relationships, and to gain memorable experiences in a community nestled in the mountains of southwest Virginia. They had friends, family, and plans for their futures. They had unique passions and interests in life. What follows is each of their stories.

CHAPTER 9

Tributes

Ross Abdallah Alameddine

by Duncan Vick

Twenty-year-old Ross Alameddine, like each of the thirty-two victims of Monday's tragedy, was a unique component of Virginia Tech's tight-knit community.

He was the kind of lighthearted jokester who put everyone around him in a better mood. Charismatic and extremely outgoing, Ross had a presence that was felt in every one of his classes. He was always willing to share his mind with the class, and weighed in on just about every topic.

In a major such as English, where often a student will only get out of the class as much as he puts in, Ross almost always put forth one hundred percent.

Brent Stevens is an English professor who had Ross as a student for three semesters. He remembers Ross as an outstanding class participant who loved sharing personal stories and experiences in class discussion.

"He talked in every class I ever taught him. He was just such an imaginative kid. He is the kind of student you count on showing up. I remember it was harder to get students to talk when he was absent, to get conversation going in class. He talked about his life, his emotions, and offered deep insights into the materials.

"He put himself out there in front of thirty-five people, most of whom he did not know. It took me years into my teaching before I was comfortable doing that, and here was this nineteen-year-old, helping us to understand what we were reading and viewing with his unique perspective," Stevens said.

Stevens also recalled a night when he was forced to bring dinner to the 7 p.m. class he had with Ross.

"I had to bring fries and a burger to class one day, and I remember Ross looked at me, took out his cell phone, and asked if he could order a pizza."

That was the kind of levity Ross brought with him everywhere he went. He especially had a gift for bringing laughter into the classroom.

Whether it was through his jokes, astute comments, or humorous anecdotes, Ross was the kind of classmate who made school a little less bland, and a little more engaging.

Ed Weathers, another of Ross's English professors, remembers him as an intelligent student who, according to Weathers, "always smiled, even when he wasn't feeling well."

"He had just recently declared English to be his major, and he would have been good at it, since he wrote in a fresh, honest, lively, witty, idiosyncratic voice. He liked to make people laugh. On the first day of my class, he wrote that he was trying to choose between English and French as a major, and that my class would be the deciding factor. 'No pressure,' he wrote. And of course I laughed, as he wanted me to," Weathers said in an email remembering Ross.

Weathers also mentioned a project Ross was working on that utilized his gift for humor in a way that could benefit Tech.

"For his final project in Professional Writing, Ross proposed to write a feasibility report that looked into the possibility of making and selling Virginia Tech products that 'have humor and parody in mind.'

"He wanted to sell these products—especially wisecracking T-shirts—through a computer retailer. He wanted people associated with Virginia Tech to have souvenirs that made them laugh," Weathers wrote.

It would have been a fitting project for Ross, a person who brought so much laughter and joy to the lives of people fortunate enough to have known him.

Ross's sister, Yvonne, expressed her pride in her brother and his influence here at Tech in a message sent on Wednesday.

"My brother is a spectacular human being, gifted in every way. I'm so happy he impacted others' lives so positively and I'm so proud of him," Yvonne wrote.

Bryan Griffith, former classmate who worked on a project with Ross: It was nice working with him because he was very smart, and I could rely on him to not just sit there and me do all of the work. . . . He was very witty and smart about the jokes that he told. He was able to joke and everything, but he was also able to cut it off like a switch, like a light switch, when he actually needed to get down to work. He wasn't afraid to talk to anyone before class. Everyone would be waiting for the teacher to show up. He didn't just sit there and not talk to people. He would talk to everyone around him. He wasn't quiet; he was very sociable. He didn't want people to get the wrong idea about him that he was just a smart guy in class or that he was just sucking up to the teacher by answering questions in class. . . . I think I'm going to miss the fact that we had so much in common and that we didn't get to spend more time together. I think what I will miss the most about him, him speaking so passionately about what he likes that you find it interesting—even if you weren't interested in it before.

Tarek Alameddine: Ross was a distant cousin to me; I actually had never been able to meet him. My experiences only consist of the call from my father in which he told me of Ross. . . . Our family tree branches from the same place in Lebanon. Even though I had not known of Ross until the shooting, I still was hit hard with the news. Ross was able to rally family and make an impact even after his passing.

Leah Robinson, Virginia Tech student, said to the *Roanoke Times*: He said the trick was to not take anything seriously, so spending time with him always put a smile on my face. . . . The man had a sense of humor.

Christopher James (Jamie) Bishop

by T. Rees Shapiro

"I know, I'm a true geek," Christopher James Bishop, German instructor and one of the Hokie fallen, confessed in his blog in July of 2005.

To those who may not have known "Herr Bishop," as he was known by his students, it could be puzzling to understand: Who admits they are an actual "geek"?

But to those who were graced by the dynamic presence of Bishop, such an admission was the essence of his laughable, intuitive, and easygoing personality. He was a comic-book fiend, a lover of horror, and a technology buff. He might have been a "geek" by his own admission, but to everyone else he was an amazingly down-to-earth and "cool" guy.

Bishop, a Pine Mountain, Georgia, native and University of Georgia Bull Dog twice over with a bachelor's in German and a master's in German linguistics, was head-over-heels for languages; he was fluent in German, but had a working base of Italian and Spanish as well.

Will Bright, who took a class taught by Bishop in the fall of this year, described how he and Bishop could talk about anything.

"He was carefree, and full of energy," Bright said. "He was from a different mold." Everyone who spoke of Bishop reiterated the same: Bishop was unique, refreshing, and very passionate in every aspect of his life.

"I've never had a teacher, never had a friend like him," Bright said. "He was always attentive to his students; they were his number one priority."

Mary Paddock, an assistant professor in the German program, started her career at Tech the same year Bishop and his wife, assistant German professor Stefanie Hofer, began theirs.

"He was the kind of person that when you were with him, it was as though you were his best friend," Paddock said. "Like you were the only person in the world. He could connect so easily, and made an effort to do so."

Bishop's roots in the mountains of Georgia were obvious from his love of the outdoors. He was an avid hiker and was very eco-sensitive.

When he and his wife moved from Chapel Hill to Blacksburg, they made an effort to move close to campus so they could bike to work every day; and they did, rain or shine.

"He was very concerned with the environment," Paddock said. "He was conscious not to make things worse in the world."

As passionate as Bishop was for languages and the environment, above all else he held one love at what he called "a near religious level": art.

"He was really artistic in every facet of his life," Paddock said.

Bishop's early love of comics and graphic novels sparked his interest in art. Heavily inspired by Neil Gaiman's *The Sandman*, and Frank Miller's work on *Daredevil*, Bishop at first thought he wanted to pursue a career as a graphic artist. While he later realized his talents lay more heavily elsewhere, he continued to pursue his passion. Memory39.com was Bishop's online portfolio, where he updated and displayed his dabblings of art in the form of digital media. Bishop was an expert in Photoshop and an excellent photographer, and combined these to create colorful and evocative pieces.

Rob Deane, a sophomore Architecture student, gallery director for XYZ, the Virginia Tech student-run art gallery, had met Bishop a few times at Stamtischt, a get-together for students which Bishop organized in downtown Blacksburg restaurants to practice social German with one another. Deane, an artist himself, was thoroughly surprised by the power of Bishop's talents from his website, and mentioned that Bishop might have been soon on his way to re-enrolling into college art classes to more seriously delve into the world of artistic creative expression.

"He was a talented artist," Deane said, "and by the nature of the way he presented his art, by its setup, it was an obvious expression about himself, and what he cared most about."

One of the images that pops up on the screen when you peruse his portfolio is a pair of sapphire irises that belong to Bishop's "Fräulein," Hofer. He met her while studying abroad in Germany at the Ruprecht-Karls-Universität in Heidelberg.

"He would mention his wife almost every class," Bright said.

"He was crazy for her," Paddock said.

Bishop was a "jack-of-all-trades." He could design a top-of-the-line webpage, and also discuss German literature. Perhaps he might strum on his guitar and hum a tune, and later get lost in the gorgeous Blacksburg countryside tubing in the New River while thinking of new artistic ideas to display on his website. His relaxed personality and passion for teaching and education will be sorely missed by the members of the Virginia Tech Foreign Languages department. Not because they lost his incredible abilities as an educator, but because they lost an incredible friend.

Ezra "Bud" Brown, mathematics professor: One or two times a week, I would take my lunch over to the Foreign Languages and Literatures department's lunch table, and Chris was usually there. He was a familiar figure around campus: a tall, thin guy who wore granny-glasses and rode a bicycle practically everywhere. A Georgia lad, "Herr Bishop"—as his students knew him—was a friendly fellow, easy to talk to, interested in his students, and just a real presence at the lunch table. Chris was part of the scene. He loved talking about teaching; I was also from the Deep South, and I had spent a year in Germany, so we had lots to talk about!

Derek O'Dell, student: [He was] my inspiration for making it to every 8 a.m. and 9 a.m. lecture, spring semester 2007. I've never been more inspired to learn. Herr B, as many of our classmates called him, would make PowerPoint presentations for every class. These were no ordinary presentations; as you came into class each morning, you would be greeted by a picture of Herr B's favorite comedy styling, ranging from David Hasselhoff to Carrot Top. It really brightened the morning for most of the class who were still relatively asleep. He knew how to teach well and his students reflected that. I had taken five years of German in high school and was taking this second semester of elementary German class as a prerequisite for the intermediate German class. I was well ahead of the first semester German students, but Herr B caught up to all that I had learned in high school about three months into the semester. I was astonished at how fast he was moving things, but also at the same time how quickly the students could pick things up. He had a way of challenging us without our knowing it. Looking back on everything that happened in that class, I know I'm a better person for having met

Jamie Bishop. He has an exuberant personality that could bring a smile to anyone who would take a few minutes out of their day to talk with him. He would help anyone who sought his help, and he would even reach out to those who were struggling in his class. I'm glad I had the pleasure of meeting Herr B; I just wish I could have known him better. I know there will never be a person that will have the profound effect on my life that Jamie Bishop had. He will be greatly missed by all those who knew him. It's still hard to believe that I won't be able to see him again.

Brian Roy Bluhm

by Michelle Rivera

Friends remember Brian Bluhm's big smile as well as his unique and infectious laugh. "He had a very characteristic laugh, everyone knew it," said Ricky Castles, a good friend of Bluhm's and a PhD student in Computer Engineering. "You could pick it out in a room of a hundred people. It was just the joy he had."

Recent stories about the Civil Engineering graduate student never fail to mention his devotion to his faith and the Detroit Tigers. He was passionate about sports, and he was never without his navy blue baseball cap with the old English *D* on the front for Detroit, the faded color a testament to how much he wore it.

Angela Jones, Bluhm's older sister, remembers the last time their family was together. Angela, her husband, Justin, Brian, and their parents, Dennis and Beverly, had gotten together the Wednesday before the incident to watch the Tigers and Orioles play in Baltimore.

"That was the last time all five of us were together," said

Jones. "And it was the first time we'd seen a grand slam in person. We were all excited."

Bluhm was also active in and very dedicated to the church and inspired many of his fellow Christians.

"Brian was a Christian, and first and foremost that's what he would want to be remembered as," said Michael Marshall, close friend of Bluhm, to the Associated Baptist Press.

However, sports and his faith were not his only passions. Many who knew Bluhm revealed that he loved his family and friends very much.

"Brian was a great brother," said Jones. "I wouldn't have traded him. He was someone I could call and talk to . . . I not only lost a brother but a friend."

Brian was also known for his compassion and ability to reach out to friends.

"Brian knew I was going through something one time," said Castles. "He put his arm around my shoulders and asked, 'Hey, man, you all right?' And he looked at me, just waiting for an answer because he really wanted to know how I felt."

Dan Cecchini, Bluhm's good friend and senior Finance major, recounted a similar memory.

"You just knew he had your back because his caring was so genuine," he said. "He made a conscious choice to be a friend you could always count on."

Justin Jones, Bluhm's brother-in-law, said Bluhm was the first family member he met when he first started dating Angela Jones. Justin Jones had been nervous because he'd heard that Bluhm was a good reader of character. He sat down and watched the Detroit Redwings hockey game with Bluhm, however, and soon became comfortable.

"He's someone that when you'd sit down, get to know him and talk with him, he'd give you the shirt off his back," Justin Jones said. "At the end of the day he's one of those guys you love to be around and hang out with. He's one of the best guys I've ever met and I feel honored to have known him."

Castles lived down the hall from Bluhm and remembered a time when he'd been sitting in his room and a knock sounded on his door. He got up, and when he looked out into the hallway, found no one. However, at the end of the hall was Bluhm looking back with his big grin.

"It was his way of saying, 'Hi, I was thinking of you,' " Castles said.

"Brian took the time for every one of his friends no matter if he had something to do."

Bluhm also cared for his students. He was a teaching assistant in the freshman Engineering course for three semesters.

"Just from talking to his students and knowing him as a TA, I know he took the time and genuinely cared for his students and all the past students he had," said Castles.

Peebles Squire, sophomore Political Science major, had Bluhm as a TA. "Brian was a great guy, exceptionally tolerant, worked very hard to make sure everyone in the class was on the same page, and he always put up with my smart-ass comments in his class," he said.

"[Brian] could hardly go anywhere on campus without being greeted by one of his students," said Cecchini. "He took interest in them all. He always sought to be a servant heart, and that is an enduring inspiration for me and many others."

"We miss Brian dearly," said Angela Jones.

Castles said Bluhm was an optimist when it came to sports. When a baseball team is down, the fans often turn their baseball caps inside out to show support and make them rally caps. Bluhm always used to do this to his cap for Tech sports teams, the intramural teams he coached, and for the Detroit Tigers.

"I can see Brian up in heaven with his hat inside out on the top of his head," said Castles. "He knows Tech is down right now, but he also knows we're going to rally, pull together, and come back stronger."

Tommy McDearis, pastor, Blacksburg Baptist Church: Brian Bluhm was a graduate student at Virginia Tech. Also one who was intellectually gifted, Brian was a dedicated Christian and a dedicated Detroit Tigers fan. With a smile and a laugh that could instantly fill a room with joy, Brian always wore a Detroit Tigers baseball cap. He would turn his cap into a "rally cap" when anyone needed a bit of a rally in their lives. If Brian ever had a bad day, I never witnessed it. Always upbeat and jovial, Brian loved his family, Christ, and life with a passion.

Hannah Barnhill, a friend from Roanoke, said to the *New York Times* in an email: He would light up whenever he met someone new, and he loved to joke around. . . . He had a memorable laugh (more of a chuckle) and a huge heart. He was a person of faith, a loyal friend, and a Hokie till the end. He deserved every good thing in the world, and we are all shocked and deeply saddened to have lost him.

Angela Antonucci, Virginia Tech student, said to the *Washington Post:* We gave him hard times about things. He was such a Hokie fan, and always at every game. He had these bright orange pants he'd wear. They were bright orange. Like the kind of vest somebody would wear cleaning up litter on the side of the road—that kind of orange. . . . He was very full-spirited and very friend-spirited.

Ryan Clark

by Meg Miller

Ryan "Stack" Clark is described by people who knew him as having the best smile and the best laugh around, as well as having a special knack for giving the best hugs.

"His laughter, his love; [he was] a guy who could make you feel incredible," said senior Jeananne Tiffany about her co-worker. "He was an inspiration to a lot of people."

Living true to the Virginia Tech motto, "That I may serve," Clark served as a leader and friend to many of his fellow Tech students. He was a personnel officer for the Marching Virginians, a member of the service organization Circle K, a resident adviser in West Ambler Johnston Hall, and a staff member of the Imaginarium, the program resource room for residence hall staff located on the third floor of WAJ.

Clark was also a triple major, in Psychology, Biology, and English, and wanted to pursue a doctorate in Psychology with a concentration in Cognitive Neuroscience after graduating.

Tiffany, who worked at the Imaginarium with Ryan, said that one thing that really said a lot about Ryan's personality was how much time he put into being an RA and a member of the Imaginarium staff.

"We were open twenty hours a week, and I would say Ryan was in there fifteen hours a week just to be around the employees," Tiffany said. "Others always came before himself, and he got joy out of helping others."

Tiffany said that everyone in the Imaginarium teased him for the amount of time that he spent making bulletin boards for his hall. She said that it was required that the RAs make one board a month, and Ryan would usually make four or five a month.

"He loved doing stuff for his residents," Tiffany said. "He talked about [them] all the time at work."

Tiffany said that Ryan was a perfectionist when it came to his bulletin boards, and the staff was always scared of messing up when they were helping him.

"He was very detailed on coloring—he was a perfectionist on coloring," Tiffany said.

Tiffany recalled a time when Ryan had to leave for a staff meeting and left it up to her to color the Daffy Duck he was working on for a bulletin board. After being extremely careful in trying not to mess it up, she realized that the bow tie was the wrong color.

"We freaked out and had to cut another one out to replace it," Tiffany said. "He never found out until we told him months later."

She said that Ryan would send her emails and instant messages when she was having a bad day and was one person who could make her feel incredible.

"The thing I miss most about Ryan is his hugs," Tiffany said.

The Imaginarium wasn't the only place Ryan put in a lot of time and dedication. As a fifth-year Marching Virginian, Ryan was not only a baritone player, he was also a beloved leader.

Matt Bartley, a sophomore trumpet player in the Marching Virginians, said that he had only known Ryan for a short amount of time before he roomed with him at the ACC basketball tournament in Tampa this year.

Bartley said that since a lot of his friends didn't go on the trip, Ryan "really went out of his way to make me feel comfortable with his friends, and be a friend."

Dave McKee, director of the Marching Virginians, said that as personnel officer, Ryan ran the records of everyone in the band and was often the first person a new member interacted with. He said that Ryan was as extraordinary a person as he had ever been around at Virginia Tech.

"He always made people smile, always brought out the best in people," McKee said.

Ryan was also a leader outside the Virginia Tech community. He worked at Camp Big Heart, a camp for children and adults with disabilities, during his summers at Fort Yargo State Park in Winder, Georgia.

Jaclyn Price, a fellow employee and a student at the University of Georgia, said in an email that she met Ryan two summers ago when he was the music director and she was a unit leader for a cabin of boys. She said that Ryan was someone she would never forget.

"He made me feel welcome at the camp, and he is the reason I wanted to come back the following year," Price said. "He just made you so happy when you saw him, and he made me laugh all the time."

Carrie Johnson, RA for fourth floor West Ambler Johnston, agreed that Ryan was definitely a memorable person. She said that he would come in her room and talk about anything and everything.

"You could hear him laughing, hear him coming from a mile away," Johnson said. "[His laugh] was definitely contagious." Ryan was always very complimentary of others, but very critical of himself, Johnson said. She said that he always blamed himself when one of his residents got in trouble, and that he loved his residents.

"Ryan was a hero, he was just doing his job," Johnson said. "Few of us would have been that brave."

Taylor White, Virginia Tech student: We were talking at the couches in Squires where music majors and those involved in music usually hang out in between classes. I could tell he was a very nice guy. I remember I said something, who knows what, but he laughed and lightly punched my arm. To think this guy I was just laughing with last week is gone . . . is just unthinkable . . . unbelievable. I may have not known him for long, but I will miss him. I've missed out on the chance to get to know him better. Actually, now that I think about it, I have been able to get to know him better . . . through everyone talking about what an incredible guy he was.

Brant Marlett, friend: Ryan was one of the first people that I met and talked to at Virginia Tech. I remember walking up the hill from the parking lot next to Owens Dining Hall on move-in day with my parents lugging all my stuff and seeing him for the first time; seeing his wide and warm smile and his bright eyes light up as we shook hands and exchanged greetings. . . . As we became closer and closer friends, we discovered that we each had this same long-sleeve, supersoft, baby blue Banana Republic T-shirt. And we would always joke to each other and say, "Now don't wear my shirt today," and laugh about it. Or when one of us would wear it and the one who wasn't caught the other wearing it, we would say, "What are you doing wearing my shirt? That's my shirt!" . . . Ryan was a beautiful person, so full of life and wonder and charisma, and I will miss him dearly as I'm sure all of his friends and family everywhere do.

Andy Mager: I knew Stack for a few years, and the simple memory I have of him is his smile. Ryan Clark's sense of humor and vibrant spirit for life was infused in every band member he interacted with. His amazing ability to live and love everyone who came in contact with him will be his legacy at Virginia Tech.

Austin Cloyd

by Kevin Cupp
Planet Blacksburg

Mahatma Gandhi once said, "Be the change you want to see in the world," a quote lived up to by Austin Cloyd.

Cloyd, a freshman at Virginia Tech double majoring in International Studies and French, grew up in Austin, Texas, and moved to Champaign, Illinois, and later to Blacksburg. The moves followed her father's teaching career, which most recently landed him at Virginia Tech, teaching Accounting and Information Systems.

"Austin was the most wonderful daughter in the world," her father, Bryan Cloyd, told the *Chicago Tribune*.

Cloyd was best known for her altruistic nature. She aspired to help bring peace to troubled parts of the world by working for the United Nations. She spent four summers on missions with the Appalachia Service Project, repairing homes for people in need in Kentucky. This project inspired her and her mother to create a similar program where she lived in Illinois, called the Champaign Urban Service Project.

"She learned that the impoverished do not have a voice," her mother, Renee Cloyd, told *USA Today*. "She wanted to help create justice in this world."

She also spent time at a medical clinic in Mexico, helping with prenatal care.

She loved working with children and helped with vacation Bible school at her church and child care in her community.

Cloyd also taught preschoolers to swim and served as a lifeguard in the Virginia Tech McComas Hall Student Recreation Sports Center, where she was recognized as an outstanding employee.

Her swimming supervisor, Katherine Frasca, told the *Washington Post* that Austin was the kind of person who would take on extra work without complaint. That kind of work ethic led her to become a dean's list student in the Honors program at Tech.

While learning about the Honors program at Tech, Cloyd discovered that Honor students march to Lane Stadium with a band of pipers and drummers when they graduate. She was excited about this privilege and looked forward to the day when she would march to the tune of pipes and drums. Because of this, Jack Dudley of the University Honors Program said her parents arranged for a lone piper at her funeral.

According to the *Chicago Tribune*, Cloyd's influence is still being felt at Centennial High School in Champaign, where she and her mother coached a park district basketball team.

She was one who remembered birthdays and loved giving people gifts. Many of her friends were unable to return the favor, as her nineteenth birthday was only a week away from the incident.

Her family, friends, and the Virginia Tech community will never forget the young girl with bright red hair and striking smile who selflessly helped so many.

Matt Nipper: I met Austin in fall of '06 through a friend named Pearl Blevins. We found out we both went to Blacksburg High School, and she always talked about our hosting a party in the woods behind the high school and bringing back everyone from that high school, like a reunion back there. She also was about to move next to a quarry and talked about how we should go rock-climb it this summer. The fondest memory I have of her is a strange occurrence. On St. Patrick's Day night, me, Will, Eric McDearis, and our friend Tony went downtown. The very last stop was Souvlaki to get some food. I ran into her and her friend Allysa while I was there, which was weird because they where supposed to go to a party hosted by that SGA organization or whatever it was that they where a part of. They ditched it and went there, and I often think fate found us there, and the coolest part was I asked for a hug before they left, which is odd of me I guess, but I'm thankful for that being the last time I saw Austin. I did get to hug her goodbye and left her on good terms. She also always talked very highly of all her friends in Champaign and Texas, and the ones she made at BHS.

Tyler Miller: I met Austin Michelle Cloyd in the fall of my senior year at BHS. I walked into school late around 9:30 or

10:00. I walked to my locker and there was this tall girl with striking red hair standing there. I was about to ask if I could just get to my locker and be on my way when she said, "Someone wrote something really awful on your locker . . . and I just don't think anybody should have to read that." Austin had chosen to be late to class so that she could do something meaningful and nice for a complete stranger. That is who Austin was—a completely selfless person who not only would but wished to do and serve others without the need for anything in return.

Jocelyn Couture-Nowak

by Amie Steele

Joie de vivre.

In English it translates to "the joy of life," which is an expression many students have used to describe French professor Jocelyn Couture-Nowak.

In fact, when John Welch, sophomore International Studies major, sat down to write a eulogy for Couture-Nowak, he was worried he "wouldn't be able to adequately capture Madame's *joie de vivre*."

"Madame," as most of her students called her, left quite an impression on the students she had in class over the years—one of energy and cheer.

"There was never a frown to be seen," said Welch, who had Couture-Nowak as an instructor for his Intermediate French class.

Couture-Nowak's love for life spread into her teaching and onto her students. Many students have recalled times when her energy was contagious and spread to them.

"I had Madame my freshman year of college for Intermediate French. I remember being really intimidated walking in on my first day, a little freshman in a mostly older class. But as soon as Madame waltzed in she breezed by with a 'Bonjour!' in a bright and colorful outfit, and I knew right away that I would just love her class," said Lauren Morrison, a junior English Literature major.

"It turned out to be two of the best semesters that I ever had at Tech. She made coming to that ten a.m. class so much fun," Morrison said.

Couture-Nowak often taught morning classes, which meant early rising for a lot of students. Somehow, though, she found a way to spread her enthusiasm to her heavy-eyed pupils.

Welch said in his eulogy for Madame last Tuesday, "No matter how tired we were from studying the night before, and how much we didn't want to get up and go to such an early class, we did, because we know that Madame would be there greeting us at the door with a bright smile on her face and a lively flash in her eyes."

That sort of energy first thing in the morning is rarely seen on a college campus—especially in early-morning winter classes.

"Students would come in half asleep because class was so early, but they wouldn't stay asleep for long, because she would greet you energetically at the door," said Luke Sponholz, a senior.

Couture-Nowak, known for her carefree style, often came to class in bell-bottomed jeans; it was said your head turned if you saw her wearing a dress. This sort of relaxed personality and style was different from her teaching style; she took teaching French very seriously. Madame was dedicated to making sure her students left the classroom having learned something.

"Her teaching was almost frenzied, because she had so much to teach with not enough time to cram in everything she wanted to teach," Sponholz said.

Couture-Nowak wanted all students to learn French because she loved the language and she wanted to pass it on, her students said. She not only wanted her students to learn the language—but the culture, too.

"We had a party at the Cranwell International Center . . . so that we could make traditional French crepes. She was right there with us in the kitchen singing little French and Canadian tunes, and helping us flip the crepe just right," Morrison said.

Couture-Nowak made every attempt to make her classroom more than a classroom. While she made students experience French culture, she also made the classroom feel like a family. On days that Montgomery County schools were closed, she would bring her daughter, Sylvie Couture-Nowak, a student at Blacksburg Middle School, to class with her. "She made us a part of her family and we loved her for it," Welch said.

Her family, friends, and students remember her for her spirit, love of nature, and dedication to the preservation of her francophone heritage, but above all else her dedication to her students.

"She was not just an instructor, she was a friend," Welch said.

Lloyd Mapplebeck, assistant professor, Horticulture, said to *USA Today*: I've never met anyone who didn't love Jocelyn. She was a high-energy person, very enthusiastic. When she got involved with something, she put a lot of energy into it.

Suzanne Couture, aunt, said to the *Washington Post*: She was always swimming and cross-country skiing. She was full of life, and she was dead-set against any kind of violence.

Sue W. Farquhar, associate professor, French, said to the *Chronicle of Higher Education*: She was a spark of energy in our department, radiating joy of discovery, and always expressing dedication to her students. . . . French culture, especially French-Canadian culture, animated her teaching and was the key to inspiring her students to love French.

Kevin Granata

by Michael Berger

Professor Kevin Granata was a devoted professor, colleague, and father. Kindness and unselfishness defined his life and characterized his actions through his final hours. According to a memoriam released by the College of Engineering, Granata first and foremost protected students on that fateful day by escorting them into his office before he attempted to locate and potentially stop the situation.

This was how Granata lived. A leader in biomechanics research, he sat on numerous engineering science and mechanics committees, oversaw graduate students, taught undergraduate classes, and still found time to share his life with his family.

The memoriam stated, "Professor Granata's greatest passion and pride was his family, especially his wife and children. He was also an athlete. He rowed crew at Purdue, participated in biathlons and triathlons, and was an avid runner and cyclist. He loved coaching his sons' lacrosse teams."

"With so many research projects and graduate students, he still found time to spend with his family, and he coached his children in many sports and extracurricular activities. He was a wonderful family man. We will all miss him dearly," said Professor Demetri Telionis in an Associated Press interview.

After joining the Tech community in 2003, he had been considered one of the rising faculty members in the Engineering department. Specifically, Granata worked on movement dynamics in cerebral palsy as well as musculoskeletal movement, control of low-back pain, and the technological development of legged walking robots.

Granata was an integral part of Tech's biomedical partnership with Wake Forest University, which has also stated its condolences and sadness for the loss of such a distinguished professor and friend.

According to the memoriam, Professor Granata was born and raised in Toledo, Ohio, and received undergraduate degrees from Ohio State University in Electrical Engineering and Physics. He later earned a master's degree in Physics from Purdue University. Thereafter, he worked in the Applied Physics Laboratory in Maryland. He received his doctoral degree in Biomedical Engineering from Ohio State University and then worked in the Department of Orthopedics at the University of Virginia, where he was the director of the Gait Laboratory.

Granata is survived by his wife, Linda; his two boys, Alex and Eric; and his daughter, Ellen. Granata stood out in his chosen academic field as well as on a personal level, as those who knew him will never forget. In an interview with the *Lafayette Journal & Courier*, Sandy Formica, a graduate secretary in the Purdue Physics Department, said, "You remember people like that because they stop in and say hello to you. That's just the type of person he was."

Dr. Ishwar Puri, professor and head, Engineering Science and Mechanics: Kevin simply would just walk into my office! And he knew that I didn't like the word "boss" because it was a four-letter word. But he'd come in and say, "Hi, boss." He'd watch the grimace on my face. You know, there are no bosses in academia. "Boss" is a four-letter word that I dislike. He'd see me in the corridor and shout across the parking lot, "Hi, boss."

John Chermak, neighbor and Virginia Tech Geological Sciences professor: I feel very badly now for Kevin's family, because that's really tough. They've done a great job. He's been a great mentor for all of them, and now all of sudden it's been ripped apart. We've always joked that we were living next to the

Cleavers. They're absolutely unbelievable in terms of their family unit. Their kids are the type of kids that play with my kids even though they're older than mine, you know, just the type of kids that would always come over and say hello. We play games, the type of kids you like having around. Kevin, as you could imagine, being a researcher as he was, he didn't have a lot of time for idle chat, but he was always very friendly, willing to help where I needed help with whatever it happened to be. He was always interested in me and my family. He was kind, a good neighbor, a nice man. Again, he'd be outside playing catch with his boys, you know, lacrosse all the time. They built a pool, and everything you'd want to see in a good family. He would do it all for his kids and his wife, that's for sure.

Brad Bennett, former colleague at the University of Virginia's Kluge Children's Rehabilitation Center, said to the *Washington Post:* He was a scientist, a hardworking scientist, trying to understand things. . . . He was great to brainstorm with. He was the first guy in the morning and the last guy to leave at night.

Matt Gwaltney

by Robert Bowman

As a second-year master's student with the Charles Edward Via Jr. Department of Civil and Environmental Engineering, Matt Gwaltney, of Chester, Virginia, had dedicated himself to his research and to helping future engineers as a teaching assistant.

Gwaltney received an undergraduate degree from Virginia Tech in 2005 as a civil engineer, focused on environmental and water resources engineering, according to Tech's environment innovations website.

Gwaltney was nearly finished with his master's degree, as he studied Small Watershed in Blacksburg, as well as Stormwater Management.

In addition to his own research, Gwaltney was a teaching assistant for three different classes, including Fluid Mechanics, Measurements, and Engineering Exploration, a freshman class.

Andrew Smith, a Civil Engineering student, remembers Gwaltney's dedication through labs for civil engineers in CEE 2814: Measurements.

"One lab, [Gwaltney] stuck it out with us through a thunderstorm and two hours of rain, just to help my group along and made sure we finished," Smith said in a Facebook memorial group.

Christine Vineski, one of many students who knew Gwaltney as a graduate teaching assistant for Engineering Exploration, remembers Gwaltney's concern for his students.

"He was so helpful with anything we had problems with and he answered any questions we had within seconds," she said. "He was always concerned about everybody's success in the class. He always asked questions that would make us think."

Dominic Liss, a freshman Engineering major, recalls a time when Gwaltney went above and beyond to help him finish a class project. Liss had a difficult time finishing a project, but Gwaltney was willing to come into the office whenever Liss needed help with the assignment.

"He didn't come off as a teacher, but as a friend who was there to help us," Liss said.

Jayme Maddox, another student in the class for which Gwaltney was a TA, notes his enjoyment for educating.

"I know that if someone can actually, [as] a college student, come to a Friday class and enjoy it, that's an amazing accomplishment. . . . He treated his students like they were his friends and made us feel comfortable in the class. . . . He quickly became my favorite educator at Virginia Tech and continues to retain that title," wrote Maddox in an email interview.

Chris Hawkins remembers his days with Gwaltney when the two lived across from each other in Pritchard Hall.

He said that Gwaltney was "always smiling and had an almost unreal sense of being positive about everything. He loved sports, was a huge Braves fan, and never missed a VT football or basketball game."

Gwaltney, an avid sports fan, and the sports editor of his high school newspaper, was often seen playing basketball.

On a post to a CNN article, his longtime neighbor, Chris Bonham, also of Chester, wrote, "I remember years ago when we would play a pickup basketball game in his driveway, or get a bunch of guys to play football in his backyard, or when we would play home-run derby."

In a life filled with research, teaching, and sports, Gwaltney will best be remembered for the always-visible smile on his face.

Dale Clark, high school baseball coach: Late in the season [his junior year], we were playing our rival school up the street, and it was sort of for bragging rights. We weren't in any tournament or anything, and Matt pitched a three-hit shutout. We won 14–0, and everything just went right that game. He was hitting his spots with his pitches and getting his curveball down there. He just pitched the game of his life that day. . . . The thing that stands out for me about Matt was that we can be in one of our team meetings, which was either at the beginning of a practice or at the end of a practice, after a game the day before, and we would be talking about the things we did well and the things we needed to work on. I knew some of the kids might be looking at their feet, but you knew they were sort of listening. But every time I saw Matt, he had that solid eye contact with you. You can tell that he was taking in every word you said. . . . Matt knew when to play around, and he knew when to work. And it was mainly work. He just worked at his game tremendously. He played basketball, too, and it was the same way with basketball. . . . He was a leader on the team by the way he carried himself. I know especially with basketball, he wasn't a great player in either sport, but he was just a competitive player. He could make everybody around him so much better. People didn't slack off because they were around Matt.

Erin Simon, childhood friend: Initially, I thought he was just a neighborhood kid to play with. Because our neighborhood was so small and so new, there weren't a lot of children, so basically we all felt like we were a microcosm of a family. We all knew each other, went to school together, played after school together from morning until night. He was just part of our family of neighbors. . . . My fondest memory of Matt would be when we would play HORSE in his driveway, I was never good. Matt was a basketball player; he played all throughout elementary school to middle school to high school. When we'd play HORSE, I'd always miss the shot, so he just looked at me and laughed. I kept saying, "Come on. One more time! One more time! Just let me try again before the game is over!" He would say, "It's been over!" He would just smile and laugh at me. I also remember him riding a bike to his pool with a towel around his neck. I always saw him with a basketball or a baseball glove on his hand when we were outside playing.

Kevin McCain, friend: In general, what I remember him most for is the dynamic of our friendship and that we spoke often. He was the constant hard worker, not necessarily the perfectionist, but everything we did in life was the polar opposite, yet still we were best friends. He was the person who worked hard with hours of studying. On the other side, we had some similarities. Our nature was similar. The way we interacted with people was with the same kind of humor. But the thing that really stood out about us is that we realized how really different we were, but in a way, that made us stronger as friends. . . . I had a class with him every year from middle school through high school. He was your perfect student, very attentive. He picked up on everything quickly. He always asked questions that people didn't think of but everyone needed to know. He was helping out the class in any way he could. He was very close with his parents, his family, and his extended family as well. He had very strong familiar bonds with them. He was an only child, so he meant the world to his parents and family as well.

Caitlin Hammaren

by Laurel Colella

Caitlin Hammaren's family and friends remember her as an amazing daughter, sister, resident adviser, and person.

"Caitlin had a way to make everyone feel as if they were her best friend," said friend and suitemate Rochelle Low in an email interview. "She was always there for you whenever you needed her, and had a smile and laugh that were contagious under any circumstance."

Originally from New York, Hammaren decided to become a Hokie after learning of the previous positive experiences of a close family friend.

"Her family really wanted her to get out of New York, something different, go somewhere safe, ironically," said Liz McClendon, Hammaren's big sister in the Kappa Kappa Gamma sorority.

"She was just one of the most outstanding individuals that I've had the privilege of working with in my thirty-one years as an educator," said John P. Latini, principal of Minisink Valley High School, to *Time* magazine.

During her high school years, Caitlin enjoyed riding her horse, Poet, and was the president of her school choir. It was her love of singing that inspired her to join a choir her freshman year at Virginia Tech. She also took on many leadership and service positions in the community, including her involvement with her sorority, and her decision to become a resident adviser.

"Caitlin decided to become an RA after seeing what a difference our RA made in the dorm the previous year," Low said. "Caitlin wanted to be close to everyone in the building and make them feel like they could come to her for anything, anytime, and they always did."

Kelsey Hawes, freshman suitemate, described Caitlin as someone who cared for her residence hall.

"She always put others before herself and would hold off on her homework or her priorities and obligations to help somebody else," Hawes said.

Her service to the resident life community is evident through the dedication she showed toward her position as an RA.

"She did special programs every Thursday night with another RA called Finding Flavor in Peddrew-Yates," McClendon said. "They did all different types of things just for anybody who wanted to come. One time they made ice cream out of liquid nitrogen, sometimes it was just bringing in a picture from home and talking about it and just sharing stories."

Caitlin enjoyed spending time with her residents and friends. Her enthusiasm for life was evident, and television classics such as *I Love Lucy* or *The Pink Panther* could always be heard blasting from her room. During the holidays she embraced singing and dancing to 'N Sync Christmas music and Mariah Carey's "All I Want for Christmas Is You."

The dedication Caitlin showed toward community involvement carried over into her passion for success in school. She had recently decided to add a French major, in addition to her major in Interdisciplinary Studies and her minor in Social Change. Caitlin also showed interest in the possibility of attending law school after graduation.

"She could have done pretty much anything," McClendon said.

Caitlin was a fun-loving girl with a passion for family, friends, and getting the most out of life. Her energy was contagious to all who knew her, and her love for humanity and making people happy was infectious. Caitlin was very close with her family, as experienced by Low, who went home with Caitlin over Thanksgiving break this past year.

"We spent half of the break making cookies, shopping, decorating chocolate, and spending time with her family. It was one of the best times of my life, and I will never forget her family and their traditions and love for Caitlin," Low said.

Tommy McDearis: Caitlin Hammaren was a girl who seemed to sparkle when you looked at her. Always smiling, Caitlin loved singing. A star in her high school chorus, she was the kind of person who made others feel better just by being near them. A resident assistant who was a constant helpmate to the students in her dorm, she was studying French and International Politics. Caitlin had big dreams for the future, she had the drive and the intelligence to make them come true, and all her dreams included God and the greater good of humankind.

Martha Murray, superintendent, Minisink Valley Central School District, said to *USA Today*: She was more than a real role model. She would encourage the kids to be positive when they were grumbling. . . . She certainly was one to sing [in the choir] with a smile on her face.

Jeremy Herbstritt

by Drew Jackson

Jeremy Herbstritt was a man of energy. His mother, Peggy Herbstritt, told CNN's Wolf Blitzer that from the time he was born, on into graduate school, Jeremy only slept a couple of hours a day.

The days were simply too short for him, but the liveliness of his character stretched these days as tight as they could possibly stretch, tighter than most will ever see them stretched, until he had exhausted that day's goal and prepared for the next.

Before entering Virginia Tech's civil engineering graduate school in June of 2006, Herbstritt, a Pennsylvania native, earned two undergraduate degrees from Penn State University, one in biochemistry and molecular biology in 2003, the other in civil engineering in 2006.

Civil engineering professor Panos Diplas was Herbstritt's adviser at Tech. Diplas and Herbstritt worked closely together on a research project set on the lower Roanoke River in North Carolina, focusing on the effect of reservoir releases on the river.

"Jeremy was very energetic, very inquisitive, and a person that was always here to help others," Diplas said.

According to Diplas, Jeremy was able to give the Roanoke River project a major push.

"He was very capable of making contacts with others, trying to find the necessary information, and he was incredibly resourceful locating people and information of benefit to the project," Diplas said.

"Jeremy had the capacity to make everyone around him better."

It was this ease and care that drew people toward Herbstritt.

A close friend, Electrical Engineering graduate student Ken Stanton, said that he first met Herbstritt at a party Stanton threw for people in his building.

"Jeremy made a Kramer-like entrance, blasting in the door, and immediately began chatting. He lit up the room, got to know everyone, and made quite a few friends that night," said Stanton in an email interview.

Stanton went on to describe Herbstritt's manner of conversation.

"He would talk up a storm, sharing stories, talking about random topics, and always wanting to learn what you cared about and were interested in," he said.

As an example of his selflessness, Stanton cited Herbstritt's willingness to drive car-less international students on errands. "If you asked him for help, he would drop what he was doing, and if you didn't ask him for help but needed it, he would give it too," said Stanton.

Herbstritt possessed a passion for running, and he himself ran several marathons. This passion was one instilled by Jeremy and similarly possessed by the rest of his family. On the Monday of the shootings Jeremy's parents watched as his sister Jen ran in the Boston Marathon. Stanton recounted a story told by her. "She says that Jeremy's legs ran the last few miles of the race, as she hit a wall at the twenty-mile marker, but found a sudden boost a short time later."

Aside from running, he enjoyed hiking, biking, kayaking, and anything related to the outdoors. He was said to ride his bike to school whenever possible. It is this love and energy for the outside world that Herbstritt planned on translating into a career.

"Jeremy was very much interested in environmental issues, and this was certainly within that area of the project he was involved in," Diplas said.

Stanton talked of Herbstritt's career pursuit.

"Jeremy loves the outdoors, and preserving it. He was highly dedicated to his work in civil and environmental engineering, and wanted to pursue a career in water resources protection," Stanton said.

He was described as caring, hardworking, hilarious, and random, a man steadfast in his pursuit of a goal, to whom the word *no* was an impossibility. To friends he was a great listener, an inspiration. Stanton, though, said these past-tense verbs are inappropriate and unnecessary.

"You may notice I talk about who Jeremy is in the present tense—this is intentional, as he still lives inside of each one of us who got to know him. Jeremy used to live upstairs above me—now he lives up above all of us," Stanton said.

Alexis Bozzo: I'll never forget the night I met Jeremy. . . . I was not planning on going out that night but my best friend Michelle Braunstein convinced me to join her after a social she had at Hokie House. When I arrived I saw my friend Ken Stanton. . . . He was playing pool with a friend of ours named Sean Wilson and Jeremy was looking on. Ken introduced us all and that is when the magic began. Jeremy talked to me for about an hour at Hokie House with his arm around me the entire time while I leaned into his lanky body so I could hear every word flowing out of his handsome lips and smile. We then continued onto Champs and Jeremy continued to talk to me, I clearly remember his lips moving rapidly that night. Every now and then he would let me get a few words in, but I did not mind because I was just touched by how he released his real identity on the first night I met him. After leaving Champs we went our separate ways at which point Jeremy gave me his phone number and I gave him mine. I ended up calling Jeremy, because he was very busy with graduate school and he always told me how he was too nervous to call me. Hence, he was glad I made the call even though he talked to me for about an hour before finally asking me to come over for a movie. From that point on, we were inseparable and even when I was in Richmond interning this spring semester I made many trips to Blacksburg and Jeremy drove his infamous red jeep to Richmond. He could not make it for Valentine's Day, but he sent a huge vase of flowers to the General Assembly and wrote a very sweet note that I will cherish forever. All of my coworkers said, "You have a very sweet boyfriend and are quite lucky to have such an amazing person in your life."

Gaurav Bansal: Jeremy was a pretty loud guy, loud in a good way. He's really energetic, really friendly, and had a different style of talking than anyone else I've met. . . . He was always running, or hiking or biking—some athletic activity. I went running with him once, and the only reason I didn't go with him again was because he smoked me. He was always like, "We should go running!" I used to run cross-country in high school. So I was thinking, "Yeah I'm pretty good, maybe I can keep up with him." So we just went running once on Huckleberry Trail. I was dying and he was like, "Come on, come on, just keep going!" I told him, "I'm not running with you anymore. I'll run on my own." He was just really uplifting to everyone, made everyone feel better about themselves.

Peggy Johnson, professor and head, Civil and Environmental Engineering, Penn State: I first met him when he took a course [Hydraulic Engineering] from me in 2005. He and his friend, Heather Wittmer, used to sit in the front row every day. They always made me laugh because they were always smiling, laughing, and telling funny stories. Jeremy wore a smile whenever I saw him. My first impression of him was that he was a super nice, warm, happy person. . . . He seemed to really enjoy life. Running was one of his favored activities, and he was happy to run with his friends and family, regardless of the speed. He was such a warm and kind person. I never once heard him say anything unpleasant or say unkind words about another person.

Rachael Hill

by Katelyn Lau

Rachael Elizabeth Hill enjoyed taking trips to Disney World with her family, having long talks with her friends, and attending classes and football games with her fellow Hokies.

But throughout her short life, Hill left a strong legacy—one of joy, love, kindness, spirituality, fun, humor, and encouragement to all who knew her.

Hill's friend of thirteen years, Christina Neulen, noted that all of these things and more seemed to "radiate from the inside of who she was to everything else."

"She just affected everyone else, and that's something she still has now. That's not temporary," Neulen said.

Hill attended Grove Avenue Christian School, a small private school, from kindergarten through her high school graduation.

She was known there for her love of God, volleyball, piano, shoes, movies, French, reading, friends, and family.

"Her parents were her two best friends," said Andrew Cannada, Hill's friend since kindergarten.

Her volleyball coach, Anna Reinstein, explained, "Rachael's mother drove her to school every day, even after she got her license, because they valued that time to talk and be with one another."

Hill was a competitive volleyball player and captain of her high school team, said Amanda Cannada, another of Hill's friends.

Maria Gillian, a Biochemistry major and Hill's friend and roommate at Tech, remembered meeting her for the first time at volleyball.

"I had transferred to the school and didn't know anyone, and she was just a sweetheart and as nice as can be. She made me feel like I had known her for years, even though I had just met her," Gillian said.

She was a leader on the volleyball court as well.

"She used to write little notes to each of the girls on the team, encouraging them and always including a scripture," Reinstein said. "We always had a good volleyball team, but if we would be in a game and things weren't looking good, Rachael had a way of bringing the team back around and bringing them to a win."

Hill was also dedicated to playing the piano.

"She would always play, even in school," Andrew Cannada said. "She usually had a free period and she would play the piano, and you could hear her through the halls."

Friends spoke often of Hill's smile, and Reinstein noted, "She had a beautiful smile that could really just make your day. She had a great way of sensing when people were having a difficult day and knew how to minister to that."

Fellow student Tre Becoat recalled Hill's kindness toward him when he was a newcomer at Grove Avenue Christian School in a *Richmond Times-Dispatch* article.

Hill burned him a CD titled *Tre's Entertainment Mix* for Christmas last year, and Becoat said in the article, "I felt like she had gotten me the most expensive thing she could have."

Reinstein, also Hill's English teacher, remembered a time when Hill's class was making sleeping bags for the homeless. "A lot of the kids, especially the boys, just couldn't even figure out how to thread a needle, much less put it into a piece of fabric and pull it through. And Rachael had so much patience with the kids who just couldn't get it. . . . And I was thinking about how patient she was in trying to help them do something that was just so simple, but without making them feel bad about not being able to do it."

Friends remember her for the conversations, the movies, the trips, and the time spent with a girl who seemed to take joy in all life offered her.

"[Rachael was] one of those people who was always good to talk to," said her friend, Anu Kuriakose. "We could talk for at least two hours about everything . . . and I'm just going to miss our long talks."

Hill's parents even took her and the four other senior girls from Grove Avenue Christian School to Disney World during the summer of their senior year, and her friends recalled "having fun acting like kids for a week" and just how much Hill loved it there.

Her friends said that after she graduated from Grove Avenue Christian School, Hill's prayers led her to Tech.

Gillian said she was leaning toward a major in Biochemistry and Nanotechnology. "She was contemplating going into research for that; she really wanted to discover a cure for Parkinson's and cancer. She found it fascinating, because chemistry breaks things down into the smallest level, and she found that was a good way to see the handiwork of God in a way that most people don't understand or appreciate," Gillian said.

Above all, those who knew Hill felt that she would want to be remembered as someone devoted to the Lord.

"She lived her life for the Lord," friend Amanda Cannada said, "and I think she would want people to come to know the Lord through this whole event."

"I know that Rachael will want people to remember her as a fun-loving person, who put Jesus Christ first in her life and enjoyed every moment she had on earth," Kuriakose said.

"I'm waiting to see my best friend again. I know she is with the Lord," Rachael's mother, Tammy Hill, said in a *Richmond Times-Dispatch* article. "If she had the choice of coming back or staying, I think she'd stay."

"I'm so thankful for that last tender hug against my cheek where we said, 'I love you, I love you,' and she left," said Rachael's father, Allen Hill, in a *Richmond Times-Dispatch* article.

Larry Taylor, chemistry professor: Office hours at VT have never been well attended from my experience. Less than five people out of two hundred show up on any given day. Rachael was usually one of the five. Thus, one word to describe her is *motivated*. She was determined to do well in chemistry. She wanted to make sure that she knew how to do all of the problems that I assigned in each chapter. She even found practice quizzes provided by the text publisher, and she would come to have me go over the answers and solutions each week. She was tenacious in a quiet, shy way. I found her to be pleasant, polite, easily communicates, and mature for her age. Each time she visited me (which was three times per week), I would probe a little more in order to learn more about her. At twenty years of age, I feel that lots of students are very negative and have little hope for the future. The description of college students as "clay pots" has always spoken to me. Rachael appeared to have hope and a spiritual foundation that would have served her well in the future.

Mark Becton, pastor, Grove Avenue Baptist Church, said to the *Roanoke Times:* Rachael was a young woman of high character, strong integrity and deep faith in her walk with Jesus Christ.

Marie C. Teodori, former science teacher and mentor, told the *Chronicle of Higher Education:* [Rachael] always loved science. . . . It was not enough for her to know the facts of science, she wanted to know: Why these facts? What does this mean? And how can this be useful?

Emily Hilscher

by Kim Berkey

"Well, let me give you the story of how I met Emily," wrote Rowan Webster in an email message.

Webster, a friend of Hilscher's, continued, "I moved to Rappahannock County about three years ago. . . . I decided to visit some schools in the area. . . . Rappahannock High was a small public school in the middle of the county. While I was walking through the halls, hearing about their athletics, sciences, etc. I was excited to learn that culinary classes were something that the school featured and asked for a chance to check them out. Opening up the door, I was greeted by the delicious smells of baking. A girl, with brown hair pulled in a ponytail, wearing a white apron skipped up to me, and thrust a chocolate cupcake right under my nose. 'Want a cupcake? What's your name? Mine's Emily.' That's just how she was. Unafraid, unassuming, generous and welcoming."

This smiling, welcoming, brown-haired freshman from Woodville, Virginia, will be greatly missed by those whose lives she touched.

"She was a wonderful kid—warm, sensitive, outgoing, and happy," said family friend John McCarthy to the *Roanoke Times*.

Hilscher, an Animal and Poultry Sciences major, loved all animals. Horses were no exception. The *Roanoke Times* said she began showing horses and rode hunter/jumpers over fences. The *Roanoke Times* also interviewed trainer Moody Aylor, who regarded Emily as one of his daughters. He recalled Emily riding as early as age nine at Old Mill Stables in Woodville.

"She was a beautiful, grown-up person," said Aylor. "She was the most mature person I've ever known at that age."

The maturity blossomed in college, impressing students and faculty alike.

"Emily Hilscher was a wonderful student to have in class—bright, cheerful, thoughtful," said freshman composition instructor Nick Kocz in an interview by the *Chronicle of Higher Education*. One day, to demonstrate interview techniques, he asked her questions in front of the class. "She made it seem fun," he says. It was the moment the students "really began to gel as a class."

"Emily taught me to have faith in in-class unstructured student demonstrations," wrote Kocz. "I'd feel grateful if even one of my children grew up to be the person she was."

"[She] was always very friendly," said her friend Will Nachless, also nineteen. "Before I even knew her, I thought she was very outgoing, friendly, and helpful, and she was great in chemistry."

A statement released by superintendent Robert Chappell said, "We extend our thoughts, prayers, and sincere condolences to the family of 2006 RCHS graduate Emily Hilscher, her many friends and her teachers as we all mourn the loss of this bright, talented young lady. No words can completely express our collective community sorrow upon the untimely, tragic passing of this child."

No death caused by violence is ever natural. However, Emily may have had a gift, a presence that some may never grasp in a full life—she had people who loved her and she loved them back unconditionally. She was herself and made impressions on people by being just that—a thoughtful, welcoming, generous, smiling person . . . and so very much more.

"She loved her friends, and they all still feel the same way. After the tragedy at Virginia Tech, I was approached by many reporters. Some asked me if Emily's friends were planning on constructing some sort of memorial to her," wrote Rowan.

He continued, "The love of her friends, the fact that she touched so many lives so deeply, is the greatest monument any person could ever hope to have built in remembrance of their life. We don't need a big stone to keep her in our hearts. . . . It's not just my loss; it's all of ours."

Erica Hilscher, sister: Emily lived and breathed horses, started riding at five or six years old. . . . She rode, did trail rides, trained, and even pony raced and fox hunted . . . She loved to cook and took every opportunity she could to learn and test out new recipes. . . . She was an avid snowboarder in the winter months, taking up skateboarding in the spring (was still learning). . . . She was a fun-loving person, who always managed to have a good time. She could brighten anyone's day by a joke or just by being her. She was stubborn, but was also very intelligent. She had a free and imaginative spirit and never hesitated to meet someone new and make them feel at home. She had friends of all types, whether they be rockin' punks, horsemen and women, or guys on the soccer field. Young and old, it didn't matter. She loved life. Emily and I were not just sisters, but best friends.

Joy Sours, former art teacher: She had a smile that lit up the room and the most beautiful blue eyes you've ever seen. From the first day I met Emily her freshman year I knew she was something special. She had a wonderful talent in art. She was always making the coolest things, i.e., Capri Sun purses, belts out of bottle caps, hemp bracelets, and anything she could out of duct tape. Emily was voted (her senior year) by her friends as the most talented and best eyes. This was so true. I can't even tell you how many years I taught Emily because she was always in my room (usually from another class), I lost count. She was such a special girl and touched my life in so many ways.

Lisa Maloney, high school classmate: There were far too many to count but there were so many little times that I will never forget. Like seeing her on the road, and having her flag me down, then sitting in the back of her pickup truck eating peach ice cream cones from a local store. Seeing her and her horse at the stable as I drove by, however it was always hard for me to remember not to honk so I wouldn't spook her horse. We spent our sister's junior prom night together, because we were too young to go. Swimming in her pool, and those famous dinner parties we used to throw before homecomings every year. . . . She was the most caring, sweetest girl, but toughest at the same time. She wasn't afraid of anything and inspired us all. She genuinely did not care what other people thought of her, she did her own thing and she probably didn't know this, but it was one of her most admirable traits.

Anne Pallie: She showed up at Old Mill Stables as so many other children have because she wanted to become a rider. We all loved her and Moody, who never imparted his very special knowledge to anyone else that I know of, took her under his wing and taught her an ocean of knowledge about horses, riding, veterinarian work. She was his pupil and his sidekick. . . . Emily and her Mom would spend hours grooming their horses—they called it "beauty parlor" and I always loved watching them. Early on out on the hunt field one day, she couldn't control her little Arab horse Sadud, so I came back from the main field, got in front of her and she followed me for the rest of the hunt. That was when I knew more than she. Not many years later, there came a time when I couldn't get my horse over the course and Moody said, "Smiley, get on Slim and get him over those obstacles." She did. He always called her Smiley. It was the perfect name for her.

Jarrett Lane

by Caroline Black

For the first time, twenty-two-year-old senior Civil Engineering major Jarrett Lane was on the verge of breaking out of his familiar surroundings and continuing his extremely promising life. Becoming a Civil Engineering major at Virginia Tech in Blacksburg was certainly a huge accomplishment, but being less than an hour's drive away from home in the small town of Narrows, Virginia, it still wasn't quite venturing out into the great unknown.

Huge accomplishments are what marked Lane's life, beginning with his domination of both academics and athletics during his high school career. The small town of Narrows is one where everyone knows their neighbor's business, and at Narrows High School, everyone knew Jarrett Lane.

"He was the kind of guy that, once you met him, he was like part of your family—the whole town knew him," David Dent, an internship supervisor of Lane's as well as a family friend, told the *Roanoke Times*. "He was always the guy that the other ones looked up to."

Lane was passionate about sports, and lettered in four varsity sports during his high school career. He put his whole heart into football, basketball, track, and tennis.

But for Lane, that wasn't enough. Being naturally competitive, he was never one to shy away from a challenge. He put more of his seemingly endless energy into his academics, and graduated as the valedictorian of his high school class. His success at Narrows meant he could finally continue on to pursue his dream—attending college at Virginia Tech.

"He had so much pride in Virginia Tech, he loved being here," said junior Marketing major Amanda Bishop, who was close friends with Lane ever since they had a class together her freshman year. "He had a lot of pride in everything he did, because he put so much effort into it. He was so hardworking."

Bishop remembers how they clicked through their shared love of sports and competition. "We played just for fun, and we also played intramural sports together the beginning of this (spring) semester," she said. "My freshman year we had a class together, and we used to play horse after class every day. We were so competitive, but I'd always beat him. One time he beat me in horse, and we didn't play again for like a year."

Through all his sporting pursuits, Lane remained steadfastly dedicated to his academics. As an Engineering major, he had a full and intense course load, and had even begun an internship with Virginia Tech's Site and Infrastructure Development the spring of his junior year, where he hoped to begin using his engineering skills to help improve the quality of life for others.

"He was very confident in himself and the things he did," said Bishop, "but was still always so fun-loving and full of spirit."

By his senior year at Tech, he was already taking graduate-level courses, and had begun looking at engineering graduate programs throughout the country. His stellar résumé landed him prestigious offers from all around the country, and Lane had recently chosen the University of Florida for his graduate studies.

"Over spring break he went down [to Florida] for a few days, and he met some of the students that were in the grad school there . . . and he loved it down there, loved the weather and loved the school," Bishop says. "I talked to him the weekend before he left, and he asked if I wanted to go down there with him. He planned to go apartment shopping the last weekend in May."

It didn't hurt that Lane was also offered a full scholarship and graduate assistantship to attend Florida.

Lane worked impossibly hard his entire life to achieve all that he had, while still managing to find time for friends, sports, and even his strong Christian faith.

Many friends and mentors recall Lane's strong faith, with a friend posting on his Facebook page, "It was a privilege to have known you. You were such a great guy and I have many fond memories of which I will never forget! From going out as a group to eat before the high school dances to goofing off at track practice and many more.

"You were a very great athlete, student and great Christian example showing others that you could do anything with Christ."

Mike Stevens, WDBJ-7 sports anchor: Unlike some of the victims who had traveled halfway around the world to attend Virginia Tech, Jarrett had simply driven twenty-eight miles down Route 460 from his home in Narrows. For the people in his Giles County hometown the fact that he was set to graduate with a degree in civil engineering this month and then attend graduate school at the University of Florida was anything but a surprise. After all, Jarrett had a 4.0 grade point average in high school, was the valedictorian of his senior class, and starred in football, basketball, tennis, and track for the Green Wave. He was one of those rare high school athletes who kept his mouth shut and led by example. You know, the kind of kid leading the conditioning drills both before and after practice.

Craig Moore, Site and Infrastructure Development coworker, told the *Roanoke Times:* We were always kidding, picking on one another. If you left your desk with your email up, you might later [find] out that he'd invited someone to a [fake] meeting using your email.

Robert Stump, Narrows High School principal, told the *New York Times:* He was always one of the hardest workers. . . . One time, after he'd had a good basketball game, he went up to the coach and said, "Coach, what do I have to work on so that we can be better?"

Brian Todd Lusk, basketball coach and neighbor, told the *Chronicle of Higher Education:* You picture it in your head, and you're probably picturing this muscular guy, but that's not the way Jarrett was. . . . Jarrett was just a skinny little kid. But he had the heart of a champion.

Jenny Martin said to the *Baltimore Sun:* What summed him up best to me was that he was a good Christian. . . . He wasn't afraid to declare his faith in front of his friends. Do you know how special it is to find a young person like that? Someone even the adults could learn from?

Matthew La Porte

by T. Rees Shapiro

Cadet Matthew La Porte's tenure in the Corps of Cadets, and as a student at Virginia Tech, was tragically cut short April 16, but his legacy of leadership, excellence, and an easy smile will be carried among their numbers for decades to come.

La Porte played the tenor drum in one of Tech's greatest traditions: the Corps of Cadets Marching Band, the Highty-Tighties.

"Matt was a kind and generous person highly respected by his bud class and the administration as well," said Major George McNeill, director of the Highty-Tighties. "He was quiet and soft-spoken but always had smile when he greeted you. He was a very talented cello player and percussionist in the Highty-Tighty Band. His conga playing in the jazz band will certainly be missed. Whenever those congas are played we'll all think of Matt and his musical talent."

His friends from the HT-platoon could only agree.

"He was a really good guy," Cadet First Lieutenant Kyle Ellington, his platoon leader in the Corps, said. "He was one of those guys that sometimes you just had to shake your head and laugh at."

Ellington described one of La Porte's most famous acts. La Porte would don his white T-shirt, extra-tight Levi's, classic Converse high-tops, leather jacket, and, then, to top it off, his signature "Aviators," sunglasses that covered his face.

"We all called him 'The Fonz,' " Ellington said. "He liked to joke around, and just be a goof."

Cadet Supply Sergeant Nathaniel Boggs was La Porte's roommate [that] semester, who smiled when he thought about La Porte.

"He'd even wear those sunglasses inside, and when it was nighttime," Boggs said.

But despite his joking personality, Cadet La Porte was held with serious respect among the Corps community.

He consistently challenged himself, was the epitome of peak physical condition, and was enrolled at Tech on an Air Force scholarship.

"La Porte was in AFSOPT," Ellington said. "Which is Air Force Special Operations Preparation Training. It's a program for those who select it in the Air Force ROTC. The cadets have to complete a variety of extreme physical tasks, which include a 1,000-meter swim, a 1.5-mile run, pull-ups, push-ups, sit-ups, and flutter kicks. But that's not all, the entire course goes on for three weeks, and it's constant physical exertion."

La Porte was also a fire team leader in charge of two freshman cadets in the Corps, and as Ellington pointed out, was the number five AFROTC cadet in the country last year.

Boggs noted La Porte lived with just the bare necessities, and was very easy to live with, but one aspect of La Porte's personal tastes did take some getting used to.

"He loved grunge metal," Boggs said. "At six a.m. he'd roll out of bed, and turn on that music and blast it at the top of the speakers. Dream Theater was one of his favorites."

His teachers admired his dedication in the classroom. Nikki Giovanni endearingly called him "Matty." Paul Heilker said no words could describe the amount of respect he had for La Porte, that he was a rare find.

But his buddies had a different name for him.

"We affectionately called him 'Space Cadet,' " Boggs said. "He'd walk around always looking lost; it was pretty funny."

Boggs described La Porte's favorite midnight pastime, a trip for a late meal at Taco Bell.

"He'd come in at two a.m. after getting some T-Bell, he loved the stuff," Boggs said.

He was just an ordinary college student, Ellington recalled, but was revered as an extraordinary guy.

La Porte's motto is still inscribed on the Highty-Tighty webpage. It's a quote from Thomas Jefferson: "I have sworn upon the altar of God, eternal hostility against every form of tyranny over the mind of man."

Mrs. Barbara La Porte, the mother of the fallen, had only this to say: Hearts of kindness invalidate evil.

Captain Andres Howell, assistant professor, Aerospace Studies: Matt [La Porte] was a student in my class. I taught him for two semesters, including the spring semester. He was someone who, especially in the spring semester, was working very hard to become an officer in the Air Force. He was joining different organizations to improve his physical fitness and to improve his physical training. . . . Sometimes in life, you really figure out what you want to do, and it seemed to be that was the case for him. He was on his way to field training this summer to become an officer in the Air Force who was preserving a second lieutenant spot for him. It's definitely a tragedy for a young person like that to be lost in senseless violence like this. But I've had talks with him asking him if he really wanted to do this, if he really wanted to be an officer; he was kind of a quiet person, it was hard to understand if he was actually wanting to be here, and he always reiterated that yes, this was something he really wants to do, he wants to become an intelligence officer in the Air Force and he was committed to it. So I guess his personality was a little reserved, but committed once he knew what he wanted to do and we definitely noticed that he was committed this spring semester. He had a perfect physical fitness test score, he led a lot of his peers in physical fitness activities.

Bryan Schamus: This whole thing hit home when the casket was rested in front of the altar. I'm Catholic. I'm a singer. I'm a music minister. I've had the experience of singing at a funeral in a cathedral. But never have I felt what I did on April 25, 2007, in St. Mary's Catholic Church in Blacksburg, Virginia. This was Matthew La Porte's funeral mass and burial. I was okay that morning. Gathering my musicians together. Making sure everyone had a ride to the church. Making sure our hymnals made it over there. Everything was okay. Once we were there I had to make sure everyone had a seat. We rehearsed with the choir from St. Mary's. My musicians had a laugh over the music director from the church, who was yelling at her singers to do a better job. We were loose, somewhat relaxed and ready to go. Then we stood up and sang "Be Not Afraid," a song by St. Louis Jesuit Bob Dufford. The refrain to the song is:

Be not afraid.
I go before you always, come follow me.
And I will give you rest.

In verse 3, one line is:

Blest are you that weep and mourn, for one day you shall laugh.

And as we finished the song, friends of Matt La Porte, members of the Corps of Cadets, the group he was a part of, carried his casket to the altar and rested it down. I looked at the kids who carried it in. I looked at Matt's parents. I looked at my friends around me. And then I looked again at the casket. And really for one of the first times since April 16, I lost it. He was a college kid, a Hokie, just like me. And he, his body, was in that casket. I couldn't make any sense of it. It wasn't like he was sick or did something stupid. He just woke up, got dressed, and went to class. I do that every day. Sitting in the front pew were Matt's parents, brothers, sisters, aunts, uncles, and his grandma and grandpa. Grandparents should not have to attend their grandchildren's funerals. That isn't the natural process of life. But they were all so strong. Especially his parents. They were rocks that the rest of the church leaned on. Weird how that happened. I'll never forget that day. And I'll never forget Matt even though I never really knew him. He had just started coming to events at the Newman House, which is Tech's Catholic campus ministry. He probably came to mass on Sunday. He probably listened to my choir sing. He probably listened to me lead the congregation in song. I never knew him. A friend of mine at Newman, Ty Biagas, told me that he had a long conversation with Matt earlier in the year at a blood drive hosted by Newman. Matt had expressed interest in helping at the next one. Little did he realize that the next Newman community blood drive would be the day after his funeral.

Dear Lord,

May Matt rest in peace and may you continue to stay and to keep watch over Matt's family and friends. May Matt's spirit continue to be a part of the Hokie Nation. May we all be reminded of just how fragile life is and may we all find the strength to live each day to its fullest. We ask this through you, Christ our Lord, Amen.

Dr. Yannis Stivachtis, assistant professor/director, International Studies: Matt was here recently because he wanted to decide whether to pursue a major in International Studies or Political Science. He was very much interested in working for the National Intelligence Agency . . . he was a very ambitious person. Of course he wanted to help his country, in these difficult times after 9/11. He wanted to be useful. And I'm confident he would have been an excellent officer. He was a very smart person and hardworking as well.

Ashley Brohawn, friend: I went to his funeral, and the entire Corps marched out for the burial. A few of his friends from high school who were at VMI came down, and they were marching with the Corps as well. And his bud class, they have white cords to symbolize what company they're in, and band company is the white cord. All of his bud class took off their white cords and put them on the coffin to be buried with him. The Highty-Tighties had their band banquet, and that's usually when the freshmen get their awards and their "congratulations—you're finally in the band, you're not rats anymore." The Virginia Tech Corps of Cadets alumni of the Highty-Tighties came up and they gave out pins to the Highty-Tighty alumni who graduated. They gave Matt one and he was actually the first active Highty-Tighty to ever get one because they just started it and they're going to give him another one his year of graduation, too. Matt's roommate brought his plaque, his Highty-Tighty plaque with him, kind of as a symbol of him being there with him; that was very emotional.

Cadet Lieutenant Colonel Jon Kaczanoski: He was goofy. He always pushed himself to the limit, physically, he never complained.

He started to open up the weekend before [April 16] on the Air Force Special Operation Prep Team . . . it wasn't enough. We joked that he was in the Italian Mafia and that he looked like the Fonz.

Captain Christopher Andersen, AFROTC/assistant professor, Aerospace Studies: He was a quiet student but spoke up when he had an opinion, but generally a quiet student. He had interests in Air Force special operations and training, preparatory team. He did not participate his freshman year, but his sophomore year he did. That was something that gave him a lot of pride, actually that caused him to be a little more outgoing and a little more dedicated to Air Force ROTC. He just saw the bigger picture as being a part of a military organization. But special operations training gave him more of the confidence he needed to be a valuable member of the team, which is sometimes something that is missing in the freshman class. . . . I saw him being not the most outgoing extrovert I've come across in my career, but he would have been a good officer nevertheless because he cared about people, and that's first and foremost is caring about people. . . . The Lord had a plan for him, it was just an honor for me to give back to this young man's life. I've talked to many of his friends and his friends had told me that he came here not so much a spiritual individual but had left having a spiritual side that was helping to guide him, so I was proud to hear that.

Henry Lee (Henh Ly)

by Michael Berger

Some of us are born to smile and Henh Ly, who friends lovingly refer to as dorky or a goofball, was able to spread his joy of life and passions to those around him with a simple smile.

"He always had a smile on his face," said Satima Cordova, a senior at William Fleming High School. "You could have the most horrible day, everything could go wrong and then when you saw his smile everything would be better, his smile is very powerful. By looking at his face the world can tell he was a great person, marked for success."

Those who knew Henh describe his work ethic as intensely devoted, but add that this focus pales in comparison to the love he had for his friends and family.

"He's a very stressed-out person but just about school work," said Linda Pham, a freshman Business major at Virginia Tech. "Other than that he had no other worries in the world. He liked to organize us and get people together on breaks, and even though he always said he didn't want to be the organizer, he'd always end up making the calls."

Pham said that she and Henh spent a lot of time together in the fall, going to lunch or going to the different activity fairs, leaning on each other for support as they got a feel for college. For two people who had been around each other since the fifth grade, Pham said that it's just a weird feeling because he'd always been a person in her life that was there for her.

Cordova, who was aware of Henh's friendly reputation long before she knew him, ended up being Ly's senior prom date. Because of a long wait for larger tables in the Olive Garden reservation line that night, Henh and Cordova's group chose to split up, giving Cordova the opportunity to really get to know the kind of person Henh was.

"My family is very sacred to me, and Henh felt the same way about his," Cordova said. "The love for his family was totally different than the love for his friends. He kept his family separate from his friends, but he was always there for both."

Henh is the second youngest in a family of ten children who immigrated to the United States from Vietnam in 1994. With the strength and determination that defined Henh, he quickly became a top student and was a model of work ethic and motivation.

Whether it was an academic competition with his fellow classmates (which they concede they barely ever won), pushing a friend to rediscover their passion for the piano together, or just encouragement to fight those bouts of procrastination that we all face, Henh would do it with a smile on his face.

"He was very competitive; he got a lot of individual scholarships, which is impressive," said Ashlee Murphy, a freshman at the University of Richmond. "The first time I met him he was building an origami crane, and he had to fold over a hundred pieces of paper for this project; it just showed his dedication and creativity."

From hundreds of Facebook wall messages, it is clear that Henh was a rock for so many people. He was unselfishly loyal to his friends and family, but more importantly, his accomplishments were an inspiration to all those around him. So many of his friends turn to his senior graduation speech in which he said, "If I can do it, everyone can do it."

"I don't want to make him sound like a superhero, but whenever you were in class with him, you just knew you were going to have fun when Henh was around," Murphy said.

Susan Lewyer Willis, William Fleming High School principal, told the *New York Times* about the formal awards ceremony during Ly's senior year: Every other award was "Henh Ly, Henh Ly." It was so cute. . . . We all anticipated Henh Ly. When I was shaking his hand for probably the twelfth time, I said, "Henh Ly, stay up here with us." He said, "Okay." He had a huge grin on his face.

Nathan Spady, former hall-mate, told the Associated Press: [Henry was] an extremely bubbly guy, always ready to go.

Joe Lee, his brother, told *USA Today:* He was the smart, quiet kid in the family. . . . The family relied on him to fix [our] home computers. I don't know who'll do that now.

Liviu Librescu

by David Grant

For Christina Krohn, battling through Liviu Librescu's Solid Mechanics course was a dual engagement. First, there was the course material. Second, there was the professor's accent.

"I went to see him during his office hours on the first week of the semester. I couldn't understand a single word he said," said Krohn, a senior Engineering major who is deaf. "He was so determined that I understood everything. He would repeat everything over and over until I understood every single word. He kept doing that all semester whenever I talked to him one-on-one. He would write them down if I still didn't understand him. He never gave up on me."

Slain on April 16, Librescu, a professor of Engineering Science and Mechanics, leaves behind a legacy far greater than his slight build. "He's a giant. This is a giant of a man," said Richard Benson, dean of the college of engineering.

Born in Romania in 1930, Librescu was deported by the Nazis at the onset of World War II, sent first to a labor camp in Transnistria and then to the Jewish ghetto in the city of Focşani. Saved by local townspeople, Librescu, a Romanian Jew by birth, became a scientist but struggled under the oppressive regime of Nicolae Ceausescu—his refusal to join the communist party and his support for Israel ended his career at the Bucharest Institute of Applied Mechanics.

That was until a personal intervention by Israeli prime minister Menachem Begin led to his 1978 immigration to Israel, where he taught at Tel Aviv University.

He and his family came to Blacksburg during a 1986 sabbatical. They never left—both his sons would attend Virginia Tech.

As an academic, Librescu had few peers.

"I've only been here two years, but I've known him for many, many years before that because of his research," Benson said.

A grader in his fateful Solid Mechanics course, senior Engineering major Matt Dunham found Librescu's academic demeanor a careful mixture of demanding and caring.

"At seventy-six he was still passionately working on many research projects when he probably could have been retired and enjoying the sun somewhere," Dunham said.

As a man, Librescu's peers may be fewer still.

In the rough-and-tumble world of allocating funding dollars, Librescu was more often than not a peaceful observer. Uri Vandsburger, professor of Mechanical Engineering, recalls one of his first projects at Virginia Tech fifteen years ago. Then an associate faculty member, Vandsburger set out on an ambitious venture: approaching groups like the Department of Defense for funding on a significant project. When disagreements arose over funding priorities, Librescu was content to let others do the arguing.

"He didn't take part in this. . . . He sat quietly when everyone else was squabbling over the budget. He has seen much more significant things in life. He liked his profession but talking about money that hasn't even arrived yet wasn't [important]," Vandsburger said.

As with Krohn, Librescu's interaction with Dunham left him feeling uplifted.

"He spoke straight with you and told you exactly what he felt. He told me that I had a responsibility to live up to and he was right. . . . He truly cared for his students and wanted them to succeed. I remember seeing how sad he was then I would give him a paper back with a poor grade," Dunham said.

It was this compassionate side that kept Christina Krohn out of Norris Hall on the morning of April 16. Her grandfather passed away on April 15 and Krohn had asked Librescu for an extension on the homework due that day. Librescu emailed her an hour before class telling her not to attend that morning.

When gunman Seung-Hui Cho made his way to Norris 204 early on the morning of April 16, it was Librescu who blocked the door with his body, ordering his students to flee by jumping out the windows.

"We heard gunshots in the hall and as they were coming closer a student stuck his head out the door and saw what was happening. The next thing I know I'm leaning out the window and Professor Librescu was against the door," said Caroline Merrey, a senior Engineering major. "I really don't think me or my other classmates would be here if it wasn't for him."

Of the approximately twenty students present that day, only graduate student Minal Panchal was killed. Librescu's selfless reaction was unsurprising to those who knew him.

"I've seen in my life, people which I thought were very strong, very macho and whatever, and when the time comes they dig themselves underground. And I've seen people who I didn't think much about and they behaved like you would not expect," said a friend on the faculty who spoke on the condition of anonymity.

"He didn't have time to think about it. It happens and you react right away. Either because you were trained to do it this way or because it's in your blood. When you are under fire, and I am telling you from experience, you don't have time to think. You react right away. As much as I know, he was never trained as a soldier or someone who would carry weapons, he was never trained in how to react. But still he reacted."

Some pointed to his history as a Holocaust survivor as responsible for his immediate reaction.

"He was a Holocaust survivor, I am a Holocaust survivor, and our feeling is 'Never again,' we will never allow someone to do something that we will not defend," said Robert Heller, a former Engineering, Science and Mathematics colleague of Librescu's and a Holocaust survivor.

Librescu's history as a Holocaust survivor was rendered even more tragic by the date of his death: April 16 is Yom Hashoa, the day in which Jews all over the world remember the horrors of the Holocaust.

In remembrance of Librescu, Vandsburger submitted a motion to the faculty senate that would create an award for professors who exemplify service to students.

"Not service to the community, not a teaching award, but someone who gives his whole soul to students. He had his heart in younger people. . . . The last time I saw him, a week before he was murdered, he asked about our children. He always wanted to talk about my boys, his boys," Vandsburger, who has three sons, said.

After a Jewish funeral in Borough Park, New York, on April 18, Librescu was interred in Israel on April 20.

Dr. Ishwar Puri, professor and head, Engineering Science and Mechanics: Liviu would come into my office. He was very European, very proper. He'd really call me Ishwar, but when he came to my office, he'd knock on my door and say, "Professor Puri, may I come in?" And I say, "But of course." He shut the door. We had long discussions about the meaning of scholarship. This man was a scholar. He was an applied mathematician. All he needed was pencil and paper! This is a man who was a giant in the professional community. He was famous in a number of different communities. He went through the Holocaust, but he was such a tolerant man. People from every part of the world wanted to be a colleague for his research. From Islamic countries, secular countries, Christian countries. And when you think of people and when you think of their beliefs and how they dress and where they came from, you stereotype them into certain boxes. And this was a man of just incredible tolerance. I hope we have more like him in the world. We'll find that a lot of problems are going to dissipate.

Ezra "Bud" Brown: Liviu Librescu of ESM was a Holocaust survivor, only to be killed by a madman on April 16. The date April 16 is observed in Israel as Yom Hashoa. In the United States, we call it Holocaust Remembrance Day. The motto of Virginia Tech is *Ut prosim*, which means "That I may serve." That day, Liviu embodied the ultimate expression of *ut prosim* when he barricaded his classroom door against the gunman, buying time for his students to escape, and knowing that the gunman would undoubtedly shoot him through that door . . . and the gunman did just that.

Joe Librescu, son, told *USA Today:* [My father] barricaded the door and blocked the shooter from entering. . . . This was typical of him. He did not fear death and at all times tried to do the right thing. . . . He died in the city he called home, where he loved what he did and what he stood for, and in front of his students, to whom he had dedicated his entire life.

Muhammad R. Hajj, Virginia Tech engineering professor, said to the *Chronicle of Higher Education:* I'll miss the way he says good morning, good afternoon, he smiles all the time. . . . He talks to you, and he's interested in what's going on with you. It will be hard to forget that way.

G. V. Loganathan

by James Carty

The King of Fluids. Dr. L. These are just a few of the names by which Dr. G. V. Loganathan was affectionately known to his students and colleagues. But no matter how they addressed him, they all knew him first and foremost as a brilliant educator.

Born in the southern Indian city of Chennai, the fifty-three-year-old Loganathan began his days as a civil engineer at Madras University, where he earned his bachelor's degree in 1976, and continued on to get his master's from the Indian Institute of Technology two years later. He then pursued and received a doctorate from Purdue University in 1982 and promptly began his twenty-five-year tenure as a professor at Virginia Tech.

"He was the ideal professor in my mind," said colleague Randy Dymond, associate professor of civil engineering and director of the Center for Geospatial Information Technology. "He gave us a role model to look up to in terms of the way he handled his classes and his students."

Loganathan was known by students and colleagues alike for his high degree of organization and expert knowledge of subject matter.

"He came to class prepared every time," said Todd Hunter, a sophomore Civil Engineering major. "There was not one class period where he came to class unprepared. He was one hundred percent every day."

Loganathan also displayed a genuine concern for the success of his students in the classroom. "He was kind and smiling in doing his best to ensure that every student could follow and understand the materials in class clearly," Juneseok Lee, a PhD student who worked under Loganathan for five years, said in an email.

"He made everything so obvious," Hunter said. "If anyone was confused, he would stop and go over a problem again from the beginning. He made it so that everyone knew what they were doing and why they were doing it."

Loganathan's passion for knowledge was the driving force behind his teaching.

"The best part about Dr. Loganathan's class was that he didn't just teach the class, he learned from it, too," Hunter said.

His excellence in the classroom was rewarded with numerous awards and accolades, including four Certificate of Teaching Excellence awards from the College of Engineering (1992, 1996, 1998, and 2001), Dean's Award for Excellence in Teaching in 1998, and the 2006 W. E. Wine Award for Excellence in Teaching.

One of his defining characteristics was his kindness and concern toward all of those he encountered. Dr. William Knocke, head of the Civil Engineering department, characterized Loganathan in a tribute speech as "a gentle and humble man who treated all he encountered with respect and compassion."

This assertion was personified in Dr. Loganathan by one instance in particular, when colleague Randy Dymond's father was diagnosed with terminal cancer.

"He volunteered to take over my classes immediately," Dymond said. "He was a true giant." Such selflessness and sacrifice was par for the course for Dr. Loganathan.

On the morning of April 16, 2007, G. V. Loganathan passed away, a victim of a tragic event that has left a mark on [the Virginia Tech] campus and all those who call it home that will remain for years to come. However, Dr. Loganathan left a mark of his own. You have to look close to see it, but there isn't any doubt that it's there. It's right in plain sight.

Right there, in the hearts and minds of all of his colleagues, in the thousands of students he taught over his twenty-five years in Blacksburg, and most of all, in his family.

It's as complex as the water distribution systems he specialized in during his career, and as simple as a friendly smile or familiar embrace. His legacy will continue on, so long as there is something to be learned, some problem to be solved, and some person to help.

While it does, so too will G. V. Loganathan live on, a brilliant educator, devoted family member, and friend to everyone possible.

Dr. William Knocke, Virginia Tech Civil and Environmental Engineering department head, said to the *Washington Post:* It probably was six years into my tenure as department head before I got him to call me anything but Dr. Knocke. It was only after I refused to call him anything but Dr. Loganathan that he said, "Okay, all right."

Joseph Tomlinson, student, told the *Chronicle of Higher Education:* He knew right away if we didn't understand [material he was teaching], he had no problem going back and trying to get us to learn it. . . . I've had few teachers work as hard as he did.

Monica Tiburze told the *Richmond-Times Dispatch:* He was all about educating us. I remember him always being very open and supportive and willing to work with you if you were stuck on something and making sure you understood. . . . I don't think he had a mean bone in his body. . . . He always said, "Hi," always had a smile for you. . . .

Partahi Mamora Halomoan Lumbantoruan

by Rosanna Brown

Partahi Mamora Halomoan Lumbantoruan, a PhD student in civil engineering, may have been quiet and reserved, but was never afraid to stand up for what he believed regarding Indonesian politics.

He was originally from Indonesia, where his mother and father still live.

Curt Nuenighoff, a friend from Blacksburg, always enjoyed talking with Lumbantoruan, or Mora, as most people knew him. "I know a lot of people describe Mora as a shy person . . . but I always found him really engaged and a great conversationalist," said Nuenighoff.

Chang Jo, a Virginia Tech graduate student, recalled seeing Mora in the library the Saturday prior to April 16. "He was working in the library as an assistant."

Jo always found that "his smile is really peaceful, he always smiled at people."

Very often Jo would see Mora shopping at the Oasis World Market.

Mora was quite the chef during the international street fair held in downtown Blacksburg on April 14. Rhondy Rahardja, an industrial and systems engineer, said that Mora was the "grill master" when the Indonesian Student Association (ISA) were providing the Indonesian specialty called *satee.*

"He did all the cooking, that's why it tastes great," Rahardja said.

This year, Rahardja said, the ISA was more organized during the street fair, and both he and Mora were able to enjoy watching the belly dancers who were a part of the show.

Eileen Hitchingham, dean of the library, was able to recollect the many times she saw Mora working in the library.

While at the library, Mora could be seen shelving, studying, or reading for his own delight. "He liked to learn about the Indonesian culture," Hitchingham said.

For Hitchingham, a memory which truly captured Mora's

good nature was a photo of him at a baseball game. "He is just laughing in a sea of orange," Hitchingham said.

Pupung Purnawarman, a Tech graduate student, had known Mora for three years. "To me Mora is one of the nicest friends I have ever met," Purnawarman said.

Purnawarman would always see Mora in the library as well. He remarked how no matter what Mora was doing, he would always be the first to say "Hi!" when he came into the library. Mora was "very caring and attentive to everyone," Purnawarman said.

Purnawarman recalled when they were picking up Mora's belongings out of his room, and he remembered how neat and orderly everything was, especially his socks.

Purnawarman also said how Mora had a love for military movies because of his background. Mora's mother, Soegiarti Lumbantoruan, and father, Tohom Lumbantoruan, were both in the military in Indonesia.

Purnawarman also emphasized how humble Mora was.

When they jokingly asserted that Mora should be president of the ISA in conversation, Mora kindly stated that there would be someone better than himself for the job.

Rahardja can still picture Mora wearing his khaki pants, polo shirt tucked in, and a maroon hat. He can still hear Mora talking about the Indonesian cabinet and his love for politics.

"I talked to him a lot about politics, but yet I never won," said Rahardja with a grin.

The serious face captivated many with his humility, political fervor, and good nature.

"He was loved and he was known and we will miss him," Hitchingham said.

Soonkie Nam, classmate, told the *Roanoke Times*: He was very shy and calm. . . . He had a lot of thoughts inside. He was very sincere. He was like my older brother. . . . He told me he was not accustomed to traditional American behavior . . . [and would] ask me how to act so he did not make others uncomfortable.

Dr. Marte Gutierrez, thesis adviser, said to the *Chronicle of Higher Education*: I tried to dissuade him from taking a PhD because of the time it would take and all the effort. . . . But he told me, "Dr. Gutierrez, I really need this, this is what I want to do."

Lauren McCain

by Janelle Frazier

Lauren Ashley McCain wrote on her MySpace profile: "The purpose and love of my life is Jesus Christ."

A powerful statement indeed, but one that becomes more poignant when written by a twenty-year-old who was one of the victims killed during her German class in Norris Hall on April 16.

McCain, a freshman International Studies major born in Midwest City, Oklahoma, lived her life for Jesus from her first day at Virginia Tech.

"When my group first met, I would always go around the circle and have each of my freshmen answer a few questions, one of which was, 'If you could pick one thing about yourself that you would want everyone in the group to know, what would it be?' " wrote Elizabeth Sullivan, a junior Interior Design major and McCain's summer orientation leader, in an email.

"While most of my group would answer with simple things like 'I have a dog,' or 'My favorite color is blue,' I'll never forget Lauren's answer—without hesitation, she said that she loved Jesus. That was the most important thing about her and she wanted everyone to know," she said.

In addition to her faith, McCain had a passion for international students. An active member of Campus Crusade for Christ (Cru), she also worked closely with Bridges International, which provides international students with a Christian language partner.

"Lauren was a bright light in our family," said McCain's aunt Judy Magouirk, in an email to the *Roanoke Times*. "She participated in five different international Bible study groups. She leaves behind a loving family who will miss her dearly."

Her parents, Sherry and David McCain, plan to create a scholarship fund for an incoming international student to Virginia Tech.

McCain also had a heart for adventure and loved new challenges, as well as helping others.

"One of my favorite memories of her was when Cru went on its annual Fall Retreat to Rockbridge last October," said freshman Biology major Sarah Olmstead, a member of McCain's Bible study. "There is a ropes course that's pretty high up in the trees, and I am deathly afraid of heights. Lauren offers to go first to show me how simple it is, so I let her. She breezes through it in two minutes flat, and as I take the next half hour to cross the ropes inch by inch, she is standing underneath me encouraging me to keep going, laughing between encouraging words, but nonetheless telling me that I could do it."

David Bounds, former pastor, Restoration Church: She had strength of character that I believed was beyond her years. . . . The last time I saw Lauren, her and Abby (her little sister) were standing on the pew beside her, lifting her hands to the Lord and worshipping. . . . They did a lot of things together, especially worship in the back of the church. That was Easter. . . . I think that will be a lasting memory for me. It was always good to see Lauren, she was the same, she was consistent.

Leonard Riley, pastor, Restoration Church; family spokesperson: Lauren had an uncanny ability to approach people with the gospel of Jesus Christ, she loved the Lord Jesus, she made no bones about it, she was very bold with her faith. She was consistent with her walk with the Lord. She was one of those unusual young people. I used to say she's every pastor's dream for young people to have a young person like her in the youth group that kids would follow and saw her as being that consistent person in her walk with Christ.

Dr. Yannis Stivachtis: Apart from being her instructor, I am also, or was, or have been, her academic adviser, because I'm the director of the program. She was this lady that was usually passing outside the office and was waving all the way, somewhere, smiling. She was very open, straightforward, very good student.

Amy Yates, friend: Lauren came as my date to prom. There wasn't any guy that I really wanted to go with, and since she was homeschooled, she didn't really have a prom. So we thought that it would be fun to just go together and hang out with the group. We had a blast with our moms helping us get ready. All of us were piled in the bathroom putting makeup on. Lauren and I were both very strong-willed. Our parents even tell stories about us being extremely strong-willed children. Our first and almost only argument was over a picture on the back of a movie case. We argued and got upset with each other for about thirty minutes because neither of us would back down. In the end, we realized how stupid it was and apologized. Later, we were able to laugh and joke about it.

Marissa Macri, friend, in an email with *Daily Press* reporter Mike Holtzclaw: Lauren was also one of the smartest people I knew. She had such a knowledge for everything—and not even just knowledge, almost more like wisdom. She was most definitely very, very wise beyond her years, and I fell in love with that. I always loved to hear her opinion on things and, yes, sometimes our opinions would differ, but she stuck with what she believed. That made her even more amazing to me, to have such faith in what she believed. I wanted that so bad.

Derek O'Dell: Lauren sat in front of me and to the left one seat. We would often be assigned partners when group work was given (almost every day). I would learn about her through broken, softly spoken German. She wanted to go into dentistry, and aspire to great things. I always thought she was shy and reserved, but this was only because she was cautious with her German. Almost a perfectionist as things go, and for her to speak a grammatically incorrect sentence would be unacceptable. Little did I know, until I saw her outside of class, she was probably the most outgoing person that I have met. She greeted me with a huge white smile and a loud "Hello, how are you?" Completely unexpected from the quiet person who I knew in class. For then on, I knew that Lauren would be one of the people who I would want to know better. I learned more about her from our group work in class, all in German of course. She was a devout Christian and a caring person.

Daniel O'Neil

by Rosanna Brown

"He was a normal kid. . . . He was a good musician and a good student. . . . He always wanted to excel. . . . He really persevered when he liked something," said Bill O'Neil, Daniel O'Neil's father.

O'Neil had two loving parents, his sister Erin O'Neil, and a great group of friends from high school in Lincoln, Rhode Island. His father was always a role model for him.

"He really looked up to his dad, he did a lot of things his dad did, like go to Europe," said high school friend Amanda Burbank.

Daniel went to high school at Lincoln High. It was there that he was involved with his high school drama program in what was called the "Variety Show" with many of his friends.

His tenth grade English teacher, Lise Robidox, said that O'Neil "was a delight to have as a student." Robidox remembered how he was always appropriately funny in class and made his peers laugh.

"He was full of high spirits . . . he sparkled," Robidox said.

After high school he went on to Lafayette College in Easton, Pennsylvania, where he received his degree in civil engineering. While at Lafayette, O'Neil was a part of the art society and was in a student-run theater group called the Marquis Players.

Daniel studied abroad in Belgium his junior year at Lafayette. While his host family was never able to teach him French, Burbank was always willing to help him translate since she took French in high school.

Throughout his life Daniel was also committed to his music. Bill O'Neil knew his son's passion for the liberal arts and science.

"He just loved playing music, he wanted to be an engineer," said Bill O'Neil.

One of O'Neil's musical inspirations was the Beatles.

"Dan was obsessed with the Beatles, all of us were," Burbank said.

O'Neil posted his music on his MySpace page, myspace.com /residenthippy.

On his MySpace page, O'Neil wrote, "So these are some songs that I've written over the last couple of years, and recorded through the microphone that came free with my computer. To be completely honest, they don't sound that bad, considering."

The last time Burbank saw O'Neil was when she visited Virginia Tech in February. They worked on some covers together and continued to work on music even when the visit was over. They would send one another files over the computer and piece together their music.

Burbank said Daniel had already purchased his ticket for Bonaroo [a music festival in Tennessee] that summer to see Damien Rice, one of the musicians she and O'Neil had covered.

While recollecting memories about his son, Bill O'Neil said his most cherished memories were "times that we spent down at the ocean." The family would go on a vacation with a large group of friends ever since O'Neil was young.

"Those were really wonderful days," Bill O'Neil said.

Amanda Burbank and Mike Truppi from Lincoln, Rhode Island, had many fond memories with Daniel as well.

Their large groups of friends were so connected, they even went so far as to make baseball T-shirts for the entire "team." His nickname on the back of his shirt was "Danatee." Burbank explained that at that time O'Neil was charmed by manatees and would have many jokes regarding the animal. His position on the pseudo baseball team was "resident hippy" in homage of his webpage.

In reminiscing about all the good times he spent hanging out with his good friend, Truppi thought of one evening in particular.

"One night we played cards from four in the afternoon until seven in the morning," he said.

"Most of the time we would just hang out with no particular goal in mind," Truppi said.

There may have been no particular goal, but there certainly was a lot of coffee for all of those late nights. The entire group loved going to Dunkin' Donuts.

Truppi thought about how O'Neil would call him on many

occasions to discuss a book he just read or just because he was thinking of him.

"You could talk to him about anything and it was always an engaging . . . conversation."

Truppi said that one of O'Neil's favorite writers was *Fight Club* author Chuck Palahniuk.

O'Neil came to Tech as a graduate student in pursuit of a master's degree in environmental engineering. Truppi explained that while he was at Tech he would occasionally make the commute to Roanoke to buy a coffee from Dunkin' Donuts for a taste of home.

Burbank and Truppi both knew O'Neil was committed to having a good time and to loving his friends and family.

"He always made everything really fun," Burbank said.

Even though Daniel may have left, his spirit still lives on.

"For somebody who believes in souls he's not really gone . . . we may not see him but we can feel him if we reach out," Robidox said.

Allison Quensen Blatt, adviser to the Arts Society at Lafayette College, said to the *Boston Globe:* He wrote songs, and typically folky stuff but a little wacky. . . . He was a free spirit. . . . Nobody batted an eyelash. . . . It was like, "Oh, there's Dan with his guitar."

Rob Harkness, Lincoln High School classmate, told the *Washington Post:* He was very intelligent, open-minded, and talented, a naturally bright person and a Renaissance man. . . . His character and virtuousness was unparalleled to anyone else I knew. His future held only promises of success, and he was someone to aspire to be like.

David Brandes, Lafayette College professor, said to *USA Today:* [Daniel] was a special student and a special person—

energetic, passionate, and full of humor. . . . [He was] not a typical civil engineer.

Juan Ramon Ortiz-Ortiz

by Alexandra Hemenway

The family and friends of Juan Ramon Ortiz-Ortiz, twenty-six, a civil engineering graduate student, have been grieving over the loss of his life since April 16.

"He was an excellent student, an excellent friend, an excellent husband, an excellent son, and he always tried to be a better person, to improve himself, without knowing that he was already excellent," said Ortiz's wife, Liselle Vega Cortes.

Before coming to Virginia Tech, Ortiz was a student at the Polytechnic University of Puerto Rico in San Juan, Ortiz's country of origin.

Ortiz was the president of Polytechnic University's chapter of the American Society of Civil Engineers. Ortiz also tutored younger students at the Polytechnic University. Ortiz graduated from Polytechnic University in June of 2005 and after working for a year, he came to Virginia Tech in the fall of 2006.

"My husband was a person that enjoyed life to its full extent," Cortes said. "He lived each day with energy and happiness as if it was the very last and transmitted that feeling to every person he met."

According to a memorial posted by CNN, the family neighbors in San Juan remember Ortiz as "a quiet, dedicated son who decorated his parents' one-story concrete house each Christmas and played in a salsa band with his father on weekends."

According to an article in the *New York Times,* Ortiz's ultimate goal was to become a teacher. He was a teaching assistant in Norris when he was killed.

"He was an extraordinary son, what any father would have wanted," Ortiz's father told the Associated Press. Ortiz and his wife, Cortes, met at Polytechnic University and both decided to attend Virginia Tech after graduation in order to earn a master's in civil engineering.

"We lived each day of our marriage as if there was no tomorrow and he gave always his very best to make me happy," Cortes said.

Iveliz Ortiz Cordero, cousin, told *USA Today:* He's an excellent son, an excellent cousin, an excellent brother, and an excellent human being. . . . He lived to help other people.

Dr. William Knocke told the *Richmond-Times Dispatch:* I know that he and his wife had to work hard to improve their English before they came here. And I know that Dr. Loganathan felt he was a fine [graduate teaching assistant] and found him very dedicated.

Minal Panchal

by Laura Massey

Minal Panchal came to Virginia Tech for a master's degree in Business Design to bring that passion back to her native country of India. Panchal, twenty-six, was killed on April 16, depriving Borivli, India, of the plans she had already begun to make for them.

Panchal's father, Hiralal, died in 2005 of a heart attack, and she wanted to follow in her father's footsteps in architecture, according to CBS. She attended the Rizvi College of Architecture in suburban Bandra, with an ambition of joining a top architecture firm.

Her thesis at Rizvi was titled "Children's Museum: An Environment for Development of Children at Borivli." Having already gotten a science degree from Mithibhai College, she demonstrated clearly that work was her passion.

Self-described as "not political," according to the *Times of India*, she was known for her willingness to help others.

Sarcastic with a dry wit, Panchal had several loves in life, as stated in a *USA Today* profile and several blogs. She was an architect, a nature lover, and a reader. One of her favorite books, *To Kill a Mockingbird,* instills the lesson "It's a sin to take the life of an innocent being."

In her spare time, she played cricket and enjoyed mint chocolate chip ice cream.

Panchal is survived by her mother, Hansa, currently living in India; her aunt; and her older sister, Kavita. Her last rites were performed at Odenton, Maryland, near Baltimore. Her funeral was attended by Ronen Sen, Indian ambassador to the United States.

According to Rediff India Abroad, there are plans to build a children's museum in memory of Panchal and her work in Borivli.

Asheem Deshpande, part of a welcome committee that greeted Minal her first semester, told the *Roanoke Times:* We saw some museums [in Washington, D.C.], had dinner, had some fun. . . . We wanted to go ice-skating but decided not to because it was cold. . . . She wanted to see the waterfront [while they were in Maryland]. . . . I couldn't understand why, but she did. There were six, seven friends that night and we went out there and saw that.

Neeta Bhivankar, childhood friend, told the Indo-Asian News Service: She was a brilliant student and warm and friendly. . . . She always wanted to excel academically and wanted to make it big in the field of architecture.

Vibhuti Sarmalkar, former classmate, told *Headlines India:* We used to keep in touch by email. . . . Minal wanted to follow in her father's footsteps as an architect. She was so studious and her room was full of books. She was polite and always a true friend to us.

Chetna Parekh, friend, said to the *Richmond-Times Dispatch:* She was a brilliant student and very hardworking. She was focused on getting her degree and doing well.

Daniel Alejandro Perez Cueva

by Kevin Anderson

Daniel Alejandro Perez Cueva was described by his sister as a "very happy, weird person." The twenty-one-year-old junior international studies major from Woodbridge, Virginia, who was shot and killed during his French class in Norris Hall, emigrated to the United States from Peru with his mother and sister in 2000, and attended two community colleges before coming to Virginia Tech.

"He was always determined and stubborn," said Mariella Lurch, Perez's older sister, who lives in Washington state. "I know God must have had a good reason to take him."

Prior to coming to Virginia Tech, Perez attended Woodbridge High School for two years, C. D. Hylton High School for two years, Miami-Dade Community College in Florida for one year, and Northern Virginia Community College for the next.

Perez entered Hylton High School as a junior in the English to Speakers of Other Languages (ESOL) program.

"He was very well liked in the ESOL club," said Ginette Cain, Perez's ESOL teacher, who now teaches at Gar-Field High School in Woodbridge, Virginia. A former principal stated that he remembers he had stood out from the other ESOL students.

Perez enrolled himself in honors classes that catered to social studies, and a year later, Cain received word from Perez's counselor that he wanted to go to college.

"He was an extremely dedicated student," Cain said. "You don't often see these students have a goal to go to college and study."

Perez ran track and played tennis in high school, but he excelled most at swimming. One year he made regionals. In college, Perez continued with his swimming endeavors, but not competitively.

"We always swam twice a week," said Megan Mirmelstein, a sophomore International Studies major at Tech who was also a close friend of his.

Mirmelstein said that the two of them did everything together and that they shared many of the same classes. She had just met him at a Model United Nations conference at Georgetown in October.

"He always made me go to class," she said. "He was very motivated and hardworking."

Mirmelstein said that her favorite memory of their friendship was when he visited her at her hometown of Virginia Beach to meet all of her friends, and the two would walk along the beach.

"He was always smiling and happy and loved everything," Mirmelstein said.

Perez was also a member of the International Relations Organization.

Lurch stated that her brother had enjoyed listening to the Goo Goo Dolls and bands from the punk genre. She remembers him joking around and dancing around in his underwear in the hallway of their house while swinging his arms.

"He was a good photographer and took pictures all the time," she said.

In high school he made a collage with his sister depicting the 9/11 terrorist attacks and was placed in an independent-study class for photography.

"God needed his angels back so bad," she said. "We are so proud of him."

Dr. Yannis Stivachtis, assistant professor/director, International Studies: He was a very good student; he was very active within the International Organization. He wanted to contribute to the college and he was a very kind personality, always smiling. He was the right person to serve the position. And Daniel was very active in the organization; he's done many things. So he had leadership skills, incredible social skills, he was an excellent student.

Hugo Quintero, best friend, told the *Roanoke Times:* Anything he put his mind to, he accomplished it. . . . He's a guy who not only dreams, but also makes dreams come true. . . . He was like a brother to me. . . . I told him, "Hey, when I get married, you're going to be my best man." He was like, "Thanks, man. You too."

Ashley Wheelock, Woodbridge Senior High School classmate, wrote in an email to the *Chronicle of Higher Education:* Daniel always had this megawatt smile that radiated wherever he was and made others around him smile. . . . He was the type of person that would take the time to congratulate and encourage others.

Erin Peterson

by Teresa Tobat

Erin Peterson was always the one who led the cheers and pumped the team up before games for Westfield High School's girl's varsity basketball team. That voice has been extinguished, but her spirit is still burning bright.

Basketball was an integral part of Erin's life. Standing tall at six-foot-one earned her the nickname "Big E." She played on the JV team her freshman year and then varsity for the remainder of her career. She was cocaptain her senior year. For coach Pat Deegan, it was an easy decision to make. "Some years you get lucky and have an Erin," said Deegan.

A guidance counselor at Westfield led a session where students wrote down anecdotes about Erin. Deegan recalled three of them:

One girl had just transferred to Westfield as a sophomore and didn't have anyone to sit with at lunch, until Peterson swooped in and told her, "You're on the basketball team. You can sit with us."

The second girl had been crying at her locker when Peterson asked her what was wrong and then comforted her by walking her to class.

The third girl was a fellow basketball player. Over winter break, Peterson had returned to sit in on a practice. But she had just forgotten one crucial element of her game—proper basketball shoes. The team was doing a block-out drill, which according to Deegan, "is one of the toughest things in basketball. It rewards aggression and favors the stronger, more aggressive players. Well, during these drills, no one wanted to go up against Erin. If kids could block Erin, they could block anyone in the state."

One girl just happened to knock Peterson down because she lacked balance without the right shoes on. "Time stopped," said Deegan, but then Peterson jumped back up and exclaimed to the player, "Way to go!"

Peterson continued to stay involved at Tech. She was a freshman international studies major and part of the honors fraternity Phi Sigma Pi's pledge class. She was also copresident of the Empower Program, which serves as a way for minority girls to increase self-esteem and develop leadership skills.

Her enthusiasm for basketball didn't wane either. Peterson was part of a girl's intramural basketball team in the fall and the spring. Both of her teams won the intramural championships and went undefeated all semester.

"She loved the game. You could tell that in her intensity. She had such a love for basketball and a love for life. She gave a lot of encouragement if you were down," said freshman and Communication major Jen Libbares.

Libbares and Peterson had played on rival teams in high school and were able to play on the same intramural teams in college.

Anna Richter, who had played sports with Erin since fourth grade, will never forget who Peterson's biggest fans were.

"Your mom and dad made sure they were heard when cheering for you in the stands. I'll never forget the sounds of their voices during the hundreds of basketball and soccer games we shared. I love you so much Erin," wrote Richter, a freshman at WVU, in a Facebook comment for the group "Remembering Erin Peterson and Reema Samaha."

Family also played an integral role in Peterson's life.

"She was an only child and very close to her mother and father. They were a very close-knit family. She'd call her parents daily when she was at college," said Tracy Littlejohn, Peterson's cousin.

That same close-knit family brought Peterson to church and it was there that she developed a relationship with God. Both Richter and Littlejohn said that Peterson "believed in the power of prayer."

The strongest testament of Peterson's faith is from Peterson herself. A paper that is dated November 14, 2006, was placed on Peterson's Drillfield memorial and was there on Thursday, April 26, 2007. The title of the piece was "Losing a Loved One and Gaining a New Perspective." In it, Peterson describes how the death of her great-grandmother was a defining moment in her life because it made her "mentally stronger" and that "my faith in God became exponentially stronger as well. All my life, my family has told me to trust in God and believe that He had a plan for all of us, but it wasn't until that day did I actually believe it. That day I had to let her go and believe that she was going to a place where she would not feel any pain. It was almost as if when she died she left some of her strength with me."

Dr. Pat McCarthy, adviser for Westfield High School's newspaper, *The Watchdog*: She was bigger than life. She could have been intimidating because she was six feet tall, but she never was. My favorite memory of her is laughing with her, seeing that face smile. I'd kid with her and she'd kid right back. She was always willing to look at the bright side of things and was a sweetheart; she stood out for that.

Ashley Anderson, friend and coworker in "Gateway" admissions program: You were such an amazing person. Erin, you always had this big smile on your face that brought this glow to a room when you walked in. You always had encouraging words for anyone. Every time I hung out with you it was always a good time. As I was reading your obituary, I realized how much you and I have in common. It was kind of crazy. My mom and I went to your funeral together and she noticed the same thing, the big smile, the strong love for family and friends, and the homebody attitude as well. . . . I just want to thank you,

Erin, and every other person in my life that has touched me in some kind of way.

Ishraga Eltahir, editor in chief of *The Watchdog:* If I could describe Erin in three words, I'd say, dynamic, great presence, and amazing. She would come back to say hi to us when she was home. I think she wanted to reestablish her connection with everyone and let you know that she may not be at Westfield anymore, but she would never leave you.

Michael Steven Pohle Jr.

by Ryan McConnell

His friends described him as a goofy giant who would set his alarm to wake up early on Saturdays to catch the morning cartoons, but made sure to do fifty push-ups before they started, and someone who always put the needs and concerns of others above his own.

Michael Steven Pohle Jr., twenty-three, was the kind of guy who knew every quote from every movie or TV show and had a memorable laugh, yet still had a quiet determination about him that friends described as admirable.

The senior from Flemington, New Jersey, was just months away from graduating with a degree in biochemistry, and had immersed himself in the job search process.

Among other pursuits, Pohle was the head bartender at the Nerv Restaurant & Lounge, and also played midfield for the school's club lacrosse team.

Nathan Milunec and Sean Simmons were club lacrosse teammates with Pohle, and roomed with him during trips for away games.

"He was always proud of how hard he worked," said Simmons, a junior Accounting and Information Systems major. "Even though he never directly said it, you could just tell that he was proud of the work he was able to do in his really hard classes."

Simmons and Milunec recounted a time in which a large group of them organized a kickball game, and Pohle showed up with enough Kentucky Fried Chicken to feed the whole group, and refused to be compensated for it.

"He always cared about other people before himself, and just trying to make other people happy all the time," said Milunec, a junior Civil Engineering major.

The team held a moment of silence in honor of Pohle before their Southeastern Lacrosse Conference tournament game, and wore stickers with Pohle's initials on their helmets along with black ribbon stickers.

Pohle was a graduate of Hunterdon Central Regional High School, and the school lowered its flags to half-staff, and also observed a moment of silence at the end of the day on April 18 in honor of Pohle.

"Michael was a beloved member of his graduating class at Central. A well-respected student athlete, he was a valued member of the football and lacrosse teams during his time with us. As we remember this outstanding young man, our hearts go out to his family and friends who are suffering a tremendous loss," said a statement on the school's website.

In addition to the tributes during tournament play, the club lacrosse team also created an award in his honor to be given to the player who shows the most dedication off the field.

Derek O'Dell: Mike worked as a bartender in the restaurant/bar The Nerv. He seemed to like his job and enjoyed telling stories about his weekends and nights there. He was the only other Biology major who was in the German class.

Joel Nachlas, Virginia Tech lacrosse coach, told the *Roanoke Times:* He was just a guy that was happy to be around and happy to be doing whatever he was doing. . . . He was just upbeat in all situations.

Marcy Crevonis, fiancée, told the *Washington Post:* We were the same person. We shared the same thoughts. We finished each other's sentences. . . . He could bench-press like four hundred pounds. . . . He was a tough guy on the outside, but he was romantic.

Bob Schroeder, Hunterdon Central Regional High School lacrosse coach, told the *Ashbury Park Press:* Even as a youngster, he was a hard worker. . . . He was a model student. He wanted to please people. He wanted to do things the right way.

Julia Pryde

by Caroline Black

Julia Pryde lived most of the twenty-three years of her life trying to do the best she could for others. One of her biggest passions was the environment, and she devoted her entire academic and professional career to helping improve and protect it. In the middle of her master's program in biological systems engineering, Pryde was dedicated to the areas of nature conservation and natural-resource management.

Before leaving her hometown in suburban New Jersey, Pryde graduated in 2001 from Middletown High School North, where she was an accomplished athlete. She was notably active on her school's swim team.

"She was a tremendous athlete," Ken Sedlak, the school's swim coach, told her hometown newspaper, the *Star-Ledger*. "She had a great personality."

Leaving her comfort zone for the enormous Virginia Tech campus didn't faze Pryde, and she jumped right into one of its most difficult majors, biological systems engineering. Unlike most college undergraduates, Pryde wasn't shy about speaking out and working to enact a positive change in her environment. Instead of rushing a sorority or joining a sports team, she began working right away to improve the world around her.

"[Julia] was a very passionate person in terms of what she believed in," said her undergraduate and graduate adviser, Mary Leigh Wolfe, who is also a professor in the BSE program. "She was a person to not just talk about things but to actually do something."

Though she was seriously dedicated to her beliefs, Pryde was a lighthearted person at heart. Few will forget her distinct laugh, which resonated long after Pryde had left a room.

"She smiled a lot, had a wonderful laugh," chuckled Wolfe. "She was very interested in the work she was doing, but knew how to have fun too."

As an undergraduate, Pryde dedicated herself to a research project she devised and presented to the Virginia Tech administration. She was interested in improving some of the environment practices that Tech was involved in.

"One was related to the composting of food waste," Wolfe recalls. Pryde believed that the dining halls could enact a composting program in order to dispose of food waste in a more useful and less environmentally harmful way than just dumping into landfills. She worked on each part of the project personally to make sure it was just the way she imagined. "She conducted the feasibility study to determine if Tech could even really do that, both economically and environmentally."

That proposal has now been taken up by a student organization on campus, and is still going through the system.

"Hopefully something more will come of that," Wolfe said.

Pryde was very excited to see the wheels of change turning,

and would continuously send Wolfe emails updating her on the progress of the proposal.

Not one to ever waste a useful moment, in addition to her studies and her work for the environment, Pryde had a desire to share her passion and knowledge. She joined the nonprofit organization SEEDS (Seek Education, Explore, DiScover) that is based in Blacksburg. She worked with the group on a variety of projects, and was especially enthusiastic about the work they conducted with local schools, working with children and teaching them about their environment.

After Pryde received her bachelor's degree in the spring of 2006, she decided to stay in Blacksburg and continued working with the BSE department right away the next fall.

She was elected as an officer of the Virginia Tech chapter of SEEDS in 2005. In addition to her master's work, she had already taken one trip with several people, including her mentor, Wolfe.

"We traveled to Ecuador and Peru last summer," Wolfe said. "She was working on a project with me and a lot of other people as well, that is taking place in Ecuador and Bolivia."

The trip was to study watersheds in those impoverished parts of the world, to look for ways to improve the quality of the towns' water.

"She was planning to ultimately work first in South America, then probably in Africa," Wolfe said. "She wanted to really improve the lives of people there by really improving their water quality and the environmental quality of where they lived as well."

Mike Rosenzweig, fellow member of Tech's chapter of SEEDS, said to the *Washington Post:* [Julia was] a wonderful friend, yet serious old soul. . . . She rallied her friends into action and was not one to let challenges stop her from trying.

Brian Benham, Virginia Tech assistant professor, told the *Star-Ledger:* I used to tease her about having an old soul. . . .

Julia was fun, she was sincere, she was thoughtful, she was very genuine.

Abbey Winter, friend since second grade, told the *Star-Ledger*: [Her laugh] was a loud giggle. . . . You could hear her from another house down the street, laughing, and you would know Julia was in that house. . . . It was contagious.

Mary Read

by David Covucci

"I know the plans I have for you," begins Jeremiah 29:11, the biblical passage that rested above Mary Read's desk, written in soft, loopy strokes. As an added touch, Mary inserted her own name at the end. "I know the plans I have for you (Mary)."

The second part of that verse reads: "Plans to prosper you and not to harm you, plans to give you hope and a future."

The two pieces of that quote are meant to be related. But to anyone who looks at that verse and then looks at Mary's tragic end, those two parts would seem very distinct and disparate.

It makes more sense in Mary's case, because everything about her, ancestry, friends, and personality, was contrasting. But it never affected her, because like that quote, Mary had her devout faith in God as a link that brought together disassociated parts.

Her heritage is split, right down the middle. Her mother, Yon Song Yi (Zhang) is Korean. Her father, Peter Read, served in the U.S. Air Force, stationed in South Korea. There Mary was born, in Seoul, at a United States Army hospital.

It was in Korea where her bridge began. Her parents took her to a Korean Catholic church in Songtan, South Korea, about an hour's drive south of the capital. There she was baptized; there she was attributed to the Lord.

"She just gravitated toward people. She always knew what other people needed," said Cathy Read, her stepmother. "She had a lot of empathy for other people."

She needed that, because as a military child, she lived an itinerant life, moving from Texas to California to Tennessee, before finally settling in with her father and stepmother in Annandale, Virginia, in 2001.

None of that, though, could keep a wide-eyed, cherubic girl from being happy.

"You had to work hard to catch her when she wasn't smiling," said her father, Peter Read. "Even if she was upset, she would smile just a little less."

Her father believes that the principles of faith, instilled in her at baptism, brought her happiness and serenity.

"We always talked about faith, hope, and love," said Peter Read, reciting a line from I Corinthians. "That's what Mary believed in."

In high school, she could run with many different crowds. Though there were big divides among the groups, Mary seemed to have an innate ability to move across those rifts as though they were smooth surfaces.

She played clarinet in her high school band, but was still elected to the homecoming court her senior year. It's a feat that truly impressed her band-mates.

"She was what you think of when you think of the girl in band: cute, smiley, but still a band nerd," said Emily Sample, a friend from the band at Annandale High School. "But she was the first band nerd to ever be elected to homecoming court. She was the only one of us that fit in anywhere."

Her father knows why.

"Like everything, Mary had a foot in both worlds," said Peter Read. "But her faith really straddled those divides."

She came to Blacksburg in the fall of 2006, and like most

freshmen, felt lost in the morass of a giant state school. She wasn't happy and even considered transferring.

Soon though, like she always was able to do, she found a place she fit in.

In mid-October she attended a fall retreat in Tennessee with three hundred members of Campus Crusade for Christ. She'd been attending weekly Bible studies, but fell in love with the group on that trip.

"She had a desire to learn and grow," said her Bible study leader, Kami Trevillian. "That was evident by her consistency at Bible study. I'm not sure if she missed a week."

The organization became Mary's foundation. In the spring, she applied to lead her own study group.

On Monday, April 16, she was to be told of her acceptance; she would lead a group of young women trying to find their faith in God.

Her faith had led her to prosper; her place in life was to help people feel God's spirit.

And a week later, almost one thousand went to church because of her.

Afterward, the caravan to her grave site stretched a mile in length. As it left the church parking lot, it passed by her high school's oldest rival.

Any animosity between the groups was forgotten; another gap bridged as students in gym class stood along a fence, silently watching the slow-moving procession.

The caravan marched on for eight miles, unabated by traffic as police shut down one of northern Virginia's major arteries.

As it neared the cemetery, the procession turned off the main road, and cut through her old neighborhood. Scores of people stood along the route, some in maroon and orange, most in Annandale's red and white.

It ended at Pleasant Valley Memorial Park, a scant mile from her home.

There, her beloved high school band began to play. As it struck the opening notes of "Amazing Grace," the sun slipped out from the clouds and started to shine. It quickly disappeared, though. A moment, but a brief one.

There at Pleasant Valley, Mary was interred. To some it was the end of a life, one cut way too short. But to those who knew Mary best, it seemed her new life had already begun.

After she was buried, people gathered back around the band. The director, Jack Elgin, wanted to play Annandale's fight song, but could not decide what tempo was appropriate for the occasion.

Before the funeral, Mary's father came to Elgin and told him that Mary would show him the right way to do it.

She must have, because as the drums were struck and the pace picked up, the crowd began to clap.

Kazue Watlington, high school guidance counselor: Mary was a beautiful combination of academic success and personal integrity. She was adored and respected among her peers and teachers. . . . She was a positive influence on others. Her smile was contagious. She was the kind of student where I'd see her name on my door, signing up for an appointment, and I'd smile.

Kami Trevillian, Bible study leader: One of the things I loved about Mary was her goofiness. She wasn't afraid to laugh at herself or do ridiculous things. She had a great sense of humor. And her laugh was adorable. It was like a goofy giggle. One of my favortie memories with her was before Christmas break. A few girls in my Bible study and I decided we wanted to make a gingerbread house. We were determined not to use a kit and make it on our own, even though no one had made a gingerbread house before. It was a disaster, but we just laughed our way through the entire thing. We finally got it to stand, so that we could take a picture and literally two minutes later it collapsed. Mary wasn't annoyed. She just thought it was hilarious and we all enjoyed eating the collapsed house. . . . I think that it's interesting how she ended up in my Bible study. I know that God placed her in my life for a reason.

Darrin Burrell: I played in the band with Mary in high school. When we'd both be at home, we'd hang out. The first thing you'd notice about her is her smile. She was charming, sympathetic, and lively. When you were around her, you couldn't help but feel happy. She was always smiling and would give advice and also listen. . . . She was a real joy, a fun person.

Reema Samaha

by Saira Haider

Ever since Reema Samaha was two years old, she was dancing. "She got her first ballet outfit when she was two," said older sister Randa Samaha, a junior at the University of Virginia. "Even whenever she fell, she would make it graceful."

Reema took dance lessons at the Russell School from age four through high school, and was involved in Hill and Veil's belly-dance club and the Contemporary Dance Ensemble at Virginia Tech.

"It was the most satisfying feeling to know that the simple form of dance has the power to unite so many individuals, whatever their background," Reema wrote in her essay for an application to the University of Virginia last year.

The weekend before Monday's campus tragedy, Reema, a freshman University Studies major, had performed in a show for the Contemporary Dance Ensemble and organized a group to perform a traditional Lebanese line dance called *debke*. She brought in participants to dance during this performance from other international groups. She was in love with her culture, Randa Samaha said.

Another one of Reema's best qualities was her humor, said friend Chelsea Stenger, senior at Westfield High School.

"She was voted class clown in eighth grade and something similar to that her senior year in the high school superlatives," Randa Samaha said.

Reema also loved theater, which she was very involved with in high school.

Haroon Haider, friend and senior at Westfield High School, remembers her during theater work in high school, where she mixed her acting talent with dancing.

"We were the first two on the stage for a bottle dancing sequence in *Fiddler on the Roof*," Haider said. "We'd dance with each other and we'd have the goofiest expressions to make each other laugh and mess us up, but we knew we had to appear professional because we were in front of a live audience. On the inside we were cracking up, but on the outside we had to look like legitimate dancers."

Reema was nominated for a Cappie Award for best dance ensemble for that play.

She often mixed her dance talent with theater talent.

"Exactly a year ago we performed *Oklahoma!* for theater," said Haider. "She was a dance captain for the play and helped us learn our choreography. No matter who needed help, she was willing to give them her full attention. Even individually, she was there when you needed help."

Reema landed the lead role in the play *Arsenic and Old Lace* at Westfield High School.

"My favorite play of hers was *Arsenic and Old Lace*," said

friend Kristen Flanagan, a junior at James Madison University. "That was the absolute perfect role for her," Flanagan said. "She played [an old lady] named Aunt Martha. She impersonated people a lot and had different voices for people. It was funny and cute to see her as a little old lady."

Reema decided to try out for *Arsenic* on a whim and literally learned her lines the night before auditions and ended up getting the lead.

Reema enjoyed using her talents to make funny home videos.

"The biggest of the videos was one we made called 'Double Date Dinner Disaster,' where Reema played the man; she just always played a really good male," Randa Samaha said.

"We also did a spoof on *Pimp My Ride* and she dressed as a Spanish man," Randa Samaha said.

The last video was one called "Johnny Poo-Poo Pants," which is posted on YouTube.

Some of Randa Samaha's best memories of her sister come from their time together in Lebanon, where they often traveled during the summer with their family.

"There was this one night [while we were in Lebanon] where we had this huge cousin wedgie war," Randa Samaha said. "It lasted for an hour."

Getting ready for bed was another great memory Randa Samaha had, where the both of them would dance and sing.

"She was always the lead singer and I was the backup singer," she said. "When I tried to take over the lead, she would give me a look."

Reema was a dedicated student her whole life and was determined about all of her endeavors.

"She was really serious about learning French and we had gone to France over spring break and if I ever spoke English, she would get mad at me," Randa Samaha said. "When she put her mind to something she went through with it. She was very focused."

Reema had some difficulty adjusting to college at Tech.

"She had her heart set on being [at U. Va.] with me," said Randa Samaha.

Reema's plans at Tech included majoring in Urban Planning and minoring in International Relations and French.

"She was about as close to perfect as you could get," Stenger said.

Scott D. Pafumi, Westfield High School theater arts director: Everybody knew her. She was very popular, but she wasn't a really outspoken person; she was kind of quiet actually. But as you got to know her, she had a really funny sense of humor, and was one of those girls that could hang out with the guys while being extremely pretty and graceful and well liked by the girls. Those that didn't know her, well, you wanted to know her. She was really big into making home movies with her brother and sister and her friends. They just made really silly video stuff all the time. She kind of grew up always doing little theater things in her backyard. I guess a lot of kids do, but they just really got into it. I saw her passion for theater take a new level, more significantly, the start of her junior year. Making the improv team in her junior year was a big deal. She really got into all the sketch comedy and cabaret shows; she really shined in that. She was somebody who would always talk to you and commune with younger students, freshmen and sophomores. She never held herself above anyone, and in that way, she was very much a role model. She wouldn't be defined by any one aspect of herself, and she really did the most she could with her eighteen years. Her family has dealt with lots of conflict in their lives. They narrowly escaped with their own lives in Lebanon last summer when Beirut was bombed. They actually were there when that happened, and got out of there before things got really bad. These are people who really understand that this world has a lot of danger and cruelty to it, but never held back, never lived in fear but moved forward and took life as it was.

Megan Meadows: One of the words that I would use to describe Reema, is the word *Reema*. It might sound odd or cliché, but there is no one like her. Since that day I can't stop saying her name over and over, because it is so much like her: unique, beautiful, Arabic. Whenever anyone who knew her hears the name Reema, I know they will think of the exceptional and glowing individual she was. Aside from all of the focus and dedication she brought to the activities we did, having Reema around was such a joy because of the good humor and positive energy she had. There usually comes a point before a performance when everyone involved starts to doubt if it will be successful, and thinking about it now, I can never remember Reema ever giving in to this phenomenon. She was always optimistic about every performance. I guess she never had any reason to doubt the end product, because it was always the best she could have possibly made it. On top of being a performer she was also an athlete. She used to play soccer and this year I remember one of our guy friends saying how he thought she wouldn't be able to keep up with the boys at the gym and she ended up outrunning him. Reema's passion was life. Sure some passions were stronger than others, but nothing Reema did was ever done without passion. We used to joke with her about how indecisive she was, but now even this makes me realize the amount of thought that she put into everything she did—from ordering Wendy's to relationships. She was always the one up the latest at sleepovers. Once we were talking about how we felt like we were missing out on something if we fell asleep; I strongly believe she did not miss out on anything while she was alive.

Waleed Shaalan

by Omar Maglalang

Waleed Shaalan came to Virginia Tech in August 2006 from northern Egypt and settled in an apartment adjacent to the Al-Ihsan Masjid, the mosque where he spent many days reflecting in prayer with his friends. The thirty-two-year old civil engineer had been married for two years to his wife, Amira, and had a one-year-old son, Khaled. Both lived in Egypt while Waleed continued his PhD studies with a full scholarship.

"Waleed was always at home, at the mosque, or on campus," Khaled Adjerid said in a written narrative to Planet Blacksburg. "During my many evenings spent in Torgersen Hall studying, we would spot Waleed going in and out of classes he was taking, or classes he was teaching. If he wasn't studying, he was keeping the ties of friendship and kinship. Waleed was notorious for being seen at computer labs having web chats. He would video chat with his mother, his wife, his siblings, and his son. All of which loved to see his smile and longed to be with him."

Amine Chigani, who met Waleed at the mosque last fall, remembers a time during a function when Waleed showed an enduring love and desire to be back with his family in Egypt.

"One time, there was a cultural event at the Cranwell Center and a lot of people were there," Chigani said. "We were dressed up and all, and there were a lot of decorations. I had my camera, so Waleed thought that the event was a really great place to take a picture. He was always taking every opportunity to send his family in Egypt pictures, telling them that he was okay and that he was in America and that he was all right. I needed to do something outside of the event, but he comes up to me and was like, 'Amine, can you take pictures of me to send to my family?' So when we go to take a picture at the front of the wall, he stands there while I take the picture and he looks at the picture on my camera and says, 'Oh, it's a plain wall. It's nothing fancy. Let's go over there!' "

Chigani was anxious to attend to something outside of the event, but Shaalan was persistent.

"I take another picture at a different spot, and this time, he was like, 'I don't like this plant. We need to get another picture,' " Chigani continued. "I was also taking these pictures of him while he was holding a balloon and I thought he should lose the balloon. But he wouldn't! 'No, Amine, the balloon has to show!' I think I had to take several of them before I could see that he was really happy to see a picture with him holding a balloon and a nice plant in the background. Then, he was like, 'This is the one that I'm going to send to my wife!' Waleed was just a very simple guy who loved his family."

Aside from his family, Waleed was also very devoted to his graduate studies. He spent countless hours in labs, and many times, he stayed late at night in his office in Patton Hall to work on papers.

"He was an academic," Adjerid said. "Hailing from University of Zagzig, his priority was education. On the weekdays he could be spotted running from class to class, building to building, Randolph to Torgersen, McBryde to Norris. . . . Always on time, always in class. The dedication to his school and lord was untainted and undying."

An attentive student who regularly sat in the front of his class in Norris Hall, Waleed's life was unfortunately cut short during that Monday morning; however, Shaalan died with honor among his friends and witnesses because of what happened in his Advanced Hydrology class in the midst of chaos.

Civil engineering professor Randy Dymond, in an interview with the *New York Times,* said that when Cho opened fire in the second-floor classroom, Waleed was badly wounded and lay beside a student who was not shot but played dead. Cho spotted that student and attempted to shoot him. Waleed, in a selfless act, distracted Cho and as a result was shot a second time and died.

Before April 16, Waleed had already made summer plans to visit his family.

"He was so excited to go home to Egypt the last time I talked to him," Chigani said. "He even bought a plane ticket to go home to Egypt May 13th. . . . He was going to come back in the fall to bring his wife and son to Blacksburg."

Shaalan had numerous friends within the Egyptian community, and they will remember him for his simplicity.

"People will try to immortalize Waleed Shaalan in photos and heroic tales, and that is great," Adjerid said. "I, however, choose to humanize him with stories of his normalness, his habits, and his attributes that bring a smile to my face, a laugh to my side and a tear to my eye."

According to his friends, Waleed loved to cook. He enjoyed Ping-Pong. He liked chocolate cake. They were accustomed to his big grin and his wave. He attended every single event hosted by the Muslim Students Association (MSA), and he would often ask them for rides to Wal-Mart since he did not have a car.

"Waleed wasn't a police officer, he wasn't a war hero, and he wasn't a fireman nor was he a superhero," Adjerid said. "Waleed was a normal human being like all of us, who had extraordinary attributes. He may have saved one life on April 16, but even if he hadn't, Waleed will always be a hero in my heart."

Amine Chigani: During the fall semester, it was a Sunday, and I can't forget this. It just describes how simple Waleed was, very simple and naive in a good way. It was noon prayer, about

1:30, and Khaled Adjerid comes into the mosque and he sees me and says, "Did you see Waleed? I think he just got jumped or robbed or something!" . . . [Waleed] looked really confused, scared, and he was walking back and forth, mumbling. I was like, "What happened? Khaled told me that something's troubling you." He told me, "I just lost my book bag. . . . It has everything! All my immigration papers." The bag had his Social Security, the I-20, which is the most important document for an international student, copies of his passport, his wife's passport, and paperwork he had to try and get her to come to Blacksburg this next semester. Again, I told him that I realized that this was a problem, but knowing the system here, I thought that there was a strong possibility it could be solved. I can understand him, coming from Morocco myself. Like Egypt, if you lose something there, you'll lose it forever, especially if it doesn't have an address or anything. There's no such system there of a cop calling you back if they find anything with your information. He couldn't remember the last time he was carrying that bag. Then, I tried to call him and said, "Listen, if it's in the bus, believe me, they will call you!" Waleed wouldn't believe me! He kept telling me how his life was in there. His computer was in there. His wife's pictures were in there. "I'm just lost here," he said. "I'm gone." He didn't think that anyone could help him. What got me really frustrated was when he said, "My notebook is there! All my notes from my adviser's meeting, all my notes from my lecture classes are there. I'm gone. I'm going to fail!" I tried to calm him down some more, and said, "Listen, you have classmates. You have advisers who would understand your situation." So finally, we solved it because he had left it on the bus. Since he had left his information in there, they called him. The most amazing thing that I can't really forget is that, when they called him, he said that he didn't have a car. So he goes to the Blacksburg Transit office, and they gave him a ride back to his apartment.

They called a cop, and the cop gave him a ride back to his apartment. And that, he completely wouldn't believe. Whenever I saw him after that, I'd ask him, "How is America?" He would say, "It's the best country ever! A cop giving you a ride to your apartment?" He never dreamed of anything like that gesture from the cop. That is how simple Waleed was.

Khaled Adjerid, friend: [Waleed] chose his home to be next door to the mosque and was regularly seen there. We became accustomed to his grin and his wave. We felt comfortable in his hug and shake as well as his company. I would see him at the mosque as well as on campus. . . . His superhuman attributes took time to spot. His warm grin wasn't anything new. The constancy of it, the habitual smile, the luminous glow consistently emanating from his face, every time and every day, regardless of situation. That was special about him. He was a regular at the mosque; after each prayer he would run to the back of the prayer hall and wait. He would meet and greet each and every one with a smile and a wave as they trickled out. . . . Waleed was so wonderful, so amazing, so gentle and nice that none of these things mattered. Had any of these things not been present, we would have still loved him and cherished him the same.

Leslie Sherman

by Joe Kendall

People smile all the time. Leslie Sherman beamed.

And it wasn't just to show off her dentist's hard work either. Sherman was truly a font of positivity for those around her.

"She was a wonderful girl," said her grandmother, Gerry

Adams. "Very responsible, very bright, and very respectful of everybody. A smile never left her face."

Her friends also took notice of her almost permanent twenty-tooth grin.

"She had a contagious smile," wrote West Springfield High School classmate Ashley Nickle on nytimes.com. "Leslie was a sweetheart. She was funny, energized, motivated, and overall just a happy, happy person. I can't even explain how her smile just made others smile; she was just a wonderful and caring person."

Perhaps more important than Sherman's infectious smile was her love of service to others. The junior History major and West End [a Tech dining hall] employee had paid her own way to travel to Mississippi and Louisiana to help the rebuilding efforts after Hurricane Katrina devastated the area.

"That's the kind of person she was," Adams said after recounting a story of Sherman's generosity. "[She] wanted to help, the reward didn't matter. It was the pleasure of doing it, not that someone would pay her for it."

A student in the University Honors program, Sherman had also developed a deep passion for history. She was both engaging and studious, and her high school teachers recognized her talent and ability early on.

"I was fortunate to teach Leslie Sherman in my advanced placement European History course at West Springfield High School," said West Springfield teacher Ronald Maggiano to the *New York Times.* "She was a wonderful student with a creative mind and a great sense of humor. She was especially known for her beautiful smile and positive attitude. Leslie was always happy and cheerful and brought out the best in others. Academically, she was brilliant without being 'bookish.' "

In addition to being president of West Springfield's history honor society, Sherman ran cross-country all four years of high school and was beloved by teammates.

"She always kept telling me: 'You can do it. It's just another mile or two or six,' " high school teammate and Florida State student Emily Grossman told the *Washington Post*. "She cheered us all on."

In fact, friends were so touched by Sherman's hard work and exuberance that they decided to hold a race in her honor and donate the proceeds to a scholarship fund in her name.

A Facebook group started by Grossman titled "Run for Leslie," almost six hundred members strong, hosted a race at Burke Lake Park in Springfield on June 23 in remembrance of Sherman.

"It was really the first thing that I thought of when one of my old teammates called me Monday night about Leslie," Grossman told the *Washington Post*. "The first thing I said was: 'We'll have to get the team together and run something for her.' "

The willingness to preserve Sherman's legacy of good will has impressed and inspired Sherman's family.

"It means all the world, it means all the world," Adams said. "They're perpetuating the good that she wanted to accomplish in her life. . . . I've just made a pledge to myself, we're going to find every way possible that we can contribute to the kind of goals Leslie would have had."

Lisa Sherman, sister: When she and I were really young we were attached at the hip. We did everything together. Before we started going to school, she and I would play together at day care and then come home and play together some more. The year that she started kindergarten was the first time that I ever went without her. I missed her so much. I would wait for her to come home and tell me all about her day. Sometimes she would teach me some of the things she learned at school. I knew how to write my name in cursive before anyone else in my class because she taught me. She taught me a lot of things. . . . Together we had big plans. We had plans for this summer, plans for next year, and plans for the rest of our lives. This summer she would be studying in Russia and work part time when she got back. She had a list of movies that she wanted me to watch with her before she left for Russia. We planned to go to the Pink Bicycle Tea Room in Occoquan one afternoon and wear big hats as we sipped on our tea together. A trip back out to Washington state was also in our plans. It would have been just the two of us traveling together this time. She was so excited for me to transfer to Virginia Tech next year. She wanted me to go to all of the football games with her and my dad. She was even sending me information about some of the clubs that I could join and that she would be willing to join with me. I couldn't wait to get there because I knew how happy it would make her and how much more at home I would feel because of her. I wish I could have gotten there sooner.

Rebecca McMahan, best friend: Leslie, you were real to me, a breath of fresh air. You were what I wanted to be. A strong girl, who knew what she wanted in life, knew what she needed to do to get it and wasn't afraid to get her hands dirty in the process. Your drive, your intelligence, your passion, your compassion, it all inspired me. Leslie, I was so proud of you for running that marathon. I kind of doubted you at first. I wasn't sure you could do it and I think that was partly because I had already given up myself. You proved me wrong, though. You finished that marathon. You even beat Oprah. I still can't believe your dad told her that. I loved every minute of that race. I loved searching for multiple places to see you along the long twenty-six miles and searching for your smiling face in the midst of all the runners. I loved that you were still smiling. I loved running beside you for that brief stint before my lungs began to burn from being desperately out of shape. I loved screaming your name and chants. I loved that someone told you we were cheering too loud. I think he was just jealous that you had such a great cheering section. But most of all I loved how much you loved running that race and how happy you were when you finished. That's the thing I wanted for you most of all, Leslie, for you to be happy. It is what any friend would want, even more any best friend. That's what you were to me, Leslie, my very best friend.

Ed Linz, cross-country coach and Honors Physics teacher: [Leslie] was not my most gifted athlete, but she was the type of person you absolutely want to have on your team because she basically was the glue that would hold everything together, especially during difficult periods. Our team was pretty good when she was here, but we didn't win every race. You really need a person like Leslie to get everyone back focused and say that this isn't the end of the world and we're going to proceed on from here. If you had to pick a team, even if you're trying for the extra best runners in the world, you'd always pick her even if she weren't one of the best runners; she was the type of person who would make everyone better. . . . I think what Leslie taught me was there really is innate goodness in people. I do not know if I have ever seen any evidence of any ill will in her body.

James Perocco, Applied History teacher at West Springfield: When I had her in class senior year, we did this big, huge field trip to Birmingham, Montgomery, and Selma, Alabama, on the fortieth anniversary of Bloody Sunday, and one of the books that the students had to read in preparation for this trip was John Lewis's book *Walking with the Wind,* a memoir of the movement. I think that book really resonated with Leslie because she decided, after we studied civil rights, after we had met all these people like John Lewis, we walked across the Edmund Pettus Bridge, ten thousand other people singing civil rights anthems on the anniversary of

Bloody Sunday. I think Leslie understood that events like those don't just happen. They're watershed moments, and I think Leslie understood that. Leslie was a visionary. Leslie really had a bold vision for humanity, for people, for herself in a nonaggrandizing way. She took to heart a lot of what Martin Luther King Jr. said. She really took very much his message and internalized it in way that I don't think I've ever had a student or even, in a way, maybe another adult that I've talked with understand the essence of the kind of message.

Enzo Ochoa, Applied History classmate: She loved learning. She did trips to South America. She was in rigorous French classes. And then, she wanted to go to Russia as well. She just loved everything. . . . You always hear on TV sometimes about how younger generations are out of touch and are not caring. Leslie is just the direct contradiction to everything the TV says about youths now, how we don't care, how we don't vote, how we don't do anything to help ourselves. I really wish she had spent more time here in this world.

Ronald Maggiano, European History teacher at West Springfield: She was never the student who would do just enough to get by or be happy with just a B. She gave 150 percent all the time in the history classroom, and that's why we gave her the Social Studies department award when she graduated. . . . She gave a lot back to the department. Even after she graduated, she would come back to us. I saw her several times after she graduated. She would always stop in, always making a point of reconnecting with teachers. She came back to help us with books actually. We got a whole bunch of new books here. She just wanted to come in and do something. She wanted to help us get ready for the new year. That was the kind of person she was. She always gave of herself, and that's what she taught us.

Ezra "Bud" Brown: Somebody donated thirty-two trees, to be planted in memory of the thirty-two slain students and faculty. We planted the first one Thursday, May 3, in the pouring rain out in front of Main Campbell residence hall, in memory of Leslie Sherman, a member of the Main Campbell Residential Honors Community and a History major who was in Norris Hall. Her parents drove down from northern Virginia just for this event. The ten-foot tulip poplar had been planted, and a large amount of dirt from the planting hole was covered up by a tarpaulin. Several faculty, administrators, and students spoke briefly, after which we handed out four shovels and held umbrellas for any and all to put a shovelful of dirt in the hole who wished to do so. The Shermans then spoke of their daughter's love of Virginia Tech, and her eager anticipation of a study abroad in the fall, led by one of the Russian teachers. Mr. Sherman then told us that Leslie's younger sister was in her first year at UNC-Wilmington, studying oceanography, but that she was not so interested in oceanography anymore, and that she was transferring for next fall. She has transferred to Virginia Tech. And if that doesn't make you cry, then you are not my friend.

Maxine Turner

by John Rhoads

Maxine Turner will be remembered by her friends as one of the most kind, gentle, and beautiful souls to have ever walked the campus of Virginia Tech. "She was the greatest person ever," Michelle Vrikkis, Turner's roommate of four years, told the northern Virginia *Journal Gazette.*

Max, as friends affectionately called her, was anything but average. She received a 1500 on her SAT, which included a perfect 800 in math, wrote the *Star Tribune*. "I did pretty good." That is all Turner's mother recalls as her humble response to her terrific performance.

Turner gave up her time and frequently volunteered at the local animal shelter. She helped found the Virginia Tech chapter of Alpha Omega Epsilon, the national sorority for women in engineering. She was working toward a black belt in Tae Kwon Do, and she was already a master of the Zelda video games.

Turner had a sense of humor and a refreshing friendliness that made her unforgettable to people she met. "I startle easily, and she knew that, so her favorite way to get me to move was to grab [me]," recalled Robin May, another of Turner's roommates. "I would jump across the room," May told the *Rappahannock Times*.

Jason Allen, a high school friend recalls, "To me, Maxine was one of the few people in high school that had no enemies. She was always helpful. . . . She used to chew me out if I started slacking off on homework. Whenever someone said hi to her, she always had a smile, and you knew it was genuine."

"Now I know what they mean when they say someone was 'a sweetheart.' . . . No one ever had a sweeter heart than Maxine. Maxine's beauty is evident from the picture, but her inner beauty was greater," wrote Suzanne Gorey—the mother of a childhood friend.

Turner will also be remembered as a dancer. She was a member of the swing dance club in high school and was given the title "Vice President of Everything." "Maxine's infectious enthusiasm for the club was often overwhelming enough to encourage those shy wallflowers (I am referring to the boys) to come out and learn to swing dance. And in a pinch Maxine could do the male partner dance lead," remembers Martin Romeo, the sponsor of the Madison Swing Club.

Her friends think that the only thing brighter than Max's

smile and personality was her future. Maxine was only one month away from receiving her honors degree in chemical engineering. She would still receive that degree, but not in a way anyone had planned. On her Facebook profile she announced plans to work for W. L. Gore & Associates, a leading manufacturer of thousands of advanced technology products for the electronics, industrial, fabrics, and medical markets. In the description field she wrote: "Not sure what I'll be doing yet, but they are AWESOME (for those who don't know, they make Gore-Tex)."

Max would have taken her energy into that company and continued toward excellence. "There are students that have kind of a twinkle in their eye, she was one of them. She was a bright young woman with a lot of potential," Jane Gardener, who was involved in the hiring of Maxine, told the *Roanoke Times.*

Turner's father told *CBS News* that Max was determined to be a Hokie. "We tried to convince her to go elsewhere. When you get accepted to Johns Hopkins, it's a very prestigious school," he said. "But no, she wanted to go to Virginia Tech."

Turner brought with her to Tech an attitude and a personality that many students strive for.

Timothy Walker (taken from an email update to family and friends): I have found out that I did in fact "know" someone who was killed on Monday. Last Friday I went with my friend to her sorority formals. There I met many of the sisters as they all came up to say hi to her and also said hello to me. While I don't even remember what we talked about, in the two minutes we spoke, I will now never forget Maxine Turner. It just makes this even more real now that I have a name and face of someone I met just three days before this occurred.

Susan Turner, mother, told the Associated Press, commenting on Maxine's interests in life: She wasn't going to get [her black belt in Tae Kwon Do] at what she called just a sort of "black-belt factory." She really wanted to know it and really be able to do it. . . . She stood on [Tech's campus] and she said, "This is my school. I don't want to go anywhere else." She loved it. Her whole four years.

Nicole White

by Emerson Blais

A twenty-year-old junior from Smithfield, Virginia, Nicole White originally came to Virginia Tech planning on studying veterinary science. Her love of animals flourished in the form of volunteering time to hometown horse stables just to lend a hand. Among friends, her giddiness toward dogs, of which she cared for two, showed her love for animals.

This loving passion for the cuddly creatures of the world lives on today as her family asks that "in lieu of flowers, donations may be made to any animal shelter of your choice," according to Tech's website dedicated to those victimized.

Yet, despite her immediate intentions, she ultimately decided to double-major in International Studies and German. In fact, close friend and fellow redhead Melanie Weis remembers Nicole constantly grinding at her German homework. While the two shared hair color, Melanie also remembers Nicole was always up for sharing her time.

"There's been several times when something has happened to me and I just really needed someone to talk to and someone to listen, and she would," Weis said. "One night I needed a place to stay and she let me sleep in her bed. She wasn't judgmental. She'd give me advice that wasn't judgmental. And, she would go out of her way to introduce me to everyone she knew. I think redheads stick together. I'm going to miss her."

To the young men and women who knew her, Nicole was everything you could ask out of a friend, especially dependable. The *Roanoke Times* recently documented her famously friendly demeanor as a lifeguard at the Luter Family YMCA in Smithfield as well as the Gatling Pointe Yacht Club in suburban Newport News.

A devout Baptist, she taught Sunday school at Suffolk's Nansemond River Baptist Church. And these are only a few of the many integral cogs defining Nicole's life. At the same time, Virginia Tech students may have known her as a waitress at local pizzeria favorite The Gobbler.

While working there, several employees recognized her dependability, including general manager Ryan Payne, who remembers Nicole working to help out in a pinch. "She was a good worker," said Payne as if it meant everything in the world. "I mean, she would come in to work when others couldn't and just help with anything. She was a quiet girl at times and, other times, she just couldn't stop laughing. I remember she really liked my pepperoni rolls. She was a genuinely good person."

Although there isn't any easy way to have life come to an end, there are those who remember Nicole from her very beginning. The characteristics and events which punctuated her time in between have been and will be shared by those who knew her best.

Ginny Gwaltney, friend: Nicole was an average person with an oversized heart. She cared about everything and everyone. I'm pretty convinced that if Nicole had been given the option April 15 of going to class the next day and being killed, or having someone else killed in her place, I fully believe she would have gone to class. Nicole was a very noticeable person. She was very tall and had beautiful red hair. Of course she had the temper that goes with any redhead, but she was such a sweetheart it didn't matter. Her main goal in life was to help others in any way possible.

Gary Vaughan, associate pastor of students, Nansemond River Baptist Church: Nicole was a girl who was strong in her faith. She loved to share, and really I don't want to use the word debate, but she liked to communicate with people who had differences of opinion of religion; she liked to share who Christ was. She like to talk with people and to share about her relationship with Jesus, and really tried to help people understand that Christ isn't about a religion, but a relationship, and to really talk to them and really see what that meant. . . . She had a huge sense of humor. She had a real quick wit and loved to laugh. She was a person that picked up on the fun side of life.

Peter Carlson, vice president, Isle of Wight Rescue Squad; professor, Christopher Newport University: [Nicole was] a very caring young lady—had a good sense of humor, very careful that she treated people with respect. All in all a very positive young lady. . . . She wasn't exactly sure what she was going to do with her life, but it would have had something to do with people or animals, I'm sure of that. Somebody that is that young and volunteers for the community is a very impressive person in my eyes. You don't get the multitude of coming out to volunteer with the rescue squad.

Ashley Baird, friend since second grade: Nicole was very spontaneous, and very energetic. She always tried to get me out of my shell, so to speak. She was very bright and very happy; she was very interested in a lot of things. She loved animals and horses, and she was thinking about doing veterinary science, or political science, and she was interested in all kinds of things. She was talented, a little bit of an artist, a little bit of a writer, and she loved people, more than anything else. She invested a lot of time in her friends and her family. Her whole life, that's what I remember mostly about her. She was sort of a stable person in my life. She herself was spontaneous and sort of all over the place, but I always knew no matter what happened she would always be willing to listen to me. Once she's your friend, she's your friend for good.

Jessica Fansler, friend: She had a temper when people messed with her friends, but she was extremely loyal and she was extremely loving and caring. . . . Me and my roommates got in a huge fight and they basically tried to kick me out of my apartment. Nicole basically stood up for me and she took me in and let me stay with her for a whole month, no charges or anything. Then, she went over to my place to get my stuff so I didn't have to deal with my roommates, she basically got me a job at DQ, she mothered me and fed me and took care of me basically. She was always doing that with animals and people.

Epilogue: Rise Up

Seung-Hui Cho's rampage had taken a stunning human toll at Virginia Tech, but as days turned into weeks after the incident, it soon became apparent the killer had struck a major blow at another victim—the university itself.

Ashley Hall, alum: It's very hard when your heart knows it has lost something that your mind can't grasp. I do know that my school is gone. The Virginia Tech of April 15, 2007, does not exist anymore.

Gary Schroeder: I'm sure there are other ways that this has changed me that I'm not even aware of at this point in time. I could tell you that the sound that just makes me cringe now that I probably didn't pay any attention to in the past is a siren. Because that Monday, we can sit in our office and see out to Prices Fork Road, just a little snippet, but that Monday, that's all we heard. And that's all I saw, one rescue squad vehicle after another coming into town and they all turned up Stanger to get up toward Norris. So now, every time I hear a siren, I think, "Oh God, what now?"

Brittney Asbury, rising junior: There is no doubt that my life has been forever changed, and when I think back on my college career, specifically my sophomore year, this event will be the first thing I think of. Many people have asked me if I am going back, and I say yes, once a Hokie, always a Hokie. And I know that years down the road when I tell people I am a Virginia Tech graduate, one of the first questions I get will probably be "Oh, were you there that day?" But as far as I'm concerned, one person and one event will not define my school and me.

Gary Schroeder: Just as in the event of an individual's death, his or her survivors have a whole year of firsts to go through: that individual's first birthday; if he or she were married, the anniversary date; and the holidays. So the whole community has a whole series of firsts to experience, and that's going to be rough when grief bubbles up on the surface again and perhaps take hold. I guess, ultimately, what I would like this community and the larger community to remember about April 16 is what happened immediately after the shootings. People talk about April 16 being Virginia Tech's "darkest hour." I think, quite honestly, in the hours after the shooting, those were Virginia Tech's "finest hours," the way that the whole community such as the volunteers, ambulances and rescue squads, and the police departments all came together to coordinate all of their efforts. The caregivers. The hospital. You name it. Everybody just knew what needed to be done from their perspective and did it. We didn't have a manual to go by. We didn't have an instruction book, but we all did it. And I think that's the thing that I would like to see people remembering years down the road is how this one community really came together in the face of an awful, horrible tragedy.

Ishwar Puri, professor and chair, Department of Engineering Science and Mechanics: It's important in life not to analyze an event simply by saying, "Why did this happen?" but I think it's very important to analyze "How should one respond?" Ultimately, how you respond defines, in a sense, what you become later. We all carry regrets. We carry regrets that something happened, but we shouldn't carry regrets that we were unable to respond to an event in the finest possible manner, in the most constructive, the most compassionate manner. We have a much smaller crisis than Katrina, but it's very important for us not to have regrets about the aftermath, because those regrets then are ultimately self-inflicted.

Allyson Klein: I was paralyzed with fear on the events of April 16. Fear of the gunman, fear for my friends who might have been in the building, fear for the lives of those victims shot, killed, and wounded. But not once was I scared of being a Hokie. With all my heart, I truly believe that what happened at my campus community, in this day and age, could happen anywhere . . . but it happened here. The events of that day will never, ever be forgotten—but neither will the convocation, the vigil, and the memorials that followed. Neither will the flowers lining the Drillfield, the tears students wept together, the embraces shared around the community, and the national and even international outpouring of love and support that ensued.

Ashley Turnage, alum: Everything about me changed that day, every single aspect of my life, past, present, and future changed. This is the part where I get foggy, because, as I said, I cannot commit to any one emotion for too long. I have tried to think of a sentence to follow that one and have had to rewrite it three different times, to say three different things. When I have grown tired of explaining this Hokie thing to people outside of my circle, I have gone inside myself and leaned on my Hokie family, who I do not have to explain it to.

Dr. Yannis Stivachtis, faculty: History has made Virginia Tech, and we are part of this history, and being a part of history is a dynamic process, but each one of us at different moments in our lives will come to say to someone else that we have been here on this 16th of April in 2007.

Tricia Sangalang: Simply being a part of this community has allowed us to build a sense of pride and strength, even long before April 16. The spirit, the honor we feel just being a Hokie is what drives us and allows us to confidently say, "I go to Virginia Tech." I hope that this pride doesn't fade. I hope that everyone who tries to gain an understanding of what this "Hokie community" is like sees that pride. Even in the midst of tragedy, we've shown that we are not only a university, but also that we are a community. We are a family.

Ashley Hall: No one's ready for the big changes, not really. Virginia Tech did not need this to "come together." We all knew what it meant to be a Hokie. The students, professors, staff, alumni, and family of Virginia Tech will act as they always have, with pride, intelligence, compassion, and an unbelievable drive to learn. I know that the cadets and the dogs and the Frisbees will return to the Drillfield, but the innocence is lost. I hope one day we can get it back.

A big question for some in the Tech community went to the issue of lawsuits. Even though legal challenges would take time to materialize, the university soon hired an extra lawyer just to deal with the additional issues brought on by the circumstances.

Surprisingly, however, the university faced an impact that threatened to be every bit as devastating as legal entanglements. Virginia Tech's Department of Engineering Science and Mechanics itself is emblematic of the challenges the university faces in the wake of April 16.

Foremost, the incident robbed a thriving department of irreplaceable faculty and students.

Ishwar Puri: Diversity in our department makes it fragile because we lost some great individuals. Kevin Granata had a degree in physics and a degree in electrical engineering, orthopedics; he worked in a medical school. Liviu Librescu was an applied mathematician, and he was an aeronautical engineer. He started doing work in mechanics. And so when you have people who've mastered a variety of disciplines and worked at the intersections, how do you replace that? And so the question is, "What do we do?" It's not just a loss to us of two faculty members; it's a loss of two entire areas. And it's not as though you can go on the job market and hire clones because there aren't any. Individuals like these are mentored, created, helped, and produced over a lifetime.

Another huge issue involved the laboratories. The second floor of Norris Hall contained an array of classrooms. Overlooked was the fact that the first and third floors housed the offices and highly specialized laboratories of one of Virginia Tech's most lucrative research departments, Engineering Science and Mechanics, or ESM, as it is known in the university's engineering school. Set to celebrate its one hundredth anniversary in 2008, ESM is a cutting-edge interdisciplinary department, one of only three such departments nationwide, that has built a reputation for "outside the box" thinking on big topics.

Ishwar Puri: We have forty-five years worth of investment in laboratory facilities. We have very unique facilities, some of which can't be moved out of Norris Hall. They're just built into

> Norris Hall. We have this tank, which few great universities have. You can make sort of miniature tsunamis and waves and sort of put miniature boats there to do experiments on them. That's just something you can't re-create elsewhere.

The list of laboratories is impressive, including Adhesion Mechanics Laboratory, Biomechanics Laboratory, Cardiovascular Hemodynamics Laboratory, Composite Fabrication Laboratory, and Fluid Mechanics Laboratory run by the ESM department, among dozens.

Because of the crimes committed in the classrooms on the second floor, there was an immediate call in the aftermath of the shootings for Norris to be closed and torn down, or turned into a memorial to the victims. However, Puri and several researchers in the Engineering Science and Mechanics department quickly took exception to those plans. The circumstances created substantial behind-the-scenes conflict as May turned to June.

> **Ishwar Puri:** Very early on, the university said that there will never be any classes taught in Norris Hall. And yet, I have teaching laboratories there. I asked for us to return to Norris Hall. Frustrating as it is for my faculty members, my students, and myself included, the decision is not ours.

> **Ashley Brohawn:** Personally, I think they should tear down Norris. The police were saying they might close off the second floor and allow the first floor to be used, and I was like, you're not going to get any current students and probably not anyone in the near future who's going to take a class in that building. It would be nice to see like a memorial building or a memorial garden or something built, just something like that.

Theresa Walsh, student who survived in Norris 205: That's so touchy. I think there should be some sort of memorial, even inside the building. I know that might be creepy to some people or some might not want to go in there because they might think it's haunted or whatever people think.

Ishwar Puri: Let us back into Norris Hall, but don't think that we have all the solutions. There are artists, architects who can help us with this. Remove any visual reminders of what happened on that day. Don't build the memorial there. Don't wall off the second floor classrooms because a workplace is a living, breathing space. ESM has survived, it's been a department for ninety-nine years if we want it to go on for another 101 you need for it to be in a place that is a nurturing, caring, and living environment. You can't work in a mausoleum.

Theresa Walsh: If anything, I don't want them to tear down the building. That was my favorite building, ironically, on this entire campus. It was like a Monopoly hotel in the middle of this big fortress. And I just loved that building. If they do anything, do not tear it down because we need to keep it Norris Hall. Maybe they'll do something like they did with Davidson, where they tore out the inside and redid it so it was all new-looking. I really don't think they should tear down that building, and there should be some kind of memorial on either the outside or the inside of it.

Ishwar Puri: My personal feeling is we shouldn't be in the business of razing multimillion-dollar facilities. It's a luxury that we have in the United States because we have funds, but this is a multimillion-dollar facility, and really, it's a second defeat. I mean, we've been victimized once and we'll be victimized another time.

Theresa Walsh: There are a lot of administrative offices in that building and I think that they should allow [the faculty] to go in there and let them decide. I mean, I know we've gotten some money donated to the school, but do we really have time to put up another building? And do we want to keep putting buildings up on campus? This campus is just going to be buildings soon. The worst part about it is that they had just redone the inside of the building. They had just put new carpet, new desks and everything in Norris. It's a great building; it's got a bomb shelter in the bottom of it. I don't know, it should be up to the teachers that have to be in that building.

Ishwar Puri: The hard thing is recognizing that we've been forcibly removed. It's like being evicted from your home and asking, "May I go back?" when you feel in your heart that it's your home. You need a reasoned, rational approach and not emotional responses. Because what may appear at first instance to be the right decision may not be the right decision. So the debate as I wrote to Charles [university president Charles Steger] was, "Don't put the memorial in Norris Hall." The university's going to retain the building, and I must rebuild the department there. I've got to go back there. I've got to take graduate students back there who do research. And so it's this tainted building. It's tainted by the event, but now it's tainted by a declaration. And so I have the challenge of reconvening, reorganizing, sort of rejuvenating an entire community. A department, a program, is a whole ecosystem, but it's now tainted. Because some people may choose now not to go there because of the events that transpired.

Normally the concerns of an engineering department chair would fail to capture the attention of most people in the Tech community. At a university where football is king, the work of academic departments can often seem less important.

Perhaps that's the best way to explain the dilemma faced by Puri and his Engineering Science and Mechanics department colleagues. Imagine for a moment that the shootings had not occurred in Norris but in the football offices at the Jamerson Athletic Center. The football program would have been staggered, just as the department was left reeling following the deaths of both faculty and students. The football program, however, is run by highly competitive people who would have sought to recover quickly, to get back out on the recruiting trail, to continue working so that the program would not suffer in seasons to come.

The coaches would want to be back in their offices, the players in their training facilities.

In its own way, the Engineering Science and Mechanics department is every bit as competitive as the football program.

> **Ishwar Puri:** The research partners have been understanding, but I think that at some point they're going to be less understanding. And, regardless of their understanding, I think that in a year or two, when time comes to renew grant proposals, these are all competitors. So the people with the best ideas and who have done the largest amount of work will get those funded projects. At some point, we'll be expected to come up to the same level of productivity.

Even before the events of April 16 unfolded, Virginia Tech faced substantial challenges. Sensing that its future lay in the balance, the university had announced earlier in the new century an ambition to become one of the country's top fifty research institutions. To do otherwise would have meant that Virginia Tech officials were ready to concede that it was a second-class institution.

The only problem with announcing its research goal was that the university faced tremendous challenges in making that happen. It had a relatively small endowment for a university its size (only about $300 million net in 2001–02 when Tech promptly lost $30 million on investments in the wake of the September 11 attacks). Another challenge was restricted state funding for the university brought about by state government budget woes.

Research is ranked by the amount of funded research that an institution does for any given year. Johns Hopkins, with its medical school and other top-flight programs, has led the nation in recent years with an estimated $2 billion annually in funded research. Virginia Tech, meanwhile, hovered back in the pack ranked somewhere in the seventies.

> **Ishwar Puri:** I'm worried about more mundane things like attrition. There's a faculty member in this department who was recently called by another university in the South, a highly regarded university, to see if the faculty member would come and be on a short list of candidates for a position. I fear, as the unit head, that there'll be attrition. This is a very fragile department. It's also a very strong department. Its strength and its greatest weakness is that it's so unique. So these people might become targets of opportunity for other universities.

Johns Hopkins, the nation's top research institution, kindly invited Tech's doctoral candidates to come to Baltimore to continue their studies in the days after the shootings.

> **Ishwar Puri:** Johns Hopkins University offered to pick up six, nine of our students, support them through the summer, and say, "You

can come here and work on what we're doing or keep working on what you're doing with your advisers, but use our facilities." And compensate them more than we would've compensated them.

Such a generous offer would become problematic only if Virginia Tech failed to move prudently to reestablish the ESM facilities. One could extend the football program analogy to imagine Southern Cal or the University of Texas offering scholarships to Virginia Tech's top players. The loss in human resources would in turn trigger a loss in revenue.

Ishwar Puri: Depending on how you count our research expenditures, they're anywhere from about $3 to $6 million. Depending on how you count the university's expenditures, they're anywhere from about $100 to $150 million. So, if you take away 3 to 4 percent of the university's expenditures, or if you truncate those abilities to generate that kind of expenditure, you truncate the university's ability not only to develop scholarship, but to develop doctoral students, human resources in terms of master students, research opportunities for undergraduates. Suddenly, when you're talking about goals of rising in the research rankings in terms of expenditures, you start slipping in the rankings quite significantly. I think that this is a fear I have.

With the high stakes, the decisions were not easy for Puri and Scott Case, his associate. The department's faculty all responded differently to the events of April 16. Some remained distraught weeks afterward.

Ishwar Puri: Some of them are still shaken up. I think that many are now to the state of frustration, because I think if you take the tools that scholars use to advance their scholarship, then they are frustrated. I think there was understanding in the beginning. Now many of them feel that they are being kept away from their laboratories. We are a science and engineering program and we need laboratories to do research, to conduct experiments. So if you're kept away from them, your scholarly productivity declines, your ability to write competitive grant proposals declines. There's a lot of anxiety, there's a lot of frustration. Some people feel that on April 16, there was a tragedy that was inflicted upon us. But now, to a certain extent, there are some self-inflicted wounds. I think many of them don't understand why they're kept away from the building.

One of the most competitive, dedicated researchers on the ESM team was Kevin Granata. He continued leading the department in many ways, even after his death. His colleagues believed Granata would have been especially intent on getting back to work in his labs in Norris Hall.

Ishwar Puri: The person who reminded me of that was Mike Diersing. He was Kevin's brother-in-law, and he also worked in Kevin's laboratory. Mike came by this morning and said, "We've just had so many discussions about Kevin and about Norris Hall, and he just loved that building." He liked the space. He liked what he was able to do. So the best way to honor Kevin's memory is just to go back there and keep working.

The second floor of Norris Hall had been marred by the shootings, but by mid-May construction crews had repaired the facility. Already two months behind in their highly competitive, high-dollar work, ESM's research faculty wanted back into their labs at Norris Hall. The administration, on the other hand, wished to remain sensitive to families that had suffered terrible losses in the building. Even some ESM faculty had misgivings about the department's moving back into Norris.

> **Ishwar Puri:** I know it's going to be difficult for some people. What I suggested to the university was that those who are adamant about not going there get transferred to other units with the same rank and same salary. And this is very painful to me because we have a great faculty and staff. That's the last thing I want to do. When there's a sense of unity and togetherness, it's tough to break that up.

With the university intent on making the building into some sort of memorial and with Puri asking that his department be allowed to return, Tech president Charles Steger held a series of meetings on the issue. At those meetings were the widows of Kevin Granata and Liviu Librescu. The wives had also consulted the wife of G. V. Loganathan for her feelings on the issue

> **Ishwar Puri:** Linda Granata was with us when we met with Charles Steger. She said, "The best way to honor my husband is to, you know, go right on doing what you're doing." Linda said, "I spoke to Usha Loganathan, and she said, 'You know, tell those ESM people to go back into Norris Hall and crack those nano particles.' " I was struck by the enormous maturity of these women, because they don't have the time to think of themselves. One has three children and one had two kids; they've got to focus on the future. The enormous maturity of these women who've suffered loss to say that. And Linda was asked, "Do you want us to preserve your husband's office as a memorial to him?" And she said, "Gosh no! You're so resource limited in this university. I remember that when my husband was given the office, someone else was displaced." And she said, "You need every square inch that you have. And why would you want to do that?"

And so the enormous maturity of these women. I think that you honor those who fell by moving on. You really do.

In early June, after hearing the perspective of Linda Granata, the university administration announced that the researchers would be allowed to return to Norris Hall. However, the long-term options for the building and the memorial remained very much up in the air.

As for the ESM department, it seemed clear that the best way to honor Kevin Granata, Liviu Librescu, and G. V. Loganathan would be to go on working, to carry on.

In its own way, the Department of Engineering Science and Mechanics faced the many difficult choices and decisions that the university at large faced in the months after April 16. Unfortunately, there was little time to make those decisions.

Ishwar Puri: I think there are times when you have to seize the moment. If you don't seize the moment, it passes. I want Virginia Tech to seize this moment. I want it to recommit itself to its plans, its goals, its mission, and I'd like us to proceed from there. But I think that if we are concerned more about our image, more of how the world may perceive what we've done and what we will be doing, rather than focusing on fundamentals. . . . I think if the university realizes what fundamentals it has to adhere to, discovery, learning, outreach, and recommits itself to that, then we will move forward. I just want to reiterate, we cannot live with indecision. I think it's very important for not just the university administration but the university as a whole to take some leadership and some ownership in the future. Leaders in academia can only move by consensus. I think if you don't move by consensus, then you essentially lead to great strife and great discussion and great entropy, which you could've avoided and vested those energies elsewhere. People don't understand sometimes what consensus means. Consensus doesn't mean that everyone follows the decision. Consensus doesn't mean that everyone originally supports a decision. Consensus means something, an agreement that's facilitated. And that requires leadership. You've got to explain why things have to happen the way they have to happen. You've got to build consensus. And you've got to coalesce people around a consensus. I think it's very important that we reinvest our energies right now in coalescing a common purpose. And the common purpose should be around the core missions of the university, and how we can dedicate ourselves to being greater than what we were on April 15.

I think that the world will ultimately perceive us from how we reacted to the immediate aftermath of the tragedy. The world will perceive us in how we will overcome it. Take the University of Texas at Austin. If you asked people that a sniper killed sixteen people at the University of Texas in 1966, many people will be amazed. What do they recognize Austin for today? What they recognize the University of Texas is for high-quality education, it's for high-quality research, and, of course, intercollegiate athletics. And so, I think that's how the world will perceive us. First and foremost, we remain an educational institution.

Engineering Science and Mechanics is a department with 125 undergraduates and ninety graduate students keenly focused on research. In addition, the department teaches courses to another three thousand students from across the university. Its numerous labs housed in the seventy thousand square feet of Norris Hall are used for both teaching and research. With good reason, research has been identified as the key to the entire university's future.

Ishwar Puri: Why do we do research? One of the prime motivations of doing research is to act to the high caliber of human resources of the country. So, when you look at a university like Austin, or if you look at a neighbor, UVA, ultimately the world doesn't see it for its research expenditure. Ultimately, the world sees it for the high-caliber human resources it produces. And that's what we need to rededicate ourselves to—producing those high-caliber human resources. When I talk about research in my department, it's not something abstract. It's the graduate students, the doctoral students who are doing it, who will be the professors of tomorrow. They are really our legacy. It's not the three or six million dollars I'm spending in one particular year. It's those doctoral students, and that's what we need to concentrate on. How are we going to attract these individuals? How are we going to get the best minds in the world? The church on Main Street is flying flags that represent victims from countries all around the world killed on April 16. Keep those flags in mind for the future. They're going to come from everywhere. They're going to be men, they're going to be women, they're going to be white, they're going to be African, African-American, they're going to be Hispanic, they're going to be Asian. How do we make this community that vibrant community, and how do we send those people out, place them in the best places? That's what we need to think about. That's the resolve we need to dedicate ourselves to. Otherwise, I fear that we'll be stuck in this moment for a long period of time. And, you know, we'll be venting our frustrations at each other for months or even years. I hope that does not happen. As any historian will tell you, a moment in time is not that. There's always a yesterday, a today, and a tomorrow. The today is based upon the events of yesterday, and the tomorrow is based upon the events of today. If we have any regrets today, and if we carry those regrets in our hearts, then our tomorrows will have yesterdays' regrets. And therefore, our mission and our vision of the future will always be tainted by regrets. What follows tomorrow depends upon today. Today is the moment to change it and take control.

For shooting victim Derek O'Dell, "seizing the moment" is as simple as making a personal choice.

Derek O'Dell: After everything that I've been through it might be hard to think that I should be happy, but that's what I am now. After that initial week following April 16 of mourning and hardships, I began to have hope and smile as often as I could. I found something as small as a smile could brighten anyone's day that I walked past. The same hope that all of the Hokies, my family, my friends, and everyone else gave me, is the same hope I tried to convey to everyone I met. It was a simple smile that provided people with hope that we would recover, a simple smile that could become contagious and spread to everyone. That's how I have recovered and that's how I hope everyone who has read this will also recover; with a simple smile of hope.

Suzanne Higgs: My mom asked me, after she saw how hard I was taking things, if I wanted to transfer schools. Without even thinking I said, "No, why would I do that?" The thought never occurred to me. I'm a Hokie, and I will always be.

Robert Bowman: After freshman year, I knew I wanted to share my love of the school with prospective students. I became a Hokie ambassador sophomore year, and now have the privilege of helping to run the organization. One of my first thoughts on Monday was of recruiting. I was worried about the number of students who would turn down Tech because of the shootings. My thoughts subsided on Wednesday when I walked into the admissions office. Inside Burruss I bumped into two students who looked completely lost. "Where are you guys headed?" I asked. "We're looking for admissions." I led them up the stairs and showed them the office. I listened as they were told that there were no tours that week because of the shootings. "Actually, I have a free hour," I said. "Do you guys want to go for a walk?" On our way down the stairs, I learned the two guys were students from Cooperstown, New York. They said that they needed to see the campus, and thought that the shootings could have happened anywhere. In no way did it reflect Virginia Tech. They needed to choose what school to go to before May 1. On our way around campus, I deviated far from the normal route, which leads right in front of Norris. Instead, we walked through Owens, the model residence hall room in Newman, West End, and even into Cassell, the Merryman Center, and Lane Stadium. Although the tour took about two hours, and I may have missed a morning meeting, the tour was the best thing for me that week. I got to forget about Monday, and do what I do best: talk about Tech. After the tour, both guys asked for directions to the bookstore, and said they were both definitely coming to Tech. They had no doubts in their minds. After that tour, the week became easier for me. A new hope was born amid such chaos and misery.

Tommy McDearis, Blacksburg police chaplain: Now we in Blacksburg are the latest to experience an unwanted and undeserved visit by the sinister darkness of life. . . . Just as others have done for us in recent days, we must be the ones to shine the light into the darkness so those who have been briefly blinded may know an eternal truth. The light shines in the darkness, and the darkness has not overcome it. In his novel *A Farewell to Arms,* Ernest Hemingway wrote, "The world breaks everyone and afterward many are strong at the broken places." We in Blacksburg have indeed been broken, but by God's grace we will become strong at the broken places. And by God's grace we will prevail.

Sources

Ashburg Park Press
The Associated Press
The Baltimore Sun
The Boston Globe
The Chronicle of Higher Education
CNN
CNN.com
Collegiate Times
Daily Press
ESPN.com
Facebook
Headlines India
Indo-Asian News Service
NBC
The New York Times
Newsweek
NPR
nytimes.com
Planet Blacksburg
Religious Herald
Richmond Times-Dispatch
The Roanoke Times
The Star-Ledger (Newark)
USA Today
Virginia Tech Office of University Relations
The Washington Post